Gaining Ground

Gaining Ground

~

MARKETS
HELPING
GOVERNMENT

Clifford Winston

BROOKINGS INSTITUTION PRESS
Washington, D.C.

Copyright © 2021
THE BROOKINGS INSTITUTION
1775 Massachusetts Avenue, N.W.
Washington, D.C. 20036
www.brookings.edu

The Brookings Institution is a private nonprofit organization devoted to research, education, and publication on important issues of domestic and foreign policy. Its principal purpose is to bring the highest quality independent research and analysis to bear on current and emerging policy problems. Interpretations or conclusions in Brookings publications should be understood to be solely those of the authors.

Library of Congress Control Number: 2021941001

ISBN 9780815739326 (pbk)
ISBN 9780815739333 (ebook)

9 8 7 6 5 4 3 2 1

Typeset in Minion Pro

Composition by Elliott Beard

To Joan in our 40th year
We will celebrate at Yaukuve Levu and live Aloha forever

In memory of HJ and TH
102 years was not nearly long enough

CONTENTS

ACKNOWLEDGMENTS

I am grateful to Stephanie Aaronson, Alan Blinder, Richard Burkhauser, Dennis Carlton, Menzie Chinn, Robert Crandall, Jay Ezrielev, Edward Glaeser, Robert Hahn, Thomas Hazlett, Amanda Kowalski, Robert Litan, Vikram Maheshri, Richard Schmalensee, Dennis Sheehan, Timothy Taylor, and Ralph Winter for many helpful comments and suggestions. Joan Winston was especially helpful in improving chapter 18. Funding was generously provided by the Smith Richardson Foundation.

ONE

Introduction

Society attempts to solve problems through different ways of cooperation. Markets are a form of cooperation: within firms, between producers of final goods and their outside producers, and between firms and consumers. Democratic government is a form of cooperation. Each form of cooperation can substitute for or complement the other. For example, government or markets can provide urban bus transportation, primary education in schools, and other services. Interacting as complements, government may set up a cap-and-trade system for reducing pollution and then let market forces operate within that system; government may pass along some of its tax revenues to nonprofit organizations for the provision of services to the poor or the sick; and the like.

With input from the economics profession, preferences of voters, and actions of policymakers, the United States continues to experiment with alternative forms of government and market cooperation, as complements and substitutes, to solve critical economic problems. Unfortunately, we currently are in a moment during which the public's faith in both capitalism and economists is at a low point.[1] One reason for this is that neither appears to have done much to reduce the growth in income inequality that began in the 1970s. Another reason is that macroeconomists did not prepare the public for the Great Recession and could only partially soften its blow.[2] The result is that many Americans, especially younger adults who are struggling financially, are quick to reject market solutions.

However, this is a serious mistake. Regardless of what people think our public objectives should be—reduce inequality, stimulate long-term growth, slow climate change, or eliminate COVID-19—markets will be a critical part of the solution. It also is a mistake for people to think that, because they do not like what capitalism is currently doing for the poor and they would prefer a more progressive policy agenda, it would be a bad idea to use market forces to, for example, help improve the quality of public schools or urban transportation. Similarly, economic nationalists who do not like what free trade and immigration are doing to employment in certain industries and would prefer a stronger industrial policy and higher tariffs should not overlook the benefits market forces provide American workers and consumers. Finally, those with some background in economics should realize that although macroeconomics is criticized by some as faith-based because it struggles to develop an analytical model that can explain and help stabilize the economy's fluctuations, microeconomics is grounded in a widely-accepted corpus of economic theory and has accumulated a voluminous body of empirical research that assesses the effects of public policies to solve economic problems.

What economic problems do economists try to solve? A popular caricature of economists is that they always are laissez-faire and that they oppose redistribution. Although some economists are neutral on or do oppose redistribution, many conduct research on and favor government interventions to reduce economic inefficiencies such as abuses of monopoly power and negative externalities. Still other economists believe that objectives besides economic efficiency are important and necessitate redistributing income to, for example, reduce poverty. I incorporate those perspectives by summarizing the economic problems economists try to solve as consistent with American citizens' goals of: (1) maximizing their material quality of life, (2) having a chance to succeed, and (3) obtaining a decent quality of life should they face hardships, either because of the adverse household circumstances in which they were born or because of unexpected shocks.[3]

To facilitate analysis and maintain consistency with the accumulated body of research, I interpret the first goal in practice as creating an economic environment where sufficient market competition exists; consumers and workers make informed choices; negative externalities are reduced efficiently; innovation is incentivized in accordance with cost-benefit considerations; and socially desirable public goods are provided. I interpret the second goal in practice as preventing employers from discriminating against specific individuals or groups when they make hiring and promotion decisions and preventing education admissions committees from discriminating in favor of or against specific groups of applicants. Finally, I interpret the third goal in practice as providing resources to keep households' standard of living above the poverty level and providing household members with merit goods—that is, as introduced by Richard Musgrave (1959), goods that individuals or society should have on the basis of some concept of need rather than on an ability and willingness to pay.[4]

I am not aware of previous research that has indicated how to broadly characterize the goals to organize analysis and synthesize findings. Thus, I refer to the first goal and its elements, which are generally associated with economic efficiency, as economic goals, and I refer to the second and third goals and their elements, which are generally associated with economic redistribution, as social economic goals, or social goals for short.

In some cases, economic and social goals cannot be neatly compartmentalized. For example, the provision of subsidized education may be justified as accomplishing a social goal because US society believes it is a merit good. But it also could be justified as accomplishing an economic goal because it generates positive externalities through a better educated workforce that helps increase society's material quality of life. Government and market actions also may affect both goals simultaneously. Nonetheless, I distinguish between the two goals because economists use different theoretical benchmarks to assess performance. Economic goals are achieved by government interventions or market forces to produce efficiency gains, which are characterized as potential Pareto improvements;[5] social goals are achieved by government interventions and market forces to satisfy a particular goal at minimum social cost, although the goal may not produce an efficiency gain.

THEORY AND PRACTICE

Government interventions and market forces both seek to accomplish economic and social goals. However, a branch of economic theory known as welfare economics—the study of how to allocate resources to improve social welfare, which is a function of efficiency and distribution—devotes considerable attention to identifying when markets are likely to work effectively with minimal government intervention and when they are likely to fail without government involvement. The classic examples of market failure to accomplish economic goals that motivate government intervention include the abuse of monopoly power, natural monopoly, imperfect information, externalities, and public goods. Those types of market failures generate a loss in economic efficiency. Markets may not generate an efficiency loss but still may fail to accomplish social goals that require government intervention to redistribute income when households live in poverty, individuals experience discrimination in various markets, and merit goods are not provided to the public.

Welfare economics problems are often assessed in a static setting—for example, a firm has abused monopoly power, markets have failed, and government intervention, not market forces, is required immediately to address the problem. Little attention is paid to whether the government addresses the problem. However, my perspective is that welfare economics problems should be assessed in a dynamic setting because market forces can change over time to address economic and social goals—for example, the firm that abused monopoly power is eventually challenged by innovative new entrants and its market share plummets. In contrast, government behavior is static and suffers from status quo bias, meaning that policymakers rarely change their policies over time to address economic and social goals; for example, by the time the government has proposed a remedy to address the monopolist's abuse of its market power, the one-time monopolist may be struggling to survive in the industry.

A dynamic perspective also facilitates a long-run view of welfare economics where technological change plays a critical role. Consider firms that produce a product but pollute the air while doing so. Government intervenes with a command and control policy to force the firms to reduce their pollution, but the policy is inefficient because it causes the firms to reduce their production by an excessive amount, such that the benefits from cleaner air are less than the value of the reduced output. Decades later, the firms adopt a new technology that enables them to produce their output without damaging the environment. Importantly, markets often have considerable potential to help address economic and social problems even if they are not currently doing so, and that potential should not be dismissed out of hand.

Table 1-1 summarizes the different approaches, which may succeed in theory and sometimes in practice, that government policymakers and markets take to accomplish economic and social goals. To accomplish economic goals, markets rely on the actions taken by private firms and individuals; technological advance enables those agents to improve the effectiveness of current actions or to take new actions that improve market performance. For exam-

TABLE 1-1. Market and Government Approaches to Pursue Economic and Social Goals

Goal	Market Approach	Government Approach
Economic goals		
Promote competition	Firm entry and exit, price and non-price strategies	Antitrust and regulatory policies
Enable consumers and workers to make informed decisions	Advertising, brand names, and other sources of information, including from third parties	Information policies and regulations
Reduce negative externalities	People and firms adjust to reduce the costs they incur and impose on others*	Command and control policies and fees
Encourage innovation by people and firms	Financial incentives and financing	Patent protection and various R&D contests and laboratories
Provide public goods	Private investment and cooperatives	Expenditures on services and infrastructure
Social goals		
Reduce poverty	Firm training, wage policies, and charitable giving	Various policies and programs
Ensure fairness in labor markets	Competition	Antidiscrimination laws and regulations
Provide merit goods	Private market alternatives, such as online education	Taxes to fund expenditures on various programs
Encourage socially beneficial immigration	Hire skilled and unskilled foreign workers legally	Laws governing the path to citizenship

*With defined property rights, other market approaches include, for example, tradeable pollution permits.

ple, new technologies can spur additional competition, increase the amount and availability of useful information, reduce negative externalities, stimulate new innovations, and encourage firms to invest in projects that benefit the public. In contrast, government entities institute regulations and spend public funds to accomplish economic goals. This does not imply, for example, that private investors can necessarily succeed in providing public goods efficiently and that government regulations can reduce externalities efficiently.

Firms and individuals also take actions to help achieve social goals; technical advance can enable those actions to be more effective, as well. Government's approach is to enact new laws and fund new social programs that are financed by taxpayers.

THE DEBATE

As noted, government and market approaches to address specific economic and social goals may not be effective in practice, which is why the optimal mix of market and government approaches often is debated as the nation goes through political and economic cycles. Currently, the public and the policymakers do not appear to have much faith in markets. At the same time, the public seems resigned to expanding the role of government despite its negative views of politicians and political institutions.

However, the debate generally does not account for the accumulated empirical evidence on the efficacy of market forces and government policies to accomplish the nation's goals. This book fills that gap by synthesizing the available evidence and by arguing that, in contrast to current dissatisfaction with markets, American society has gained ground when government has allowed markets to help accomplish the aforementioned economic and social goals, especially when government policies have made little progress in achieving those goals. I further argue that society could gain even more ground if government removed constraints, which would enable markets to play a greater role in the process (Caplan 2019).

Notwithstanding my belief in the efficacy of markets, the available evidence does not support the view that market forces could always improve on government performance and that all government interventions should be dismantled. But the vast inefficiencies in government policy that I summarize explain why it is socially desirable for the mix of government and market approaches to change and why it is important for policymakers to be more cognizant of the actual and potential accomplishments of market forces. Policymakers may then be more willing to accept that, because of technological advances, new sources of competition, and more enlightened thinking about the private benefits of addressing social problems, times change and markets may be able to help solve economic and social problems they could not help solve in the past.

A simple illustrative example of markets helping when government performs poorly occurred when Amtrak, a heavily-subsidized government corporation, broke down en route to Washington, DC, and failed to provide food for its stranded passengers. In response, a proactive hungry passenger placed an order on his cell phone with the closest Domino's Pizza, and the delivery-person leaped over an embankment, found the passenger's railcar, and delivered the pie.[6]

Similarly, an example of market forces helping discipline firms that behave poorly occurred in April 2017 when United Airlines violently expelled a paying passenger because United had overbooked the flight. As pointed out by Antony Davies and James Harrigan (2018), within twenty-four hours, United's stock plummeted by a quarter of a billion dollars because investors dumped the stock in anticipation of a consumer boycott of United, and within days, several airlines announced they would end their practice of overbooking flights.[7] How did the government respond to United's behavior? Congress took a month to schedule hearings to investigate the matter and then took no further action.

I do not wish to convey the impression that the current lack of faith in markets and capitalism is shared by all Americans. We live in a time of heightened political differences, which often take the form of overly intense prior beliefs about the characteristics of markets and government and the appropriate policies to enhance economic and social goals. Accordingly, the next chapter assesses alternative perspectives on markets and government, and then clarifies the scope and content of my analysis.

The remainder of the book is divided into four parts. Part I examines the evidence on government policy inefficiencies in attempting to accomplish economic goals to set the stage for the discussion about the evidence on markets helping improve on government actions and on additional ways markets could provide help. Part II reviews the evidence on government policy inefficiencies in attempting to accomplish social goals to, again, set the stage for a discussion of the evidence on markets helping improve on government actions and on additional ways markets could provide help. Part III synthesizes the evidence for both goals on government policy inefficiencies and explanations of them, and on markets helping government and additional ways markets can help. The broader implications of the evidence for economic growth and inequality are also discussed.

This book was completed during a global pandemic that appears to have originated in China in late 2019 and spread throughout the United States at the beginning of 2020. The novel coronavirus is still affecting the entire world in ways that have been unimaginable; however, it has not changed the important themes of this analysis. In fact, it has reinforced them. The pandemic has required government action—stay-at-home orders, incentives to develop safe and effective vaccines, and rules about individual travel—and it also has required the power of market forces—private firms to develop those vaccines, and employers to find new ways to work in an uncertain environment. This once-in-a-century, unfortunate event has presented an unanticipated opportunity to subject the major findings of the book, which show markets assisting government, to a "robustness test" of whether they have helped government during the pandemic.

In Part IV, I conduct this test. In a post-coronavirus world, the importance of markets helping government should gain greater prominence as society reconsiders their respective roles. I conclude the book by taking a proactive approach that stresses the importance of increasing our reliance on market forces to help solve the nation's economic and social problems in light of the evidence synthesized in Part III that indicates markets can and have provided considerable help—help that should be greatly appreciated because it is very difficult to identify the source(s) of government inefficiency that could guide reforms to significantly improve government performance.

I suggest the role of markets helping government potentially could be increased if the United States government formed a major commission composed of academics, policymakers, and business people to explore how market forces could provide greater help to government to address economic and social problems and to provide specific recommendations, including conducting policy experiments. Hopefully, policymakers would find the advice useful for reforming policy that would help the US better accomplish its economic and social goals and would regularly reconvene the commission along the same lines in the future.

TWO

Perspectives on Government and Markets and the Scope and Content of the Analysis

Supporters of government approaches to economic and social problems rightly claim government has some advantages over markets that could lead to successful outcomes. For example, as part of a military objective, government can finance research and development that produces major innovations with important civilian applications. Government also can mobilize political support and allocate resources to pursue social goals, such as advancing civil rights, instituting a criminal justice system, securing nuclear storage sites, and providing military defense. Government institutes public policies that could complement markets by ameliorating their weaknesses, such as industrial plants that pollute, competitors that fix prices, consumers who are misled about the quality of a product or service, and firms that discriminate against women and minorities when hiring workers. And government creates and enforces a legal framework within which private market participants can cooperate to achieve significant dynamic efficiencies that increase economic growth and enable all members of society to enjoy a higher material quality of life.

My focus, however, is not on what government does well in theory and, occasionally, in practice, but on the broad range of areas where markets do well in practice and the additional ways they could contribute if given the chance to improve on government inefficiencies. One can deduce that the areas I do not discuss tend to be ones where government performance is satisfactory. Even so, defenders of government approaches may claim my focus is unbalanced because improved government policies could correct much inefficiency and because markets are often inefficient. It is important to assess that view.

PERSPECTIVES ON GOVERNMENT POLICY INTERVENTIONS

An extensive literature exists that proposes efficient government solutions that, in theory, could address alleged market inefficiencies and social problems. Recent examples include:

- A measured application of the antitrust laws in response to the rise of tech platform companies and the growing industrial concentration at the national level, including updating merger standards, a smarter way to get tough on dominant firms, and other ways to promote competition (Litan 2018).

- Simple and effective disclosure policies that could benefit consumers by ameliorating problems from asymmetric information that arise when firms hide important matters about their behavior or about the products they sell (Akerlof and Shiller 2015).

- Efficient emissions and carbon taxes to reduce production and consumption externalities that are harmful to the climate, the air we breathe, and the water we drink. Such taxes provide market incentives for the private sector to invent, fund, develop, and commercialize new low-carbon and low-emissions products and processes (Nordhaus 2019).

- Efficient truck pricing and highway durability investment policies that would increase pavement lives, reduce the damage trucks do to roads, and help fund the nation's highway infrastructure (Winston 2013).

- Lifetime career-loan accounts, wage insurance, and career and life counseling that would help the US workforce adjust to technological change and help less-affluent Americans raise their standard of living (Alden and Litan 2017).

- Legal reforms that make it easier to initiate class action lawsuits or require mandatory arbitration of employment issues on an individualized basis to combat pervasive hiring discrimination (Neumark 2018).
- Strategies to reduce opioid use given demand-oriented policies, such as improving access to medication-assisted treatment, and supply-oriented policies, such as increasing monitoring and regulation of opioid prescribing, have not significantly reduced opioid-related fatalities (Glickman and Weiner 2019).[1]

Unfortunately, little evidence exists that policymakers actually reform their policies by adopting more efficient and potentially more effective policies, such as those listed. And there is little reason to believe policymakers will heed Alan Blinder's (2018) plea that they improve their understanding of basic economics and use it more as a guide to good policy and less as a tool for political spin.

Some defenders of government recognize its shortcomings but assert that certain government actors are arguably anti-government and, for example, are unwilling to provide funding to improve public policies. Instead, they pursue their own ideological interests at the expense of the social interest. Government policy performance has long been criticized, and several reasons have been proffered to explain its inadequacies, which are briefly summarized in the next chapter and discussed in more detail in part III of the book. The important conclusion from the available empirical evidence is that we cannot explain the causes of inefficient government policies with much confidence and that we do not know what steps to take to influence policymakers to significantly correct most of those inefficiencies in practice.

CRITICAL PERSPECTIVES ON MARKETS

Defenders of government approaches also argue that market forces often do not contribute to socially desirable outcomes. Leading academic economists and business people are at the forefront of the current dissatisfaction with markets and capitalism. For example, Joseph Stiglitz (2019) argues that most of society's problems have been created by markets. He calls for more government intervention in the economy, especially because the economic divide, as reflected in widened inequality and increased concentration of market power, has led to a political divide, and the political divide has reinforced the economic divide. Jonathon Tepper and Denise Hearn (2019) assert that, in industry after industry, Americans can purchase goods only from local monopolies or oligopolies that tacitly collude. They are particularly concerned that political power is becoming concentrated in those firms. Ray Dalio, founder of the world's biggest hedge fund, is quoted in Mark Niquette (2019) as arguing that capitalism must be reformed because it is not producing enough opportunities for most Americans and is creating an income gap that threatens to spark conflict. And David Leonhardt (2019) quotes Peter Georgescu—a refugee from Romania who became CEO of the advertising firm Young and Rubicam—as lamenting that capitalism has been slowly committing suicide for the past four decades because the American economy no longer functions well for most citizens.

However, those views are not accompanied by detailed empirical evidence that identifies large welfare losses generated by market forces and supports the merits of government interventions. As noted, considerable doubt exists that socially desirable interventions would occur in practice.

THE MIDDLE GROUND

Scholars who call for the effective use of markets and government intervention to promote efficiency and accomplish social goals occupy the middle ground. For example, Robert Solow (2010) argues that the only legitimate questions to ask about markets are: What are their limitations? Can they go wrong? What can government policy do to protect the economy and society against market failure without losing much of either the capacity of a market system to coordinate economic activity efficiently or its ability to stimulate and reward technological and other innovations that lead to technological progress? Edward Glaeser (2019) discusses a "New Freedom" that would be guided—intelligently—toward solving social problems, with the public sector establishing financial incentives and private entrepreneurs developing ingenious solutions. The middle ground perspective concludes that society does not have to choose between a "corner solution" of either unfettered laissez faire or beneficent government, especially because basic government policies such as rules about property, contracts, torts, and criminal law underlie and enable markets by setting the framework within which firms are formed and compete to provide solutions.

While I agree with that view, I argue, based on the accumulated evidence reported here, that society can gain ground by relying more frequently on market solutions. Importantly, such a view is politically free in the sense that it is not associated with the actions of a particular presidential administration or political party because evidence does not exist that any administration or party has generally been more effective than other administrations or parties in using markets to improve government performance. For example, despite conventional views about Democrats and Republicans, the bulk of economic deregulation occurred during the Carter administration, and the effort to reduce poverty by ending policies that discouraged work occurred during the Clinton administration. When policies are linked with an administration, it is done only to clarify their timing.[2]

SCOPE AND CONTENT OF THE ANALYSIS

The effects of government policies and market forces on economic and social goals are discussed separately, in parts I and II of the book. Part III then shows how each approach may simultaneously affect both goals, intensifying the strength or weakness of a particular approach. For example, technological advance in information technology that justifies eliminating occupational licensing to address alleged information problems also can increase employment and earnings for individuals who were prevented by licensing requirements from getting jobs in those occupations.

The scope of the discussion is dynamic in the sense that different policy issues have captured the imagination of policymakers and economists over time. Policymakers were concerned about monopoly power in the late nineteenth century, although economists generally did not share those concerns (Stigler 1982). Both economists and policymakers focused much of their energies on externalities after the mid-twentieth century. Recently, some policymakers have raised new concerns about monopoly power, while economists are divided on the matter. I focus on the current state of knowledge on government and market approaches to economic and social issues, but it should be kept in mind that many of those issues are not new and have a long scholarly and institutional history.

Dynamic considerations also are important because markets can help government accomplish economic and social goals in different ways at different times. In some cases, such as enabling consumers to make informed choices and being able to choose among many alternative suppliers, markets independently help government without government taking any specific action to enlist that help. Market forces may be more effective in providing that help over time as they become more competitive and promote efficiency and innovation that benefits society. Markets may be less helpful over time if competition weakens. In other cases, government must change certain institutions to enable markets to provide greater help by, for example, withdrawing price, entry, and exit regulations, designing emissions cap-and-trade programs, and so on. Again, it takes time for government to be convinced to adopt institutional change.

Still, there are cases where markets could help government if government gave them the freedom to do so. One goal of this book is to suggest specific cases and to argue that, in general, government should consider such cases continuously as a matter of policy reform to enable markets to provide additional help over time. Finally, there are cases where, although government is not explicitly relying on the private sector to address a problem, it could apply market principles to improve social welfare, such as implementing efficient pricing of externalities, or it has done so, such as allowing school choice for grades PK–12 and reforming health insurance to expand coverage.

The idea of market forces is used in different ways. The most common way refers to the conventional demand and supply sides of a market composed of firms and consumers, with firms taking actions that benefit consumers and increase their market share. In other cases, the private sector represented by firms may pursue actions to improve their reputation among consumers (for example, by adopting more sustainable production practices), or to influence other firms (for example, to reduce pollution), or to influence government (for example, to withdraw discriminatory legislation). Finally, government could take actions that produce market-type response by consumers or firms, such as congestion tolls that discourage motorists from traveling on highways during peak periods, or effluent taxes that discourage firms from polluting rivers.

I qualify my analysis because the availability of scholarly empirical assessments of the nation's accomplishments of its economic and social goals is uneven. Generally, there is more peer-reviewed academic evidence that assesses government and market performance on economic than on social goals, and there is more peer-reviewed academic evidence on the actual effects of markets helping government than on its potential effects. Those differences suggest it would be fruitful for researchers to make a greater effort to assess government and market performance on accomplishing social goals and on the potential effects of markets helping government.

I draw on a variety of sources of empirical and descriptive evidence, including peer-reviewed scholarly books and journal articles, working papers, often from the National Bureau of Economic Research (NBER), and articles in national newspapers and magazines.[3] This evidence can be regarded as the start of a living document that will eventually be put on a website and updated as new evidence is available on various topics, thereby converting working papers into peer-reviewed scholarly publications and converting the descriptive evidence in newspaper and magazine articles into researchable questions that are analyzed in working papers and eventually appear in peer-reviewed journals.

It will also be necessary to update the evidence because, by casting a broad net, I suggest there is a wide range of actual and potential opportunities for markets to play a constructive role in enhancing public welfare. Recent examples are drawn on that are the result of technological advances that have enabled markets to help government address particular problems. Updated evidence is likely to show that markets are even more successful in helping government address those problems.

The implications of other examples may be less durable. For example, examples are presented that indicate that firms have made "generous" contributions to workers that could be interpreted as helping reduce poverty and promote education. At the same time, I acknowledge that firms provided this help during a strong macroeconomy with a tight labor market and that such help may not last indefinitely. Examples are provided to suggest that one should have an open mind about the potential for markets to contribute to a broad range of economic and social problems. Currently, some organizations, such as the Business Roundtable, and leading executives are re-evaluating firms' responsibilities and questioning whether they should strictly follow Milton Friedman's dictate to focus only on maximizing profits. Some firms appear to embrace taking a broader social role, but my examples should be qualified as not indicating a permanent commitment that the government can count on to help reduce poverty and provide merit goods. The examples suggest only possibilities and motivate speculation about whether government could encourage firms in an efficient manner to take a broader social role in the future.

Given that the relative roles of government and markets in addressing economic and social goals could change significantly over time, with markets playing a greater role, it will be important to update and expand the evidence that motivates and supports the desirability of that change.

PART I

Markets Helping Government Address Economic Goals

THREE

Why Markets Can Help Government Address Economic Goals

Markets can help government address economic goals because they do not generally share the primary weaknesses of government and the policymaking process, while government does not share the strength of markets. As a heuristic overview for comparative purposes, the weaknesses of government likely to compromise performance include:

- Resource constraints on implementing and managing a policy.
- Poor workforce morale attributable to ineffective management.
- Ideologically-based preferences of policymakers.
- Many veto players in the legal process.
- Weak incentives for efficiency.
- The absence of a culture of experimentation that could help government learn by trial and error to become more innovative.

Households and firms have built-in incentives not to be compromised by those weaknesses and to avoid the harsh consequences of failure in a competitive market setting, such as termination of employment, bankruptcy, and liquidation, by recognizing performance problems and exploring alternative approaches to solve them.

Banks, venture capitalists, strategic investors, crowdsourcing participants, and the like may assist another party to overcome resource constraints;
however, those participants generally must be persuaded that the goal and
the strategy to achieve it are sound and that the chances of success are high.
Market responses indicate whether resource constraints are a useful signal
that the goal is not worth pursuing or that the strategy to achieve it is un-
sound or both, or that the goal entails risks that third parties should consider
before they help market participants.

Market competition incentivizes private-sector firms to address poor
workplace morale and managers' ideologically-based decisions by bringing
parties together who are committed to pursuing a goal in the most efficient
way possible and to reaping the rewards of achieving it, while simultaneously
weeding out those parties who would undermine the goal's pursuit and jeopardize the potential rewards. Finally, though market participants are certainly
subject to laws and engage in political infighting, they generally operate with
fewer (uncompromising) veto players than the government does in its politically charged environment.

The strengths of markets that government does not share are the dynamic
abilities to: respond to incentives for efficiency or suffer the aforementioned
consequences of failure; make difficult and often time-consuming adjustments to respond to changed circumstances and overcome failure; and the
capability to develop and implement innovations, often by trial and error, that
enable participants to disrupt conventional activities by performing them
more efficiently or to engage in entirely new activities. In practice, markets
encourage participants to conduct many small-scale experiments where success may eventually be achieved in later experiments following failure in the
initial experiment (Manzi 2012; McArdle 2014).

Successful market participants have vision and take the long view by
making appropriate long-run investments in human and physical capital,
which government finds difficult to do because of its status quo bias and because elections have forced elected officials, who generally control the policy
agenda, to think primarily in the short term. To the extent that government
is inclined to "develop" innovations, it does so by subsidizing more of yester-
day's technologies instead of making large-scale investments in basic research
that may entail significant risks and rewards. Generally, government's policy
agenda trails current technology and is inimical to advancing technology
(Foldvary and Klein 2003).

In sum, market participants—and, thus, market forces—can help government improve resource allocation efficiency because they are not inhibited from searching for alternative approaches to overcome constraints and because they have strong economic incentives to make appropriate adjustments and develop new innovations to address problems in ways never before imagined. The primary virtues of markets—competition, incentives for efficiency, innovation and technological change, and the potential to expose government abuses and inefficiencies—will appear repeatedly in the different settings discussed in this book. Repetition can be boring, but it is important here because it indicates that a common set of tools enables markets to be versatile and address a variety of economic problems.

My 2006 book *Government Failure versus Market Failure* (hereafter, *Government Failure*) reviewed and synthesized the available empirical evidence that assessed government policies to accomplish economic goals by correcting market failures. The policies include antitrust enforcement to curtail anticompetitive behavior by firms; economic regulations to address natural monopoly and other market characteristics that prevent workable competition; policies to reduce imperfect information in product and labor markets; policies to reduce negative externalities; policies to encourage research and development; and provision of socially desirable services (public production). The remaining chapters of this part of the book briefly summarize the critical conclusions from those policy assessments and provide recent evidence to illustrate that they are still valid. The summaries help explain why and in what ways market forces could help government. Then, evidence is provided to show that market forces have improved upon or have the potential to improve upon government performance in accomplishing economic goals.

FOUR

Protecting Consumers against Anticompetitive Behavior

When a firm attempts to inflict losses on consumers by engaging in illegal conduct to monopolize a market or by abusing its market power to earn excess profits, government intervention in the form of antitrust policy and enforcement is justified to stop those actions to protect consumer welfare and discourage other firms from engaging in such behavior in the future. Market forces also can respond to protect consumer welfare by generating effective competition from existing firms and from new entrants that develop because of technological change.

ANTITRUST POLICY AND ENFORCEMENT

The evidence in *Government Failure* indicated that antitrust policies toward monopolization, mergers, and collusion have done little to improve consumer welfare. Some recent research has raised concerns that market competition has become less intense in recent years and has called for antitrust to be strengthened to restore competition and benefit consumers (for example, Jonathan Baker 2019). However, Carl Shapiro (2018) and Gregory Werden and Luke Froeb (2018), economists who have served as deputy assistant attorney general for economics and as senior economic counsel in the Antitrust Division of the US Department of Justice, have concluded there is no evidence of a recent systematic decline in competition in the United States at the level of relevant antitrust markets.

Clifford Winston (2021 forthcoming) argues that critics of markets effectively ignore that their criticisms are more appropriately directed at the ineffectiveness of antitrust policy. For example, Thomas Phillipon (2019) claims that airlines have become more concentrated at the national level; yet, he does not discuss the role of antitrust policy that allowed mergers among the major carriers that contributed to the alleged increase in concentration. He also does not assess the role of market forces by estimating the effects of the mergers on competition at the route level and on fares and service.[1]

Defenders of the efficacy of antitrust may reach unjustified conclusions. For example, Robert Litan (2018) discusses the efforts by the US Department of Justice (DOJ) to bring cases against firms that conspire to fix prices. He points out that although the DOJ has brought fewer price fixing cases over time, the fines the DOJ has imposed in cases where it has been victorious have gone up substantially over time. But Litan provides no evidence that the DOJ's actions have increased consumer welfare or have significantly deterred unlawful conduct.

In theory, criminal penalties, including fines and jail sentences, should act as a strong deterrent against price fixing by competitors. However, Tanja Gonzalez, Markus Schmid, and David Yermack (2019) find little evidence that the legal system holds managers of cartel firms that participate in price fixing accountable. Instead, managers enjoy greater job security and receive higher cash bonuses, while legal sanctions against individual managers are infrequent. To the extent the DOJ does levy penalties, they are against corporations instead of against their officers.

The implication of this evidence is not that the government should abandon its role to prevent price fixing or any other anticompetitive action; rather, it should pursue investigations that yield greater consumer benefits and not pursue investigations that yield few benefits and even cause harm. For example, Robert Crandall and Clifford Winston (2003) found that price-cost margins increased when the government and potential merger partners reached a consent decree to gain regulatory approval for a proposed merger. Opposition by the DOJ against the proposed vertical merger between AT&T and Time-Warner was characterized as personally motivated by President Trump because Time Warner owns CNN, which was extremely critical of

Trump. (Justice did not oppose the Disney–21st Century Fox merger because Fox is the parent company of Fox News, which supported Trump.) Such ideologically-based opposition could have prevented a merger that might enhance efficiency. In this case, a federal judge and appeals court did not agree with the DOJ's position, and they struck down the government's opposition to the merger.[2]

Currently, there is an outcry to regulate large technology firms, such as Google, Facebook, Amazon, and Apple. The CEOs of those firms appeared before the House Judiciary Subcommittee on Antitrust, Commercial, and Administrative Law in July 2020 and were questioned about alleged instances of aggressive and anticompetitive behavior. However, there was little discussion of the enormous benefits those firms have provided to consumers. And there was no presentation of retrospective evidence that consumers have been harmed by any of the technology firms' actions, or prospective evidence that any new government policies toward one or all of the technology firms would increase consumer welfare.

The CEOs pointed out that their firms are not monopolies and that they face intense competition, often from each other. In addition, Walmart is larger than Amazon in retail; Apple's iTunes must compete with Spotify and Amazon Prime; Facebook is losing customers to Snap and TikTok; and Google competes with Microsoft. Finally, the technology firms are increasingly vulnerable to competition from foreign competitors, especially from China.

In October 2020, the House Judiciary Committee issued a report condemning the abuse of monopoly power by Amazon, Apple, Facebook, and Google and recommending that those companies be restructured and that the antitrust laws be reformed to strengthen antitrust enforcement. Shortly after the report was issued, the DOJ and eleven states filed an antitrust claim against Google, which may be followed by suits against other major technology firms. The important issue in the Google suit is whether Google's extensive search capabilities actually are harming consumers and sellers and whether the Justice Department's remedy, if any, would increase their welfare.

MARKET FORCES

Markets generate competition from many sources that effectively complement government policy by curbing anticompetitive behavior that may have occurred otherwise and reduced consumer welfare. Markets require time to adjust to changing economic conditions to produce this outcome, but in the long run, market forces have addressed potentially anticompetitive situations by reducing entry barriers, encouraging international trade and foreign competition, challenging industry leaders, and enabling consumers to gain competitive advantages. Unfortunately, policymakers have periodically offset those sources of greater competition by adopting anticompetitive policies.[3]

Reducing Entry Barriers

Entry of additional firms into a market is the most common and effective way anticompetitive behavior is addressed and consumer welfare protected. In fact, the entry of new firms and the exit of unsuccessful firms occurs so often that the efficacy of the process is probably overlooked by most consumers. Potential entry has even more subtle effects, and the contestability literature indicates those effects may be important (Baumol and Willig 1986). But the ability of markets to generate competition is probably best illustrated by the different ways new entrants seek to overcome entry barriers and take market share from incumbent firms.

UNREGULATED ENTRY. Regulation of entry has protected incumbent firms from competition by preventing new firms from entering a market without obtaining formal regulatory approval. Because customers of the incumbent regulated firms may have to pay inflated prices or experience poor service or both, they have an incentive to explore alternative suppliers that are not subject to regulation, which could include providing the product or service themselves. For example, before the trucking industry was deregulated, some shippers who faced high regulated prices and poor service transported their own freight; thus, private trucking became a new entrant that overcame entry barriers and was not subject to price regulation. However, a firm's private trucks could not carry other firms' freight until the trucking industry was deregulated in 1980.

More recently, given that free entry cannot occur to relieve utility companies that are straining to keep up with demand and power outages, households have provided their own electricity in the short term by purchasing generators. Entry regulations limited competition in the taxi industry. But, Uber, Lyft, and other ride-sharing services have "cooperated" with consumers through apps to enter the industry. This is an example of markets taking many years before technological change facilitated entry that could generate competition that enhanced consumer welfare and helped government. One can either bemoan the time it took markets to help government or recognize, as I have stressed, that the process by which markets benefit consumers and help government is dynamic and that government is unlikely to take actions that benefit consumers while the process evolves.

CHALLENGING PATENT PROTECTION. Patents confer monopoly status on firms and protect them from competition for a specified period. Firms have tried to generate competition in such situations that could benefit consumers by "designing around a patent" to develop an alternative product that does not infringe on the patent's claims. For example, Michael Kremer (2001) indicated that firms have developed alternatives to certain vaccines that do not violate the original patent.[4]

FOREIGN FIRMS. Foreign firms provide many of the goods and services that US firms provide, and in certain US industries, they can overcome entry barriers and increase competition. For example, until the 1980s, the US automobile industry was dominated by the "Big Three," General Motors, Ford, and Chrysler, because of the large capital requirements to enter the industry and because consumers had not developed strong preferences for foreign vehicles. Following the 1970s energy shocks, foreign automobile companies got a toehold in the US market by offering small, fuel-efficient vehicles that consumers valued, and they eventually dominated sales in that size classification. Subsequently, they expanded production in other vehicle classifications, including SUVs and light trucks. Today, more new cars are sold in the United States by Toyota, Honda, and Nissan than by the "Big Three," who are now known as the "Detroit Three."

MERGER. A firm also can overcome entry barriers to serve a market by merging with another firm that already serves part of the market. For example, railroads, among other firms in network industries, have consummated end-to-end or vertical mergers to enter markets as a merged entity, thereby avoiding the possibly prohibitive expense of acquiring land and installing new track to serve additional markets, or by providing interline service that is viewed by shippers as inferior to single-line service (Winston and others 1990). Hence, a railroad serving market A to B could fully serve the entire market A to C by merging with a railroad that serves B to C. Marcin Krolikowski and Kevin Okoeguale (2018) argued that, in general, the industry restructuring that occurred in the aftermath of its deregulation was an efficient response to greater competition.

DIFFERENT TYPES OF ENTRY. Actual entry by new firms into a market usually has the strongest effect on prices and service, while potential entry also can have important effects. In addition, adjacent entry may be another important source of entry when actual and potential entries are not possible. For example, an airline may not be able to serve a route because one or both airports that comprise the route have slot or gate constraints that prevent entry. However, an airline could still reduce prices on that route by serving airports that are located close to the airports that comprise the route. Southwest Airlines has reduced fares on the route comprised of Washington, DC, Dulles Airport, and San Francisco Airport by entering the route comprised of Baltimore-Washington International Airport and Oakland Airport (Morrison and Winston 2000). Xinlong Tan, Clifford Winston, and Jia Yan (2020) estimated that adjacent competition provided by Southwest has reduced average fares 5 percent in the long run.

International Trade and Foreign Competition

As pointed out by Marc Melitz (2003), foreign competition is powerful because when a country opens its markets to international trade, the most productive firms expand their markets and the least productive are driven out by increased competition; thus, trade intensifies competition by increasing productivity. It also enhances consumer welfare by increasing product variety.

Robert Feenstra and David Weinstein (2017) estimated that the increase in US import shares between 1992 and 2005 raised US welfare by nearly 1 percent, with the source of the gain equally accounted for by the decline in price markups and by greater product variety. Mary Amiti and others (2017) found that China's imports to the United States following its entry into the World Trade Organization in 2001 reduced the price of manufactured goods paid by US consumers by reducing the price of inputs. Liang Bai and Sebastian Stumpner (2019) also found that Chinese imports reduced consumer prices. Finally, even professional sports teams in the United States have relied on foreign inputs to increase their competitiveness. For example, baseball players from the Dominican Republic and Venezuela accounted for nearly 20 percent of major leaguers in 2017.[5]

Challenging Industry Leaders

The large size and apparent dominance of tech firms have revived concerns that dominant firms may harm consumers by setting supra-competitive prices that would not attract entry in the long run that could reduce prices.

Generally, free markets do not allow any firm that has reached even near-monopoly status to have a quiet life for long because disruptive competition can emerge from firms that take advantage of technological change to challenge an incumbent firm in a different industry, and from new entrants in the same industry as the incumbent firm that turn out to be more efficient and innovative.

Vivek Wadhwa (2017) provided several examples of disruptive firms that took advantage of technological advances in other industries to challenge incumbent firms:

- Microsoft developed Skype more fully and Facebook created WhatsApp to decimate the costs of texting and roaming and caused telecommunications companies to lose a large amount of long-distance revenues.
- Netflix used internet connectivity and put Blockbuster video stores out of business.
- Uber took advantage of advances in smartphones and GPS and threatened the viability of monopoly taxi companies.
- Airbnb used similar technology to connect people with alternative forms of lodging and reduced hotel patronage.

Currently, it appears that Amazon may disrupt all forms of retail and cloud services, and Tesla, or a less well-known firm, could shake up the automobile and energy industries by making a technological breakthrough in batteries that makes it much less expensive to own and operate an electric vehicle than a gasoline-powered vehicle.

Clayton Christensen (1997) observed that dominant firms are not well-prepared to compete effectively against disruptive firms that adopt technologies developed in other industries because they are often in denial about the threat those firms pose. In 2018, Sears—the Amazon of its day—filed for bankruptcy after 132 years in business. Ultimately, the problem with Sears was that it lacked the vision to anticipate how the internet would be used to fundamentally change retailing. By 1993, Sears closed its national network of warehouses and catalog business; in 1995, Amazon shipped its first book. Walmart, the Amazon of the late twentieth century, remains one of the world's largest employers as of this writing, but it is struggling to compete with Amazon in online sales.

Alan Reynolds (2018) summarized the succession of firms that, over a number of decades, have been technology industry leaders only to be displaced by a new entrant in personal computers; internet browsing; the internet portal; search engines; personal digital assistants and cell phones; online music; and social networking. Brendan Markey-Towler (2018) theorized that both the evolutionary characteristics of markets and the organizational and behavioral factors within a firm make it difficult for monopolies to last very long. Although monopolies do not last, firms that are successful and that grow to become very large attract the attention of regulators, which may have a dampening effect on the firms continuing to innovate if the effect of innovation were to make the firm larger and more financially successful.

Enabling Competitive Advantages for Consumers

Thus far, I have mainly considered the effect that the supply side of markets, represented by individual sellers or firms, has on protecting consumer welfare. Markets also enable consumers to enhance their welfare by gaining competitive advantages, including bargaining more effectively and becoming more informed about prices.

Consumers have organized as a bargaining unit to negotiate lower prices for many products and services in markets with a small number of competitors. For example, shippers have been organized by third-party logistics firms to obtain lower freight transportation rates from a railroad. Consumers also have been organized to make bulk purchases at a discount—examples include Costco and Sam's Club—and they can join particular organizations, such as the American Automobile Association and AARP, to obtain lower prices on various services. Finally, consumers also can "create" competition where it may not appear to exist. For example, Curtis Grimm and Winston (2000) provided evidence that shippers who face limited railroad competition have obtained lower freight rates by exploiting potential geographical competition (shipping outputs to different destinations served by different railroads) or potential product competition (receiving different inputs from different origins served by different railroads).

The internet has enabled consumers to create competition by providing extensive information on alternative competitors, prices, and evaluations of product and service quality. Fiona Scott Morton (2006), for example, found that the internet benefited retail consumers by enabling them to reduce the prices they paid for new cars, term life insurance, books, and other products and services. When competition appears to be lacking temporarily, social media can discourage price gouging by providing signals for other suppliers to get their goods to the market, which would reduce excessive prices, and by publicizing the actions of offending firms, which may hurt their reputations and future sales.

SUMMARY

US industries are not perfectly competitive. Consumers suffer welfare losses from prices that are set above marginal costs and from products and services of poor quality. While those market inefficiencies may motivate intervention by the antitrust authorities, it is difficult to make an empirical case that antitrust policy and enforcement has significantly raised consumer welfare. Other government policy actions, discussed later, including entry regulations, tariffs, and patents, have harmed consumers.

I certainly do not advocate abolishing the antitrust laws on one extreme or strengthening and expanding them on the other. Instead, consistent with the evidence, my view is that antitrust enforcement should be restrained but strongly guard against: (1) horizontal agreements to fix prices or divide markets; (2) mergers that create monopolies; and (3) exclusionary behaviors by firms with market power that are harmful to consumers.

Markets have been an effective complement to antitrust policy by relentlessly developing alternative ways to generate competition from existing firms and from new entrants, who, if necessary, overcome entry barriers to ensure that monopolies are short-lived. Technological change can lead to the development of new and powerful competitors. Market forces also have enabled consumers to protect and advance their interest in obtaining lower prices and higher-quality products and services. In the long run, the forces of competition and technological change have greatly helped prevent anticompetitive behavior from being a significant threat to consumer welfare.

FIVE

Protecting Consumers When Technology Appears to Prevent Price Competition

Natural monopoly is an unusual situation where social costs are minimized when one (well-behaved) firm serves the market. Government regulation of the industry in question may be justified because competition under those conditions could result in industrywide bankruptcy or a monopoly survivor that extracts consumer surplus at the expense of total welfare. Economic regulation can, in theory, improve welfare by setting efficient regulated prices for the monopoly provider and by preventing other firms from entering the market, albeit with adverse incentives for innovation. Optimal prices could be set either at marginal cost with a subsidy or tax that enables the regulated monopolist to earn a normal return or at Ramsey prices that satisfy a break-even constraint.[1]

Natural monopolies may be short-lived, because changes in technology could enable more than one firm to serve a market efficiently. But that possibility may be masked if the industry continues to be subject to price and entry regulations, which make it appear that the industry has natural monopoly characteristics, such as scale economies, when, in fact, those scale economies reflect excess capacity caused by economic regulations. Market forces often suggest this sometimes may be the situation by showing, in limited cases, that competition could address problems created by alleged natural monopoly. New forms of competitive entry and technological change then combine to support the case for deregulating an industry that is subject to price and entry regulation. In the aftermath, market forces are unleashed and competition incentivizes firms to reduce costs, leading to lower prices, and to become more innovative, leading to improved and new products and services that greatly benefit consumers.

ECONOMIC REGULATION:
WITHIN THE US AND AT THE BORDER

Given deregulation of large parts of the transportation, communications, energy, and financial industries during the 1970s and 1980s, federal price regulations now are largely confined to agricultural commodities and international trade of selected products—neither of which are believed to invoke natural monopoly considerations. The evidence in *Government Failure* indicated that such regulation has produced large deadweight losses in the process of transferring resources from consumers to producers.

Recent research indicates that although some policymakers appear to recognize the inefficiencies created by agriculture and international trade regulations, they find it difficult to eliminate them and are, in fact, expanding them. Members of Congress have periodically introduced bills that, if passed, would have reduced agricultural commodity subsidies. However, congressional bills to eliminate subsidies have not passed; the subsidies have persisted, and the Congressional Budget Office has projected that their cost from 2017–27 will exceed $60 billion.[2] In addition, the Trump administration gave nearly $10 billion to farmers in 2018 and gave them an additional $16 billion in 2019–20 because of the losses farmers incurred from tariffs imposed by the administration on China (Reiley 2019).

The US imposed tariffs on $283 billion of its imports in 2018, with rates ranging from 10 to 50 percent. In response to the tariffs, China, the EU, Russia, Canada, Turkey, Mexico, Switzerland, Norway, India, and Korea all have filed cases against the US at the World Trade Organization, and many countries have retaliated by applying tariffs of their own. Trump also renegotiated the North American Free Trade Agreement (NAFTA) and the US-Korea Free Trade Agreement, and withdrew from the Trans-Pacific Partnership (TPP).

Recent research has estimated the costs of the increased trade protection and withdrawal from trade agreements. Mary Amiti, Stephen Redding, and David Weinstein (2019) estimate that by December 2018, new import tariffs were costing US consumers and the firms that import foreign goods an additional $3.2 billion per month in added tax costs and another $1.4 billion per month in deadweight welfare losses. Pablo Fajgelbaum and others (2019) estimate that the trade war with China has, as of 2018, generated an annual aggregate welfare cost from higher import prices of roughly $6.5 billion annually after accounting for tariff revenue and gains to producers, with consumers losing nearly $69 billion and with any employment gains failing to offset the cost of higher import prices. Aaron Flaaen, Ali Hortacsu, and Felix Tintelnot (2020) estimate that the average annual cost of the tariffs to consumers per job created is over $800,000 (after netting out the collected tariff revenues).[3] Urata Shujiro and Peter Petri (2017) argue that Trump's withdrawal of the United States from the TPP will generate significant losses because fewer US exports will reach the shores of countries that belong to the Asia-Pacific Economic Cooperation. We await research that determines whether the new United States-Mexico-Canada agreement improves US welfare over the gains from free trade created by NAFTA. In any event, Trump's primary objective of forcing China to change its policies in ways that benefited American workers and consumers, in fact, had the opposite effect.

Regulations of international transportation services continue to limit foreign competition and harm consumers. Air carriers are prevented from serving US international airline routes that are not subject to Open Skies agreements, which has resulted in an annual welfare cost estimated by Clifford Winston and Jia Yan (2015) of $4 billion. In addition, foreign airlines are prohibited from serving US domestic airline routes; that is, they are not granted cabotage rights and are prevented from developing their networks to offer seamless domestic and international travel.

Trade restrictions, as imposed by the Jones Act, also increase the cost of ocean transportation by requiring ships calling at two consecutive American ports to be built in the United States, be owned by American companies, fly the American flag, and be operated by American crews.[4] Clifford Winston (2013) pointed out that the Jones Act significantly raised the cost of ocean transportation for US shippers because the cost of US-built ships is much higher than the cost of comparable ships built overseas. The 2010 Open America's Waters Act would have repealed the Jones Act, with cost savings estimated by the US International Trade Commission of as much as $15 billion (Kashian, Pagel, and Brannon 2017), but Congress failed to pass it. Additional cost savings would be accrued from reduced highway congestion, less pavement damage, and fewer fatalities because some freight that is transported by heavy trucks on the nation's highways would have been carried over water by cargo ships.[5]

MARKET FORCES UNLEASHED BY PARTIAL AND FULL DEREGULATION

For many decades, the communications, transportation, energy, and financial industries were subject to price, entry, and exit regulation because regulatory authorities believed their technologies were characterized by significant scale and density economies that prevented those industries from becoming workably competitive and would result in either a monopoly provider or destructive competition.[6] Economic regulation, however, caused firms to operate with substantial X-inefficiencies and suppressed innovative activity.

Market forces unleashed by deregulation were an effective substitute for government regulation because they gave formerly regulated firms the freedom and economic incentive to compete more intensely by operating more efficiently, developing and adopting more advanced technology, and offering new, innovative products and services. The most efficient firms were able to substantially reduce excess capacity (the least efficient firms exited the industry) and engage in price competition while operating at close to minimum optimal scale.

This chapter discusses the scholarly evidence that has quantified the actual gains from industry deregulation and identifies several innovations that have emerged that have substantially benefited the US economy and enabled markets to substitute for or complement government policies to help achieve economic efficiency goals in other areas.[7] I take a long-run view to understand the effects of deregulation because firms took time to shed their regulatory-bequeathed capital structure and operating inefficiencies and to reduce costs and develop more efficient operations and a capital structure conducive to innovations. As firms became more efficient and innovative, the initial benefits from deregulation expanded. After discussing the actual benefits of market forces when policymakers withdrew industry regulation in favor of deregulation, I discuss the potential for market forces to generate additional benefits by substituting for remaining (inefficient) regulatory policies.

Communications Industry

The government started the communications industry on the path to deregulation by breaking up AT&T in 1982, which led to the entry of new competitors, healthy price competition, and, importantly, the development of new technologies and services.[8] The Telecommunications Act of 1996 accelerated the process by letting any communications business compete in any market and by deregulating the converging broadcasting and telecommunications markets.

TELECOMMUNICATIONS PRICES. As technology has evolved, telephony has been divided into wireless services, with effective competition among Sprint, T-Mobile, AT&T, and Verizon, and landline services. The result has been intense competition, with the price of long-distance service (interstate and intrastate toll service) falling more than 70 percent in real terms between 1984 and 2006 (Eisenach and Caves 2012). The benefits of entry into local telecommunications have varied by metropolitan area. For example, in the case of New York State, Nicholas Economides, Katja Seim, and V. Brian Viard (2008) found that entry into local telecommunications created by the 1996 act resulted in a welfare gain of roughly 6 percent of the average subscriber's bill.

NEW COMMUNICATIONS SERVICES. New communications services, which regulation had suppressed, generated hundreds of billions of dollars of annual benefits to consumers and producers, including voice mail and cellular service (Hausman 1997) and, more importantly, contributed to the development and widespread use of the internet (Litan and Rivlin 2001; Varian and others 2002; Goolsbee and Klenow 2006; and Holladay, Glusman, and Soloway 2011). In addition to studies that have used monetary expenditures to estimate the benefits of the internet, Erik Brynjolfsson and JooHee Oh (2012) estimated that the benefits of free internet services have amounted to more than $100 billion annually in the United States alone. All of the internet's benefits have been enhanced by broadband connections, which emerged in the last decade as a higher-quality alternative to a dial-up connection, with faster speeds and greater reliability (Greenstein and McDevitt 2011; Dutz, Orszag, and Willig 2012). But the cost and speed of US broadband, as compared with broadband in other developed countries, has been a matter of contention.[9]

High-speed internet service has also facilitated Over-the-Top (OTT) film and television content, such as Netflix, Sling TV, and the additional entry of streaming providers, possibly including Google and Microsoft. This content is not free, but it is highly valued by consumers, especially during the COVID-19 pandemic to watch first-run movies without going to a movie theater. OTT providers also have benefited consumers by becoming an important source of competition for cable television companies, which helps address concerns raised by Gregory Crawford, Oleksandr Shcherbakov, and Matthew Shum (2019) that cable television prices and qualities may be higher than socially optimal.

It can be debated whether at least part of the revolution in communications services may have occurred without deregulation in a regulated environment. However, there is no doubt that continued regulation would have significantly delayed the availability and increased the cost of those new communications services.

NEW CONSUMER SERVICES. New consumer services that have become available on mobile phone apps and online represent another source of significant benefits from communications deregulation. Notable examples include Tinder, with 50 million active users, who spend as much as ninety minutes per day on the app (Bilton 2014); online dating websites, which psychologists suggest promote better romantic outcomes than conventional off-line dating (Finkel and others 2012); and apps that facilitate the design of markets to match supply and demand in restaurants (Chase 2015), food trucks (Anenberg and Kung 2015), private air travel (Krupnick 2015), short-term hotel stays (Meyer 2016), and the like.[10]

Finally, consumers have derived enormous utility from the creation and growth of social media. For example, Hunt Allcott and others (2019) conducted an experiment that determines individuals' willingness to pay to access Facebook after their accounts were deactivated. Based on those valuations, the authors suggest that the annual consumer surplus gains from Facebook could be as much as hundreds of billions of dollars in the US alone. The sixty minutes that participants spend on Facebook each day, on average, is suggestive of the substantial value it provides. As discussed later, social media is helpful also in addressing information problems.[11]

David Byrne and Carol Corrado (2019) estimate the value of digital services to households based on the intensity with which they use their IT capital to consume content over networks. Digital services encompass electronic delivery of information, including data and content, across multiple platforms and devices like web or mobile. The authors estimate that innovations in digital services have contributed nearly 0.6 percentage points per year to US economic growth from 2007 to 2017.

Transportation Industry

Deregulation of transportation was aided, to a large extent, by intrastate deregulation, which occurred before the national movement took hold. For example, California and Texas airline markets were effectively deregulated. When policymakers saw comparisons of airline fares on routes in those two states with airline fares on regulated interstate routes of comparable distance, they liked what they saw because deregulated fares were considerably less than regulated fares, providing evidence that competition could work effectively in airline service. Similar comparisons and results were obtained for trucking rates.

Deregulation of the intercity freight transportation modes—rail, truck, and barge—and the intercity passenger modes—airlines and buses (Amtrak, a public corporation, continues to provide rail passenger service)—greatly improved the efficiency of their operations, reduced their costs and, thus, prices to users, and led to service innovations such as accelerated hub-and-spoke airline operations and just-in-time (JIT) freight service deliveries to optimize firms' inventories.[12] Steven Morrison and Clifford Winston (1999) estimated that consumers gained $50 billion annually from intercity transportation deregulation (in 1996 dollars), with the benefits composed of lower prices from cost reductions and improved services from operating innovations. No degradation of modal safety occurred, and there was only a modest decline in labor earnings. Deregulation revitalized a declining rail freight industry, which had experienced many carrier bankruptcies and may have become nationalized if deregulation had not enabled it to substantially improve its financial performance. Similarly, deregulation spurred the recent growth of the intercity bus industry; since 2008, its passenger miles have increased by 2 billion, while Amtrak's have increased less than 1 billion.

The benefits from intercity transportation deregulation extend beyond the transportation sector because transportation is an input to many other activities. Efficiency improvements in transportation modes have contributed to reductions in trade costs, decreases in production costs, and increases in competition spurred by the adoption of JIT inventory policies, and even improvements in scientific research, because less expensive airline flights have facilitated more face-to-face collaborations (Catalini, Fons-Rosen, and Gaulé 2018).

In combination with innovations in communications, trucking deregulation has greatly improved logistics and distribution in the United States by enabling Amazon to develop its business model of providing prompt and reliable delivery of a plethora of consumer goods; Ryder to provide idle commercial vehicles to users who want to expand trucking capacity efficiently; commercial truckers making deliveries to acquire new assignments immediately and to re-optimize their routings in real time to improve efficiency and service; and new entrants to offer digital freight apps that connect companies looking to ship goods with truck drivers.[13]

Competition in surface freight transport is likely to intensify as Amazon .com pushes into one-day shipping and continues to develop its own delivery network independent of UPS and Federal Express, which it no longer uses or allows third parties to use. Competition from Amazon has influenced UPS to modernize its operations with automated sorting and automated ground hubs, while FedEx is introducing full-service home delivery of bulky goods, including assembly. Walmart has even toughened delivery demands for its suppliers to compete more effectively with Amazon.[14] Finally, consumers have benefited enormously from the greater product variety offered by online sellers.[15]

Energy Industry

Pressures to regulate the interstate sales of natural gas culminated in a 1954 Supreme Court decision, *Phillips Petroleum Company v. State of Wisconsin*, which imposed federal price controls on natural gas sold in the interstate market (Davis and Kilian 2011). During the 1970s, price regulation created acute natural gas shortages that reflected firms' lack of incentives to explore and exploit new gas resources given that the regulated price was set below market value. In the short term, markets that are not subject to price regulation interpret high prices as a signal to explore alternative ways of increasing supply. Thus, the long-term effect of fully deregulating natural gas price controls in 1989 was to significantly reduce energy prices by encouraging technological innovations in horizontal drilling and hydraulic fracturing that enabled tremendous amounts of natural gas to be extracted profitably from underground shale formations that had been long thought to be uneconomical.

Once again, when government took a specific action, deregulation, that enabled markets to help, the combination of competition and technological change transformed an industry and increased social welfare. In 2000, natural gas produced from shale formations, or shale gas, accounted for only 1.6 percent of total US natural gas production. By 2017, so-called fracking accounted for an astonishing 60 percent. Catherine Hausman and Ryan Kellogg (2015) estimated that the shale gas revolution led to an increase in welfare for natural gas consumers and producers of $48 billion per year. Because energy affects so much of the economy, the energy boom also reduced the prices of goods, such as plastic, and helped decrease unemployment and increase wages (Feyrer, Mansur, and Sacerdote 2017). Susan Lund and others (2013) predicted that, by 2020, the expansion in energy supply would generate a 2 to 3.7 percent increase in annual GDP.[16]

Energy companies are continuing to pioneer new ways to extract oil faster and less expensively. For example, EOG Resources has created an app called iSteer, which enables rig workers at drilling sites and geologists who are miles away to share information that guides corrections of a drill bit's trajectory within minutes compared with an older process that took at least thirty minutes to make adjustments (Ailworth 2017). If other energy companies also contribute important innovations, it is conceivable that the US energy sector could seriously challenge OPEC's ability to control market prices.[17] Improvements to end a distribution bottleneck with pipelines opening in Texas to ship oil from the Permian Basin straddling Texas and New Mexico will result in a significant increase in the supply of domestic oil. The Permian Basin has become the world's second most productive oil field, and in 2018, the United States became a net petroleum exporter for the first time in seventy-five years.

Fracking has imposed social costs in terms of the deterioration in local amenities, including declines in health and increases in noise, crime, and traffic. Alexander Bartik and others (2019) assess the costs and benefits of fracking in terms of the change in both local productivity (that is, the change in real income) and local amenities. The authors find that willingness-to-pay (WTP) for allowing fracking equals $2,500 per household annually (4.9 percent of household income), and that WTP is quite heterogeneous. Grant Jacobsen (2019) also finds that fracking has benefited local communities economically, as measured by changes in wages and housing rental rates.[18]

Financial Industry

Federal and state regulations created inefficiencies in the financial industry by restricting the scale of banks, their ability to compete with one another, and the kinds of products and services commercial banks could offer. Charles Calomiris (2000) and Randall Kroszner and Phillip Strahan (2014) argued that federal banking deregulation during the early 1980s transformed the size, structure, and geographic range of US banks, the scope of banking services, and the nature of bank-customer relationships. Banks became more efficient and innovative because they operated in a more competitive environment, and they were able to diversify their risk by operating without geographic restrictions on their expansion. Consumers gained from the greater availability of loans and from improved banking services, including the allocation of capital through diversification and new indexing and pricing options (Litan and Wallison 2007).

Eliminating restrictions on geographical expansion and product lines also led to a more consolidated but generally less locally concentrated banking system that was dominated by large and diversified banking organizations that competed in multiple markets. Automated teller machines (ATMs) were developed in the early 1970s and reduced the value of geographical protections, especially for smaller, local banks. Some states decided to eliminate restrictions on branching, and Jith Jayaratne and Phillip Strahan (1996) found that banks in states that did so were able to improve their loan portfolios (allocation of capital).

Of course, the financial liberalization, integration, and wave of new financial products attributable to deregulation could also amplify economic cycles by allowing financial capital to flow from low-growth areas into booming ones, and by creating risks that investors failed to fully understand. Kroszner and Strahan (2014) pointed out that, during the 2000s, capital mobility fostered by securitization allowed funds collected from global capital markets to pay for housing booms in areas like Florida, Arizona, Nevada, and California. Had such areas been forced to rely on local pools of savings, the boom-bust cycle likely would have been smaller (Loutskina and Strahan 2015).[19]

Financial markets must demonstrate their robustness by reconciling the tension between operating in an environment that encourages innovation to foster cheaper credit and faster growth and avoiding the financial instability that may result from interconnections that accompany financial development. Kroszner and Strahan (2014) suggest that greater transparency is the key to addressing this tension, which, as discussed in the next chapter, is what markets have been doing more effectively by using advances in information technology to address problems of imperfect information.

Potential Gains from Further Deregulation

Industry deregulation occurred in a major wave in the late 1970s and early 1980s. It appeared that policymakers would take stock of the surge in competition and innovation and recognize that markets could improve on government intervention in many cases where workable competition was alleged to be infeasible. However, policymakers tend to compartmentalize, and they have continued to subject parts of the transportation, energy, and agricultural sectors to economic regulation, while President Trump introduced new regulations of the trade sector. The large benefits of industry deregulation have grown as firms have been able to take advantage of technological advances to innovate and engage in new activities. Policymakers could further enhance social welfare by eliminating economic regulations that restrict competition and innovation by allowing markets to allocate resources.

AIR, OCEAN, AND URBAN TRANSPORTATION. Deregulation of airline travel in US markets indicated that intense competition could develop and generate lower prices and improve service, especially flight frequency. Travelers could accrue similar benefits if policymakers pursued global airline deregulation by negotiating open skies agreements on all international airline routes, which would eliminate price and entry regulations, and by allowing foreign airline carriers to serve US routes by granting cabotage rights.

Winston and Yan (2015) estimated that US travelers have gained $4 billion annually (in 2000 dollars) in lower fares and more frequent flights from the open skies agreements that have been negotiated thus far, and that travelers could gain an additional $4 billion annually (in 2000 dollars) if the US negotiated agreements with other countries that have a significant amount of international passenger traffic. Discount or low-cost carriers have accounted for a large share of the benefits of domestic deregulation. Similarly, low-cost carriers that develop an extensive international route network could increase the benefits of open skies if they were free to serve any international market they desire.

Xinlong Tan, Clifford Winston, and Jia Yan (2020) analyzed the potential effect on air travelers of granting cabotage rights by first estimating the effect that the leading low-cost carrier (LCC) in the US, Southwest Airlines, and the leading low-cost carriers in the European Union (EU), Ryanair and EasyJet, have had on fares in their respective markets. The authors found that Southwest reduced fares 30 percent and Ryanair and EasyJet reduced fares 20 percent, the difference attributable in large part to entry barriers to EU airports, such as the limited availability of slots and gates, which are greater than the entry barriers to US airports. The authors then simulated a stylized example of cabotage by determining the effect that the entry of an EU LCC into US markets would have on travelers' fares assuming those markets were not served by either Southwest Airlines or another LCC or ultra-low-cost carrier, such as Spirit or Frontier Airlines, and that entry of the EU LCC reduced fares

25 percent—that is, less than Southwest's average effect on fares but more than its average effect on fares in EU markets. Under those assumptions, the authors found that EU LCC entry on US routes would provide a modest annual welfare gain of $1.6 billion because Southwest and other US LCCs provided service on routes that accounted for a large fraction of US passengers, roughly 80 percent.

However, it is likely those initial gains would expand greatly under a more comprehensive cabotage policy that would allow entry by other foreign carriers, not just by an EU LCC. Competition in a more integrated global airline market would encourage both foreign and US carriers to restructure their networks, resulting in greater entry on international routes and on domestic routes that feed those routes. The case for allowing cabotage strengthens greatly as the framework evolves from a static network to a network restructured by new foreign entrants and domestic carriers that facilitates and encourages seamless international travel. Competition under cabotage would provide additional protection to US travelers' welfare because excessive fares on domestic routes could discourage travel on international routes.

Repealing the Jones Act and deregulating US coastal ocean shipping would spur international competition in water freight transportation because a ship from any country would be allowed to call at two consecutive American ports without having been built in the United States, being owned by American companies, flying the American flag, and being operated by American crews. Cost efficiency would be improved because the cost of US-built ships is much higher than the cost of comparable ships built overseas.

As noted, the annual benefits estimated by the US International Trade Commission from repealing the Jones Act would be roughly $15 billion (Kashian, Pagel, and Brannon 2017)—a lower bound because, as in other deregulated industries, ocean transportation technology is likely to improve significantly and benefit shippers.[20] Deregulating ocean transportation would also increase competition in all modes of surface freight transportation because low-cost cargo ships traveling over a "natural" infrastructure (for example, along the US east coast) would capture some freight that is currently transported by railroads on their track network and by heavy trucks on the nation's interstate and local highways, thereby reducing congestion and pavement damage caused by trucks.

The justification for regulating taxis in US metropolitan areas has long been questioned by economists.[21] A powerful case for deregulating for-hire urban transportation has been made by the emergence of digital ride-sharing platforms, such as Uber and Lyft. As explained by Robert Hahn and Robert Metcalf (2017), ride-sharing companies connect drivers and passengers and set real-time prices to reduce excess capacity. Typically, customers use an app on their smartphones to request a ride from their origin to a specific destination. The platforms use GPS to arrange for the pickup and to determine a driver's best route, and the platform's database allows for an efficient payment system. Many urban and suburban travelers have flocked to ride-sharing services and have abandoned taxis because they pay lower fares and experience less delay and uncertainty about when they will be picked up. Hyeonjun Hwang, Clifford Winston, and Jia Yan (2020) find that travelers in major US cities have gained several billions of dollars annually from the introduction of ride-sharing. Caitlin Gorback (2020) finds that UberX's entry has caused New York City house prices to increase 4 percent by improving residents' accessibility and the area's amenities.

Taxis were regulated in most US cities because of concerns about an oversupply of vehicles that would lead to destructive competition, congestion, and a degradation of safety. However, ride-sharing companies have shown that technological advance has transformed for-hire urban transportation by enabling unregulated workable competition to be possible.[22] Taxi medallions in New York City, once marking an exclusive right to provide car hire service, now sell for a fraction of their peak value of $1.3 million in 2014, and the number of yellow cabs is now dwarfed by cars working for ride-hail apps (Hu 2017).

Similar to other industries, such as railroads, that once welcomed regulations until they created an unbearable cost burden, taxis must be deregulated to become more adaptable and to use the technology that has enabled ride-sharing companies to attract such a large share of their passengers.[23] Instead, New York City, for example, instituted a cap to limit the number of licenses for ride-hailing services in a forlorn effort to enable taxi drivers to improve their financial condition.

Other cities and states have tried to resist the ride-sharing innovation. Actions include imposing regulations that have discouraged Uber and Lyft from operating, instituting extra charges on ride-sharing companies and requiring them to pay supplementary charges, some of which may be used to fund bus and rail transit operations, and insisting, as in the case of Washington, DC, that a new ride-sharing company, Via, expand its coverage to the entire city or risk losing its license. By not deregulating taxis and making it more difficult for ride-share companies to operate efficiently, government is not fully capitalizing on an opportunity to allow markets to improve local transportation.

ELECTRICITY. The electricity industry is a case where markets have shown they can reduce regulatory inefficiencies, but no one has figured out how to completely deregulate the electricity market, including transmission and distribution, to reduce current inefficiencies and benefit consumers.

The electricity market is more complex than other industries that have been deregulated because vertically integrated utilities own both the generation assets (production) and the wires (transmission), which has meant that deregulated firms would be able to shut out competition from other producers. Firms operating in a deregulated environment also could exercise market power by withholding capacity in the short run to drive up prices without fear of entry. A fundamental technological challenge is that electricity cannot be stored to ensure that supply matches demand, so equilibrium must be achieved in real time without causing the grid to crash.[24]

Regulation of electricity markets has led to the same inefficiencies that regulation has led to in other industries: utilities have a financial incentive to overinvest in labor-saving capital facilities, which inflates their costs; they have little incentive to innovate and operate efficiently; and prices do not adequately reflect the marginal cost of service, especially during peak periods. At the same time, California has shown that it has not learned from its poorly conceived electricity deregulation in 2000–2001 that resulted in frequent power shortages, sporadic blackouts, and astronomical wholesale prices and market manipulation. Recently, California has experienced rolling blackouts, and a big part of the problem is that state regulators have left the state exposed to buying large amounts of imported electricity on the spot market during peak periods on days when there is extreme energy demand (Smith and Blunt 2020). California has significantly increased the share of its electricity production by solar energy, which falls off as the sun goes down and as people want to turn their lights on. On several days, California's imports of electricity from other states have fallen short of the drop in available renewable energy.

Regulatory reform has proceeded in steps to reduce costs by developing competition in parts of the production process that do not have elements of a natural monopoly. States have restructured the industry such that electric utilities divested ownership of transmission networks from production; however, no state has passed restructuring legislation since the California deregulation fiasco. States that had already restructured before the California crisis have not returned to vertically integrated electricity production and transmission. Steve Cicala (2015) estimated that deregulated utility plants have reduced the price they pay for coal by 12 percent, and they have shifted to more productive coal mines for a $1 billion annual reduction in expenditures. Peter Hartley, Kenneth Medlock III, and Olivera Jankovska (2017) estimated that electricity reform and retail pricing in Texas benefited consumers in competitive areas. Following deregulation, Texas households are paying electricity rates that are nearly 20 percent lower than the national average.[25]

Federal actions embodied in the Energy Policy Act of 1992 and subsequent Federal Energy Regulatory Commission orders gave electric utilities a chance to realize additional efficiency gains by requiring open-access, nondiscriminatory tariffs for wholesale electricity transmission. Firms were able to make output decisions in service areas in a liberalized environment and realize gains from trade instead of using command and control–type operations. Cicala (2017) found that by placing greater reliance on markets, firms reallocated output among existing power plants efficiently and reduced production costs $3 billion per year.

Although partial deregulation of electricity has shown that it can reduce certain X-inefficiencies, full deregulation that would generate significant gains to consumers awaits a major technological breakthrough to reduce the cost of storing electricity, enable real-time pricing to be practical, and result in an unregulated competitive equilibrium, where firms could connect storage facilities to the electricity grid (Kleit 2016).[26] Policymakers would have to reform their regulations and implement deregulation carefully to avoid a repeat of the California experience.

AGRICULTURAL SUBSIDIES. The case for eliminating costly agricultural subsidies and for allowing market forces to allocate resources in farming has become even stronger because subsidized farm families have significantly elevated their incomes above the income of the average US household by taking nonfarm jobs. The total number of US farms has continued to decline as more countries have grown food for their own populations as well as for export. Subjecting farmers to market forces without providing subsidies would incentivize them to adopt new practices and technologies to improve productivity and to be more effective competitors in the global agricultural market.

International Trade

Policymakers have reduced consumer welfare by imposing tariffs or quotas to protect certain industries and workers from competition, not to correct an alleged market failure that would lead to destructive competition or monopoly. Market forces—that is, free trade—can raise consumer welfare, but can it do so without significantly harming specific industries and workers? Markets can overcome those potential problems but are often prevented from doing so by government policies that constrain adjustments in the labor market.

Joseph Shapiro (2016) put the most recent estimate of the global gains from international trade at $5.5 trillion annually, which greatly exceeded the environmental costs due to additional CO_2 emissions. The gains to the United States from free trade tend to be smaller than the gains other countries receive because a significant fraction of US trade occurs intra- rather than internationally. In any case, Armaud Costinot and Andres Rodriguez-Clare (2018) reported that the US gains from trade ranged from 2 to 8 percent of GDP, while Gary Hufbauer and Zhiyao Lu (2017) calculated that US output in 2016 was $2 trillion greater than it otherwise would have been because of greater trade and financial integration since 1950.

Turning to specific policies, Lorenzo Caliendo and Fernando Parro (2015) found that the US achieved modest welfare gains from NAFTA's tariff reductions. Targeted reductions of import barriers could benefit consumers of specific products. For example, a provision of the Medicare Modernization Act of 2003 empowered the FDA to allow drug imports whenever they were deemed safe and could reduce consumers' expenditures on drugs. However, as pointed out by Tim Wu (2017), the FDA has not aggressively used the law to reduce drug prices.

It has been argued that the benefits from trade—or globalization—have lowered wages and employment in the industries affected by foreign competition. In fact, the expansion of trade has coincided with a slowdown in the growth of global wages. In the United States, wages and salaries have risen 2 percent annually following the 2007–2009 financial crisis, down from 2.9 percent in the five years before the crisis. Shushanik Hakobyan and John McLaren (2016) report evidence that blue collar workers in industries highly affected by NAFTA experienced wage growth that was substantially lower than the wage growth workers in other industries experienced.

The effects of US trade with China have attracted considerable attention, especially because of the ongoing trade war between the two countries. Liang Bai and Sebastian Stumpner (2019) find that, during 2004–2015, Chinese imports reduced US prices by roughly 0.2 percentage points annually. Two-thirds of the effect is driven by lower inflation among existing goods and one-third of the effect is driven by the introduction of new goods and the disappearance of old goods, implying that pro-competitive effects and variety gains are at work.

The controversial aspect of trade with China involves its effect on employment. David Autor, David Dorn, and Gordon Hanson (2016) estimated that imports from China resulted in competition that claimed 1.2 to 2.4 million US jobs between 1999 and 2011. However, other researchers have questioned those findings or placed them in a more appropriate context. Robert Feenstra, Hond Ma, and Yuan Xu (2017) argued that job losses from imports must be balanced against job gains from exports. When the authors made that adjustment, they found the net job effect of exposure to trade with China was roughly balanced. Zhi Wang and others (2018) offered an additional response by pointing out that US firms use imported inputs (for example, computers and telecommunications equipment) to improve efficiency and potentially increase employment. They found this effect caused net employment in the United States from trading with China to increase and enabled American workers as a group to experience an increase in real wages, although many noncollege educated workers experienced a decline in real wages. Finally, Nicholas Bloom and others (2019) use confidential US Census microdata and find no evidence that Chinese import competition generated net job losses. Instead, competition from China reallocated employment from manufacturing to services, and from the US heartland to the coasts. Almost all of the manufacturing job losses are in large multinational firms that expanded in services; thus, they appear to have offshored manufacturing employment to reduce labor costs and created US service-sector jobs.[27]

While it is still true that some workers have clearly been hurt by more liberalized trade agreements, the social costs may be overstated, and they should not be used as an excuse to foreclose the large benefits trade has generated. A more efficient solution would be to allow labor markets to respond fully to changes in product markets that may be affected by free trade. For example, Eric Cunningham (2016) pointed out that import competition contributed to the decline in furniture making in Hickory, North Carolina, but the Hickory labor force adjusted by producing fiber-optic cable and by working in other areas of technology. Market forces enabled Hickory to change and flourish to the point where even some furniture manufacturers transitioned into custom, high-end products.

Government policies, such as Trade Adjustment Assistance (TAA), do not respond effectively to changes in product markets and, in fact, other government policies have impeded efficient responses.[28] For example, unemployed workers could adjust to secure employment by moving to other areas of the country that have been less impacted by trade. But occupational licensing, zoning that inflates housing prices, and the like have significantly slowed labor force migration, and social policies have created disincentives for some unemployed workers to aggressively seek employment. According to the US Census Bureau, the share of the population that has moved since 1985 has declined by half, from 20 percent to slightly more than 10 percent in 2017.

SUMMARY

The totality of the evidence in this chapter supports a clear case that when competition is unleashed in a market environment as a substitute for price and entry regulations, incentives for production efficiency intensify, innovation and technological change flourish, and society gains enormous benefits. The evidence also suggests that market forces have the potential to produce additional benefits if policymakers give them the freedom to do so by withdrawing regulatory impediments to competition.

The alleged economies of scale that appeared to justify industry price, entry, and exit regulations were often created by regulatory constraints and by disincentives for firms to optimize their operations and reduce excess capacity. Deregulation, and even partial deregulation, have enabled the most efficient firms to reduce costs, operate closer to minimum optimal scale, and engage in intense workable competition. As firms have adjusted to their deregulated environment, they have introduced new innovative products and services, including but not limited to:

- Cellular service, voice mail, and, more importantly, the development and widespread use of the internet.
- New consumer services that have become available on mobile phone apps and online.
- Improved transportation network design, such as hub-and-spoke operations, and improved logistics and delivery services, such as reliable JIT freight deliveries to optimize firms' inventories, and fast deliveries by Amazon and others of a wide variety of consumer goods.
- Innovations in horizontal drilling and hydraulic fracturing that have enabled energy companies to extract tremendous amounts of natural gas from underground shale formations that were long thought to be uneconomical.
- Improved banking services, including the allocation of capital through diversification and new indexing and pricing options.

Litan (2014) puts the value of the benefits of those products and services in the trillions of dollars.

Markets also could be effective as a substitute for inefficient regulatory policies in:

- Air transportation, where regulations have prohibited US domestic markets from being served by foreign airlines and have prevented price competition and new entry on certain international routes that do not have open skies agreements.

- Water transportation, where the Jones Act has prevented competition that could be provided by foreign ocean container ships.

- Personal transportation, where taxis have been subject to price and entry regulations in most cities, and ride-sharing companies have been discouraged from operating in certain cities by regulations and supplementary charges.

- Agriculture, where unjustified subsidies for farmers are borne by taxpayers and discourage productivity growth.

- International trade, where inefficient government policies reduce US consumer welfare and limit labor market adjustments, which could reduce trade's potentially adverse effects on employment.

Finally, an innovation that could significantly reduce the cost of storing electricity could facilitate extensive deregulation of the electricity industry, which would greatly benefit all consumers by reducing costs, improving pricing efficiency, and increasing service reliability. Such an innovation also could occur in the provision of energy from alternative sources, such as wind and solar, which I discuss in the context of reducing negative externalities.

Poorly designed deregulation, as occurred in California in electricity, can undermine support for the policy when, in fact, a credible opportunity to deregulate should be explored because there are enormous costs to suppressing competition and preventing markets from providing incentives for efficiency and spurring innovations that can greatly benefit the entire economy.

SIX

Enabling Individuals to Make More-Informed Decisions

If consumers are uninformed or misinformed about the quality of a product or service, they may derive less utility from it than they expected. Similarly, workers may become injured or ill because they lack information about the health risks they encounter in product markets or their workplace. In those situations, government intervention may be justified to enable individuals to make more-informed decisions in product and labor markets. The federal government empowers regulatory agencies to direct firms to provide complete and accurate information about their products, services, and workplaces and to ensure they meet reasonable safety standards.

Markets transmit information to consumers from various sources so they can make more-informed choices. Sources include sellers' informative advertising; signals of product quality based on brand names, certifications, and warranties; other consumers' word of mouth and their reviews of a product or service; and third parties' independent and objective assessments of a product or service. Compensating wage differentials provide information about risks at workplaces. As in other areas where markets help government, technological change plays a significant role by improving the efficacy of existing sources of information and creating new ones.

GOVERNMENT INFORMATION POLICIES

The evidence in *Government Failure* indicated that government actions generally amounted to weak solutions in search of a problem because there was little evidence of large welfare costs attributable to imperfect information. The explosion of information technology during the past few decades, most notably high-speed internet services, suggests it is even less likely that information failures are eroding consumer welfare because it is much easier for individuals to obtain safety and other information about products, services, and workplaces. Nonetheless, research continues to find that information policies deployed by the government are often ineffective and impose costs on consumers, including:

- *Mandated disclosures*, which are ignored by the vast majority of consumers (Ben-Shahar and Schneider 2014; Ben-Shahar 2016; Seira, Elizondo, and Laguna-Muggenburg 2017).[1]

- *Regulations by federal agencies*, including the Consumer Product Safety Commission (Frankel 2019), National Highway Traffic Safety Administration (Ivory 2015), Federal Drug Administration (Philipson and Sun 2008; Ip 2016; Kaplan 2017; Hudgins 2019), Occupational Safety and Health Administration (Leeth and Hale 2013), Federal Communications Commission (Krause 2019); and Security and Exchange Commission (White 2017).

- *Occupational licensing*, including moderate low-income professions (Flanders and Roth 2017; Han and Kleiner 2016), lawyers (Winston and Karpilow 2016), opticians (Mills and Timmons 2018), and certified public accountants (Barrios 2018).

- *Financial regulations*, including the Sarbanes-Oxley Act of 2002 (Coates and Srinivasan 2014) and the Dodd-Frank Act of 2010 (Bordo and Duca 2018; Ferrara 2018).

There are some instances, however, where information policies and recent policy reforms have been effective and benefited consumers. At the federal level, for example, Sumit Agarwal and others (2015) estimated that regulatory limits on credit-card fees have saved consumers nearly $12 billion per year.[2] The US Department of Transportation has required airlines to give air travelers a full refund at no charge if they cancel a flight reservation within twenty-four hours of making their reservation, and has reduced the taxes paid by travelers by requiring airlines to include all ticket taxes in advertised fares (Bradley and Feldman 2020). The FDA has increased the share of new drugs approved through fast-track programs that skip or shorten major steps that other drugs must pass from 38 percent in 2008 to 73 percent in 2018 (Loftus 2019). And Martin Baily, Aaron Klein, and Justin Schardin (2017) concluded that the capital requirements imposed by the Dodd-Frank Act have made the financial sector safer today than it was before the crisis because the requirements increase with the riskiness of a loan. Currently, banks have leverage ratios that average around 90 percent compared with roughly 95 percent before the crisis, a notable change. In addition, the act provides greater transparency and oversight of financial derivatives.

At the state level, workers' compensation laws, which require employers to purchase insurance to compensate workers if they are injured at work, have provided a strong incentive for employers to maintain safe workplaces because workers' compensation insurance rates are tied to a firm's injury experience (Moore and Viscusi 1990).

Examples of potentially beneficial reform begin with Dodd-Frank, whose legal framework is still in flux a decade after the financial crisis (Tarullo 2019). In particular, the framework does not deal effectively with threats to financial stability outside the perimeter of regulated banking organizations, most notably from forms of shadow banking, including hedge funds, structured investment vehicles, money market funds, and other nonbank financial institutions. Lawrence White (2017) argues that SEC regulations of the credit ratings industry should be reformed to reduce barriers to entry and increase competition that would benefit investors.

The Occupational Safety and Health Administration (OSHA) could be more effective if it accounted for compensating wage differentials, a market response to imperfect information at workplaces that reflects workplace risks and helps reduce occupational injuries by incentivizing firms to improve safety. OSHA should inspect a greater share of small firms that are less likely to compensate workers for safety risks and that employ more disadvantaged workers, such as non-English speaking immigrants, who are less likely to receive compensating wage differentials (Leeth and Hale 2013).[3]

Finally, occupational licensing can create entry barriers to employment in an occupation and raise wages and prices and limit the availability of services. State licensing boards should reform the stringency of occupational licensing where those effects cause individuals to harm themselves because they either try to perform dangerous tasks themselves (for example, attempt to fix faulty electrical wiring) or choose to do without the service (for example, eschew dental checkups).

MARKET FORCES

By significantly reducing the cost of searching for, collecting, and distributing information about products, services, and workplaces throughout much of the world, the revolution in information technology that followed deregulation of the communications industry has increased the dissemination and content of information provided by traditional sources. The following sections highlight the new information sources and technologies consumers can use to enhance their welfare and that further complement and could substitute for some government information policies.

Improving Traditional Sources of
Information Generated by Markets

Previously, I reported evidence that the availability of retail price information on the internet has helped consumers improve their bargaining power in certain cases and, in general, pay lower prices for various products and services. Speaking from personal experience, I have benefited from information on the distribution of actual sales prices for automobiles with specific accessories to negotiate a price for a new vehicle with the dealer at the lower tail of the sales price distribution. Because dealers know such information exists, they are less able to make false claims about their prices and the cost of vehicle options.

Management consulting companies, such as Accenture, have concluded that it has become vital for a firm to develop a website that engages consumers by providing detailed, high-quality information; builds relationships through interactive exchanges; and encourages return visits by current and potential customers through the use of promotions, premium services, clubs, and other online innovations. Sellers also are applying new technologies to provide more information about their products and services on their websites. For example, Red's Best has developed a software system that electronically tracks a daily catch from the moment fishermen offload their vessels onto their trucks to develop a chain of custody, label the catch correctly, and subject it to quality control on its journey to customers. The data on its website include who caught the fish, where the fish were caught, and how the fish were caught, thus enabling consumers to make informed decisions about where their fish comes from and to significantly reduce the likelihood that they will be deceived about the quality or even the type of fish they consume.[4]

There also has been an explosion of websites devoted to forums where consumers of various products and services share their experiences with millions of potential customers and give an overall quality rating. Websites that consumers frequently consult for advice before they choose to purchase a product or service include TripAdvisor, Angie's List, IMDB, Amazon Reviews, Yelp, and the like, not to mention social media reviews on Facebook and Twitter. Such forums even can assist government efforts to provide potentially useful information.[5] Online website reviews have become so important to a firm's reputation that some managers spend considerable time responding carefully to negative reviews to soften their impact on future sales, and they even may ask the aggrieved party to contact them to resolve the matter satisfactorily.

Finally, third parties that provide objective reviews are another source of online information about the quality of products and services. Some publications, such as *Zagat* and *Consumer Reports*, played that role for many years before the internet existed, and they continue to do so online. Websites that have recently gained prominence include CNET, which publishes reviews on technology and consumer electronics, and CarFax, which provides vehicle history reports on used cars and light trucks, including information on mileage and repairs. The information provided by CarFax is undoubtedly more responsible for preventing consumers from buying a "lemon" in the used car market than are states' "lemon laws."[6]

Markets have used technology to increase transparency in other ways to address informational asymmetry. eBay was one of the first and biggest online platforms to facilitate direct transactions between private buyers and sellers. Tobias Klein, Christian Lambertz, and Konrad Stahl (2016) pointed out that eBay increased market transparency by lowering the opportunity costs to buyers to share negative experiences via detailed seller ratings (DSRs), with one to five stars, on the accuracy of the item description, communication, shipping speed, and shipping charges. The authors found that greater transparency caused sellers to improve their behavior without causing them to exit the platform, and reduced buyer regret, thereby leading to higher product quality outcomes. Similarly, Amazon has increased market transparency by allowing consumers to review (and rate on a five-star scale) products sold on their platform and provide feedback on product packaging. Reviews by individuals who purchased the item on Amazon are tagged as "verified purchase." For items sold by third-party merchants on the Amazon platform, Amazon allows customers to provide feedback (reviews and ratings) on both the products and the merchant's customer service.[7] Reimers and Waldfogel (2021) find that Amazon star ratings provide much greater benefits to purchasers of books than do reviews by professional critics in traditional media outlets.

Taxis have been able to overcharge passengers by taking a longer route to their destinations when passengers were unfamiliar with the area or were disinterested in the cost because their employer was paying for the trip. Uber and other ride-sharing companies have addressed this information problem with a transparent pricing system, which requires a receipt for the passenger with the name of the driver and a map of the actual journey. Liu, Brynjolfsson, and Dowlatabadi (2021) find that taxi drivers take longer routes that are more time consuming than Uber drivers take for matched airport routes by an average of 8 percent, with nonlocal passengers experiencing even longer routes and travel times.

Finally, information technology even is helping consumers seek redress if they believe they have been deceived. A new app called DoNotPay is being developed to allow users to sue anyone in small claims court in any county in the country for up to $25,000 without the help of a lawyer. In particular, the app aims to fight unfair bank fees, earn refunds from rideshare companies, and the like (Tashea 2018).

Allowing Markets to Address Other Information Problems
The Affordable Care Act includes a provision requiring chains with twenty or more locations that serve "restaurant-type food" to post calorie and other nutritional information. Proponents of menu labeling requirements assert that making nutritional information available to consumers would encourage them to choose lower-calorie meals and would, possibly, affect the items offered by various food establishments. The Food and Drug Administration (FDA) has not finalized a compliance date for the labeling provision, which may turn out to be fortunate, because market forces should be allowed to resolve the matter.[8]

My argument is that if consumers valued nutritional information and were willing to pay the cost incurred by food establishments to provide it, then the hyper-competitive restaurant industry would surely provide it. However, as indicated previously, little evidence exists that consumers' choices would be influenced by nutritional information. At the same time, it would be costly for food establishments to reprint menus and revise displays to include nutritional information. As a potential alternative source of information, digital ordering platforms, which have been introduced in recent years and are accounting for a growing share of food sales (Hughes 2017), can enable the market to make an efficient determination of whether to provide nutritional information instead of the government requiring it.

Because a food establishment can sell its offerings online, cost should not be a significant issue when it decides to include nutritional information; thus, establishments that think nutritional information would be informative to consumers and would help increase their sales are likely to provide it. Food establishments that do not provide such information would then suffer financial consequences if consumers truly valued it. Arguably, the FDA still should set a compliance date for the original provision in the ACA; it would impose little cost as digital ordering platforms are used more widely. However, an inflexible government regulation may prevent efficient market forces from responding to evolving consumer preferences by providing more, less, or different nutritional information.

FDA-approved medication prescription information has tended to lag behind the range of uses that medications were being prescribed for by licensed physicians. Shea and others (2018) recommended the FDA collaborate with the developers of clinical guidelines and drug compendia to evaluate existing evidence about approved drugs and to suggest updates to labeling. Given its expertise, the private sector would determine the uses of old drugs that are safe and effective, and those determinations would be adopted by the FDA. However, as pointed out by Alexander Tabarrok (2018), if it were desirable to allow private market participants to approve new uses for old drugs, then the FDA's drug approval power could be transferred to the same participants who would be allowed to approve new uses for new drugs. Similarly, it is not clear why the FDA exercises enforcement of mobile apps that could transmit useful medical information instead of allowing private users to determine the value of those apps.[9]

Fines issued by the Federal Communications Commission (FCC) to discourage unwanted information generated by robocallers to unsuspecting households have been ineffective. Fortunately, apps have been developed, including Truecaller, Hiya, and Call Control, that identify and block robocalls, telemarketers, and fraudulent calls like IRS scams. Telecommunication companies, such as Verizon, also offer free apps for this purpose.

Workplace Safety

Market forces have generated compensating wage differentials to transmit information about safety risks at workplaces that have contributed to a decline in occupational injuries for private industry. However, instead of paying employees higher wages to work in hazardous conditions, some firms recently have started to use new technology to perform dangerous tasks that workers used to perform. For example, companies, such as BNSF Railway, use drones instead of employees to inspect parts of their plant that could pose safety hazards, such as underneath a highly elevated railroad bridge. Recently, the North Carolina Department of Transportation announced it would be using a drone startup company, Skydio, to inspect its bridges. In addition to improving safety, using drones instead of traditional inspection methods could reduce taxpayers' costs of bridge inspections.

Eliminating Government Information Policies and Relying on Market Forces

By either eliminating or at least reconsidering the social desirability of some of their information policies, policymakers have begun to acknowledge that markets complement or can substitute for their efforts to address imperfect information about products and services that may harm the public. For example, a careful examination of *Consumer Reports* over time suggests that market competition has resulted in technological advances that have made automobiles much more reliable and less likely to have a serious unknown defect that threatens a motorist's safety. Accordingly, some states have discontinued vehicle safety inspections that were required for residing motorists. Alex Hoagland and Trevor Woolley (2018) found that eliminating vehicle inspections in New Jersey did not cause an increase in the frequency or intensity of accidents due to vehicle failure. Daniel Sutter and Marc Poitras (2002) concluded that the continued existence of vehicle inspection programs can be attributed to status quo bias instead of a public interest or special interests explanation.

Information has become increasingly available to assess the quality of workers in any occupation. Some states, such as Florida, are considering a law that would eliminate license requirements for hair braiders, nail polishers, and timekeepers and announcers at sporting events, and that would scale back licensing requirements for other occupations.[10] As of 2019, plumbers in Texas are no longer subject to occupational licensing and state regulations (Byrne 2019). Individuals can offer commercial plumbing services without completing agency-required education and tests.

Markets are responding to the inefficiencies caused by occupational licensing by providing some services at lower costs without harming the public. The services are not provided by licensed practitioners with a professional degree, but they give certain individuals the opportunity to obtain services they otherwise would not obtain. The following examples in legal, medical, and dental services eventually may strengthen the case for eliminating occupational licensing and for allowing markets to inform consumers about the quality of a practitioner.

LEGAL SERVICES. LegalZoom is an online technology company that provides low-cost legal services for families and small business. Through its platform, customers can access legal help for products including wills and living trusts, business formation documents, copyright registrations, and trademark applications. Low-cost services also have begun to be provided in a few instances by quasi-lawyers, who have some legal training but have not graduated from a three-year law school accredited by the American Bar Association. For example, Washington and Utah have permitted limited license legal technicians, who have not passed the bar and are not full-fledged lawyers, to provide a limited range of legal services at low cost, while Arizona, California, and New Mexico have established task forces to explore whether nonlawyers could provide some legal services.

MEDICAL SERVICES. Nurse practitioners and physician assistants outnumber family practice doctors in the United States and are the principal providers of primary care to many communities (Stange 2014). Nurse practitioners in some states can order and interpret diagnostic tests, prescribe medications, and administer treatments without a doctor's approval.

DENTAL SERVICES. Dental technicians have begun to provide services, such as whitening teeth, in nonclinical settings like shopping malls. Dental therapists can perform basic clinical dental treatment and preventative services in some states and on tribal lands with a varying amount of supervision by a dentist.

If states eliminated occupational licensing requirements, the market would determine the extent of training and supervision necessary to perform a service, and would provide information to consumers about the quality and reputation of practitioners. For example, Avvo, an online service, currently provides consumers with information on lawyers' disciplinary records and qualifications; Aaron Carroll (2016) discusses evidence that indicates that Yelp reviews can help improve patient care; and so on. As in other markets, online consumer forums and objective third-party assessments would proliferate as the market bears responsibility for providing information about the quality of a practitioner. Importantly, consumers would not have a false sense of security about a practitioner's quality that may have been created by occupational licensing requirements. And, of course, individuals in many occupations can and do voluntarily choose to obtain certification or licensing because they believe doing so provides an informative signal of quality.

SUMMARY

Government intervention to address imperfect information gained theoretical support from economists' contributions during the 1970s; for example, George Akerlof (1970) identified the potential cost of asymmetric information in the automobile market but seemed to imply by omission that the market could not help solve the problem. Government's information policies and market responses to imperfect information have occurred simultaneously, with the evidence indicating that most government interventions have turned out to be solutions in search of a problem while imposing social costs. The policy implication to be drawn from the evidence is not that government should completely abandon its role to protect consumers from the harms of imperfect information; rather, it should direct the limited resources of its agencies so they yield demonstrable net benefits to consumers.

Economic theories about information failures and the potential benefits of government information policies have become out of date, especially because, over time, markets have become more effective than government in addressing inefficiencies that may arise from imperfect information.[11] To take an interesting historical example, Edward Glaeser and James Poterba (2021) describe the market failure associated with private provision of water by Manhattan Water Company during the 1800s because consumers could not directly observe whether privately sold water was clean or dirty. Today, as a result of technological advances that have improved the transparency of product safety and the huge financial disincentives for providing unsafe products, markets have reversed that failure and gained the trust of many consumers who purchase bottled water from dozens of private firms and of many households and firms who have bottled water coolers in their homes and work-places because they are less trusting of the quality of the water coming out of the tap that is supplied by the public utility.

As noted, markets may take many years before technological change enables them to help government address an economic goal. However, this is not the case in addressing imperfect information because even before the revolution in information technology, market forces had been effective in addressing inefficiencies that may arise from imperfect information. The revolution in information technology has enabled markets to become even more effective by enriching consumers' knowledge about more products and services and by enriching workers' knowledge about more workplaces. The fact that state policymakers are evaluating and slowly eliminating some information policies is consistent with the vast improvements in information technology. Policymakers should be more proactive in eliminating the vast array of information policies that markets have superseded or could supersede if given a chance.

SEVEN

Addressing Negative Externalities Efficiently

Negative externalities are caused by an agent's production or consumption that adversely affects the welfare of others and a classic example of market failure that justifies government intervention. Government can reduce the harm caused by an externality and increase efficiency by using pricing (taxation) or quantity-based (command and control) policies to encourage consumers and firms to account for the social costs of their actions.

Market forces are not usually thought of as a way to reduce the cost of externalities. But given sufficient time, markets can reduce those costs through efficient adjustments by firms and consumers and by market designs by the government, such as emissions trading programs. As pointed out in the case of addressing other economic goals, competitive market forces that create new production and consumption technologies hold the promise of actually eliminating some externalities.

GOVERNMENT EXTERNALITY POLICIES

The evidence in *Government Failure* indicated that some environmental externality policies have been expensive successes because, although their benefits have exceeded the costs, the gains could have been achieved at much lower cost. In other cases, government policymakers have missed opportunities to generate large benefits by implementing efficient environmental, energy consumption, congestion, and airplane noise taxes to reduce those externalities.

Environment

Recent research continues to identify expensive successes in environmental externality policies. Janet Currie and Reed Walker (2019) document the significant declines from 1980 to 2015 of air pollution from carbon monoxide, nitrogen dioxide, ozone, and particulate matter. However, they stress that it is difficult to determine how much of the improvement in pollution concentration and overall social benefits can be attributed to the 1970 Clean Air Act and its amendments. At the same time, the law has imposed substantial costs that are considerably greater than the direct compliance costs, such as reductions in plants' total factor productivity (Greenstone, List, and Syverson 2012).

David Keiser and Joseph Shapiro (2019) point out that since the Environmental Protection Agency was created in 1970, the United States has spent nearly $5 trillion to clean up surface water pollution and provide clean drinking water. Many measures of drinking and surface water pollution have fallen since 1970 due, at least in part, to the Clean Water Act in 1972 and the Safe Drinking Water Act in 1974. But Keiser and Shapiro argue that large investments could be more cost effective by using more efficient market-based instruments, regulating agriculture, and exploiting returns to scale in waste water treatment.

The estimated benefits of investments in drinking water appear to create substantial health benefits that exceed their costs, but the existing evidence suggests the estimated costs of most investments in cleaning up rivers, lakes, and ocean exceed their measured benefits. Maura Allaire, Haowei Wu, and Upmanu Lall (2018) summarized health-based violations from 1982 to 2015 at 17,900 US local water systems and concluded that, in 2015 alone, as many as 21 million Americans may have been exposed to unsafe drinking water. The problem is particularly severe in rural, low-income communities because they struggle to maintain aging infrastructure and to keep up with the latest water treatment techniques.

Despite the nation's continuing problem with water pollution, Congress repealed the "stream protection rule" in 2017 to help the coal industry, thereby loosening the rule's stricter limit on coal companies dumping waste and debris in surrounding ecosystems, and eliminating the rule's requirement that companies restore damaged waterways close to their state that existed before mining began (Palmer 2017). The rule imposed costs by making it more expensive for coal companies to operate. Nonetheless, the industry should have been incentivized, for example, by an efficient tax, to account for the social costs of its contribution to water pollution, instead of receiving government protection on the grounds that environmental regulations put coal miners out of work.

Additional opportunities to implement efficient environmental externality taxes include:

- A plausible tax on carbon dioxide to avert the potentially enormous costs of climate change. William Nordhaus (2008) estimated that the net cost to the world economy, in 2008 prices, from waiting for fifty years to reduce carbon dioxide emissions to a sustainable level is $4.1 trillion. Gilbert Metcalf (2019) provides evidence that a carbon tax need not impose large costs on an economy.

- Charges for carbon dioxide emissions by aircraft, which currently account for 2 percent of global carbon emissions. Aircraft also deposit water vapor and particles at high altitudes, which form thin clouds that can heat the planet.

- An efficient pollution tax on nitrogen oxides (Shapiro and Walker 2018).

- Charges for water pollution caused by gas companies' technology of using hydrofracking to extract oil from shale rock based on the scientific evidence of the costs of radioactive wastewater and the benefits of drilling.

Efficient externality taxes, which would have to be implemented by the government, are an example where government could draw on market incentives to reduce externality costs efficiently. Thus, government could help itself accomplish economic goals with policies that correctly apply market principles. As discussed later, government also could implement an efficient market mechanism, such as a pollution cap-and-trade program, to reduce externality costs efficiently.

Energy Consumption

Government policies to reduce energy consumption have generally been inefficient. Energy consumption policies are typified by the 2009 Car Allowance Rebate System, better known as Cash for Clunkers, launched during the Great Recession with two objectives: (1) an economic stimulus to US vehicle and parts manufacturers by offering rebates to consumers who shifted their purchases of new, fuel efficient vehicles from future periods to the recessionary period; and (2) a way to improve the fuel efficiency of the vehicle fleet and reduce vehicle emissions by requiring new vehicles purchased under the program to have sufficiently high fuel economy and by encouraging consumers to replace their less fuel-efficient vehicles. Mark Hoekstra, Steven Puller, and Jeremy West (2017) found that Cash for Clunkers performed poorly in improving the fuel economy of the US vehicle fleet because it encouraged households to purchase vehicles that were only three-miles-per-gallon more fuel efficient than the vehicles they would have purchased if the program did not exist. The environmental benefits per vehicle subsidy, $253, fell far short of the average taxpayer costs per vehicle subsidy of $4,210.

The federal government also tried to reduce fuel consumption and air pollution by providing a $7,500 subsidy to consumers who purchased a pure electric vehicle (EV); supplementary subsidies also were provided by some states.[1] Jianwei Xing, Benjamin Leard, and Shanjun Li (2019) raise a similar concern about the EV subsidy that was raised about Cash for Clunkers; namely, households used the tax credit to replace relatively fuel-efficient vehicles. The authors also estimated that 70 percent of the tax credits from purchasing an EV were obtained by households that would have bought an EV without the credits.[2]

An alternative approach to reducing energy consumption is to increase residential energy efficiency. The nation's largest residential energy efficiency program is the Weatherization Assistance Program (WAP). Meredith Fowlie, Michael Greenstone, and Catherine Wolfram (2018) assessed the program based on households in Michigan who received roughly $5,000 worth of home improvements, on average, including furnace replacement, attic and wall insulation, and infiltration reduction. Importantly, the WAP pays only for energy efficiency measures that pass a cost-benefit test, based on ex ante engineering projections. Despite the bias toward beneficial investments, the authors find that weatherized homes do not have significantly higher indoor temperatures, and even when accounting for the broader societal benefits derived from greenhouse gas and local pollutant reductions, the costs still outweigh the benefits; the average rate of return is roughly –7.8 percent. The government appears to have based a program on engineering models that predict returns on energy efficiency investments that are lower than actual returns.

The states also tried to increase residential energy efficiency by subsidizing more energy-efficient appliances through the 2009 State Energy Efficient Appliance Rebate Program, referred to as Cash for Appliances. Consumers could claim a rebate if they purchased an appliance with an ENERGYSTAR (ES) rating that meets specific energy efficiency requirements. Sebastien Houde and Joseph Aldy (2017) estimated the impact of Cash for Appliances rebates on the sales of refrigerators, clothes washers, and dishwashers and found the program resulted in very small improvements in the energy efficiency of those appliance categories because most consumers would have purchased an ES-rated appliance during the period of the program without the rebates; a smaller fraction of consumers simply changed the timing of their purchase of an ES-rated appliance by a few weeks; and the rebates led consumers to upgrade to higher-quality but less energy-efficient models. In terms of cost-effectiveness, the dollar amount spent for each kilowatt saved was $1.10 for refrigerators, $0.21 for clothes washers, and $0.46 for dishwashers, which substantially exceeded the average cost per kilowatt saved of $0.06 that was found for other utility-funded programs.[3]

Congestion

After several decades of traffic growth, motorists have become so stressed by highway congestion that Daniel Kahneman and Alan Krueger (2006) concluded that, over the course of the day, individuals' automobile commutes are the leading activity for which their dominant emotion is negative. For more than a century, policymakers have ignored economists' recommendations based on market principles to set congestion prices to alleviate traffic delays efficiently. The basic idea is to set a toll based on actual traffic volumes that can be collected electronically to force motorists to account for the delays they impose on other motorists when deciding the time of day to drive and the route to use for their journey. Instead, the government has relied on gasoline taxes, which are inefficient because they do not vary by time of day and location.[4] In addition, all levels of government have experienced shortfalls in highway revenues because of improvements in vehicle fuel economy and because the federal gasoline tax has not been increased since 1993.[5]

As an alternative to efficient road pricing, policymakers have used inefficient land use policies to reduce congestion, including minimum parking requirements (MPRs), zoning, and regulations that establish minimum lot sizes. Those policies have done little to reduce congestion, often increased it, and created other costs. W. Bowman Cutter and Sofia Franco (2012) and Simon McDonnell, Josiah Madar, and Vicki Been (2011) found that MPRs, which attempted to limit congestion on local streets and curb the excess demand for parking places, have caused an oversupply of parking places and increased housing costs. Edward Glaeser (2011) and Glaeser and Bryce Ward (2009) showed that zoning and minimum lot size regulations restricted the construction of new housing units, thereby increasing housing prices and promoting sprawl by reducing residential density. Enrico Moretti (2017) vividly described zoning's effect on the San Francisco Bay Area: severe housing shortages and strong pressures for development on the edge of the region, creating sprawl, congestion, and environmental costs.

Land use controls that limit the growth of successful metropolitan areas force Americans to live in places that make it easy to build, not in places with the highest levels of productivity and job opportunities (Glaeser 2017a). Although land use controls are typically imposed by localities, they have national economic implications because, by preventing Americans from moving to certain cities with better employment opportunities than where they currently live, they have misallocated labor across the country.

Chang-Tai Hsieh and Enrico Moretti (2017) estimated that curtailing regulatory constraints that have denied hundreds of thousands of workers access to better job opportunities and housing would increase GDP by a whopping 9.5 percent. At the same time, it would reduce wage inequality because the poorest Americans would not be priced out of the most productive labor markets. Peter Ganong and Daniel Shoag (2017) reinforced this point by showing that high interstate mobility during 1880 to 1980 dramatically reduced inequality; however, from 1980 to 2010, land use regulations have significantly limited interstate migration, especially low-skill migration, and job matching. Finally, Kyle Herkenhoff, Lee Ohanian, and Edward Prescott (2018) find that housing restrictions in just two high-productivity states—New York and California—account for large distortions in the US labor market, including the decline in median wages for male workers since the 1970s.

Airplane Noise

The Federal Aviation Administration (FAA) has not attempted to reduce airplane noise externalities that lower property values and pose risks to health with an efficient tax or an optimal limit on decibels (Morrison, Winston, and Watson 1999). This policy failure has recently become apparent to households because the FAA has begun to change flight paths as it replaces radar with a Global Positioning System of satellites to guide planes. Residents of Boston, San Francisco, Culver City, and Washington, DC, have sued the FAA over the increase in noise. Phoenix brought the first successful lawsuit and had flight paths affecting the noise levels experienced by its residents changed in 2017 (Zipkin 2019).[6]

MARKET FORCES

Markets are generally thought of as the source of inefficiencies caused by negative externalities and not as a substitute or even complement for government action to reduce social costs. However, Ronald Coase (1960) pointed out that, in theory, market adjustments could help reduce the social costs of negative externalities, and possibly eliminate them in the absence of transactions costs. Examples of market adjustments include households' residential sorting to reduce the social costs of congestion, airplane noise, and pollution. The idea is that households who have the highest values of travel time, disutility from airplane noise, and highest values of life purchase houses that, all else constant, are more expensive and are closer to work, farther from a flight path, and less exposed to pollution than are the houses purchased by other households. Conversely, those households who have the lowest values of travel time, disutility from airplane noise, and lowest values of life purchase houses that, all else constant, are less expensive and are farther from work, closer to a flight path, and more exposed to pollution than are the houses purchased by other households.

Robert Ellickson (1991) argued that people frequently resolve disputes in a cooperative fashion without considering the laws that apply to those disputes. He cites two examples: one where a landowner paid to shore up an urban building whose foundations were threatened by an excavation on adjoining land, and another where rural residents in Shasta County, most of which is open range, resolved potential disputes by sharing the costs to prevent livestock from wandering and damaging adjoining property and ambling onto a road and colliding with motorists.

Markets do not always work to reduce the cost of externalities. For example, some firms pollute the air and water resources without making any efforts to reduce the damage caused by their activity. In those cases, government intervention is justified a priori, but as discussed, government externality policies in practice have missed an opportunity to use market principles to guide policies that could reduce the cost of externalities efficiently and, instead, have implemented policies that often have reduced externalities at an excessive cost.

It is, therefore, useful to take another look at how markets could help reduce negative externalities and complement government interventions by reducing their cost more efficiently. The three most promising market approaches include technological innovations that increase the availability of alternative sources of energy for households and firms that reduce environmental externalities; self-interested actions taken by firms and consumers that reduce externalities; and market designs, such as emissions trading, that give firms an incentive to reduce social costs. Government actions can enhance or limit the efficacy of those approaches.

Reducing Environmental Externalities with Alternative Technologies

Alternative technologies developed by the private sector that have the potential to reduce the use of fossil fuels and improve air quality include solar energy, electric batteries that can power automobiles with only periodic recharging, and wind energy. Some new technologies also have the potential to directly reduce air and water pollution.

SOLAR ENERGY. Solar energy has enormous potential to meet the nation's energy demands because the sun beams down a nearly limitless supply of energy every hour. The technological challenge is to harness this energy and allocate it efficiently with innovations that significantly reduce the cost of solar panels and that can store intermittent sunshine so it can be used conveniently as fuel. In addition, power grids must become more flexible so they can efficiently and reliably use the sun's energy to expand capacity during peak periods.

In many parts of the country, large combined-cycle natural gas power plants and wind turbines are the most cost-effective way to provide energy to homes and businesses. But some utilities are announcing plans to retire their old coal plants and add new capacity with larger solar arrays. Federal tax subsidies have improved the cost-competitiveness of solar, but similar government intervention could be used in the future to prop up coal-fired power plants, so solar's future should not depend on the availability of government subsidies. In fact, solar energy's recent cost trend indicates that, even without subsidies, which Congress has tentatively agreed to phase out, it could start to replace old coal-burning power plants. The cost of solar technology then could be reduced further by realizing scale economies and by new innovations.

Residential solar panels have the potential to curb greenhouse gases. They are gaining adoption throughout the world, but their growth in the United

States recently has stalled. A fundamental problem is that the cost of solar to a US household has been inflated by government policies that have resulted in excessive permitting requirements, increased installation time to meet electricity codes, and tariffs on solar panels made in China (Birch 2018). In addition, Jackson Dorsey (2017) argues that some solar installers have been able to charge high markups because many potential buyers are not fully informed about market prices. In any case, California recently has required most new houses built after January 1, 2020, to include solar panels without carefully considering that the requirement will raise the cost of housing roughly $10,000 and that the demand for solar panels and supply of solar energy has yet to develop significantly. Thus, for example, problems in satisfying peak demand for solar power could set back California consumers' long-run demand for this alternative energy source and discourage consumers in other states because of what turned out to be a premature and misguided experiment.

Technological breakthroughs could enable the solar industry to attract a significant share of energy consumption for residential and commercial use and for online platforms that connect buyers and sellers to reduce high price markups and inferior quality. Such a development could be a useful complement to government externality policies.[7] However, uncertainty exists about whether the solar industry can advance its technology. At the same time, recent government interventions are slowing the long-run growth of solar construction plants, homeowners' adoption of solar panels, and solar's share of the energy market. Policymakers should remove those obstacles.

ELECTRIC VEHICLES. Electric vehicles currently have a tiny market share, but automobile and technology companies have made at least $100 billion in investments worldwide with the expectation that the EV market share will start to grow and that EVs will eventually replace gasoline-powered vehicles. Of course, investors are focused on their returns and not on the social benefits of electric vehicles. But if engineers solve EVs' remaining technological problems to make them more commercially viable, and if the government (or possibly the private sector) provides an adequate supply of fast charging stations on the US road network,[8] then large-scale adoption of EVs is likely to occur and improve the environment by reducing the nation's consumption of fossil fuels.[9]

Growing sales of EVs depend on their having a battery that can store enough energy so the range of an EV on a fully charged battery is comparable to the range of a conventional vehicle with a full tank of gasoline, and that it becomes cheaper to own and operate an EV than a gasoline-powered vehicle. The new wave of lithium-ion batteries expected during the next few years could increase energy storage significantly. Battery costs are falling as manufacturers increase production and competition between manufacturers intensifies. EV manufacturers are reducing vehicle cost by increasing the energy density of the battery, meaning that it requires fewer raw materials and less weight to deliver the same range. Faster increases in energy density than were expected have led some to predict that it will be cheaper, even without tax subsidies, to own a plug-in vehicle than one that burns fossil fuels before 2025 (Boadway 2020; Ewing 2020). As manufacturers increase production, however, they have to avoid shortages of the essential battery ingredients—cobalt, lithium, and graphite.

The average range of EVs, currently about 200 miles compared with 475 miles for a gasoline-powered car, will continue to increase with improved batteries. For example, one study forecasts that the average range of an electric vehicle will be 275 miles by 2022 and 400 miles by 2028.[10] Drivers also will need more convenient plug-in stations and less delay in recharging their EVs. Currently, there are roughly 25,000 public charging stations in the United States, compared with about 112,000 gas stations.[11] Electricity America, a company established as part of Volkswagen's settlement for building cars with illegal software, has installed more than 2,200 fast chargers nationwide and plans to install thousands more.[12] Other startups and established infrastructure charging companies, such as ABB, also expect to be part of the effort to make fast charging stations widely available. And several automotive, utility, and infrastructure companies are testing dynamic charging, which allows electric cars, buses, and trucks to charge on the move. The process involves under-road pads that wirelessly transmit electricity to receivers mounted underneath cars and, for some vehicles, overhead wires such as those used by trams. Automobile companies, such as Renault, are testing the technology on city streets. The financial cost of modifying the infrastructure to connect roads to the energy grid is large and needs to be reduced to enable the technology to be economically viable.

After decades of alleged hype and wasteful government subsidies, the ongoing commitment of the private sector suggests that owners of electric vehicles could become notable users of America's roads in the foreseeable future and that those vehicles could contribute to cleaner air. Competition is evolving as many mainstream and luxury brands, including Audi, Ford, GM, Porsche, Toyota, and Volkswagen, are offering new EV models to challenge the Tesla Model 3, which has accounted for the majority of EV sales in the United States. It is important for government policymakers to allow EV adoption and competition to evolve without providing tax subsidies that give any company an advantage and without instituting regulations that impede the development of the EV sector.[13]

WIND ENERGY. Wind energy markets also have the potential to reduce fuel consumption. Thus far, their development in the United States has been primarily supported through a tax credit to producers based on the share of electricity they produce with land-based and offshore wind energy. Wind energy has been of modest importance in a few states, such as Texas, and of only limited importance to the nationwide development of alternative energy sources.

However, private investors have begun to finance large wind farms in places like Oklahoma, Wyoming, and Vermont, and to build a series of transmission-line projects, which would represent a major advance by bringing renewable energy from the hinterlands to urban centers such as Los Angeles and Boston (Gold 2017). At the same time, California is allowing private companies to lease deep waters adjacent to central and northern California for wind projects, with the expectation that floating windmills could begin producing power within six years.

On the East Coast, water-based windmills are being developed in Maine, and wind projects will be built off the coast of Long Island within the next five years.[14] In March 2021, the US Department of the Interior approved the nation's first large-scale offshore wind farm, Vineyard Wind, which is about twelve nautical miles off the coast of Martha's Vineyard, Massachusetts. Roughly 22,000 megawatts of generating capacity that could supply more than 10 million homes is reasonably foreseeable in the waters of the Atlantic (Meyer 2020). The development of water-based windmills is important, because land-based wind farms have been criticized for requiring too much land.

Builders of transmission lines are not eligible for federal subsidies but, like public infrastructure projects, they must endure the lengthy federal review and regulatory permitting process. If private investments in wind farms and transmission lines are profitable, then this renewable energy source will provide an increasing share of the nation's energy. But government regulatory hurdles could threaten the profitability and thus the future of wind energy in the United States.

OTHER POTENTIALLY HELPFUL TECHNOLOGIES. Researchers and technology companies also are attempting to develop new innovations that focus on ameliorating specific environmental problems. Such innovations have yet to be implemented, and they may never be, but they illustrate the potential of private-sector innovations to simultaneously meet financial goals and address environmental externalities. Some recent examples include Negative Emissions Technologies (NETs), which suck carbon dioxide out of the air (Tollefson 2018), and companies that turn carbon dioxide and unrecyclable, contaminated plastic waste into chemicals that can be used by consumers and industry.[15] Companies using carbon capture technologies to clean the air include Occidental Petroleum, United Airlines, Stripe, Shopify, and Microsoft.

Several firms are trying to address the problem that the weight of plastic in the ocean will rival that of fish by 2050. Emre Peker (2019) reports that multinationals like Coca-Cola, Adidas, and HP reuse trash fished from seas or collected on coastlines. Companies also are making an effort to commercialize supply chains that prevent plastic getting to oceans. Coca-Cola recently introduced its first plastic bottle made with 25 percent recycled marine litter. Hundreds of entrepreneurs are crowdfunding startups to recycle ocean waste into surfboards, swimwear, chairs, and backpacks. In addition, Ocean Cleanup, a nonprofit, has designed a trash collection system to capture and hold debris, especially plastic. Fish and other sea creatures are able to swim beneath it. The current prototype holds plastic until a ship can collect it. Finally, Origin Materials is planning to use sawdust to make recyclable plastic bottles that remove carbon dioxide from the air because they are made from sustainably sourced wood waste. Nestle SA, Danone SA, and PepsiCo plan to sell water in Origin Materials' recyclable plant-based bottles in early 2022 (Quinn 2019).

Actions by Firms

Market forces are providing financial incentives for firms to reduce pollution, and certain investors are putting pressure on firms for the same reason. Firms are responding by either improving their current technologies to produce fossil fuels or by using renewable technologies. For example, because major energy companies have made large investments in natural gas and are increasing output, they want to both ensure that natural gas is a significant part of the transition to a low-carbon future and to respond to pressure from investors that they address concerns about climate change. Almost all the major energy companies have publicly announced plans to reduce methane emissions from natural gas production, transportation, and consumption. The companies have yet to finalize how they will achieve the reduction, but they have signed a set of guiding principles that strongly indicates they are committed to the effort (Kent and Olson 2017). As another example, a few new US coal plants have used a carbon capture system (CCS), which removes most of the carbon dioxide from coal and then uses it to force additional oil from the ground. The carbon capture technology could also be used by existing older coal plants.

Amazon started a climate pledge whereby firms commit to being carbon neutral by 2040, which means that a company relies entirely on renewable fuels or offsets the burning of fossil fuels through carbon capture. FedEx, for example, plans to honor its pledge by electrifying its fleet and contributing to carbon capture.

The US Department of Energy has tried to expedite the benefits from carbon capture by providing billions of dollars in subsidies to companies that have researched and to the few that have used a CCS. However, the companies already have an economic incentive to use the system. Instead of providing subsidies, the government should implement a carbon tax to provide an additional incentive for energy companies to adopt a carbon capture technology. This is another example of government applying market principles to help accomplish an economic goal. Exxon has taken the lead in the private sector to fight climate change by committing $1 million over two years to promote a tax on carbon emissions because it believes a carbon tax is a superior alternative to the current patchwork of regulations and that it is a way to eliminate policy uncertainty.

Third parties also have taken actions to help reduce externalities and influence private firms to support actions that improve the environment. As an example of the former, TerraCycle receives funding from private sources to recycle "nonrecyclables" by partnering with individual consumers and firms to divert millions of pounds of waste from landfills and incinerators each month to produce recyclable products. As an example of the latter, two academic researchers have joined with the financial services firm UBS Group to develop metrics for investors that indicate how a company's actions and policies are affecting climate change and air and water quality. Investors then could indicate to the most egregious offenders that they might withdraw their investments unless the companies made a greater effort to adopt more sustainable practices. If the metrics turned out to be credible, such pressure could influence the behavior of firms in ways that might generate social benefits. Starbucks recently preempted such pressure—and undoubtedly improved its reputation among certain consumers—by committing to stop using plastic straws by 2020 and, instead, to use recyclable, strawless lids.

Finally, airplane pilots and drivers of private vehicles have used advances in technology developed in the private sector to reduce the cost of congestion and safety externalities. For example, commercial and private motorists use Waze and other traffic navigation apps that rely on GPS to avoid congested routes with stop-and-go traffic and, therefore, obtain better fuel economy. Congestion pricing implemented by the government also would reduce stop-and-go traffic and improve fuel economy. Commercial airline pilots have used Don Bateman's Ground Proximity Warning System to virtually eliminate fatal crashes into the ground or bodies of water due to poor visibility (Levin 2016a), and private pilots have used iPad apps, which provide real-time weather and other important safety information, to reduce their fatality rates (Levin 2016b).

Market Designs to Reduce Externalities

Markets for automobile and airline travel have effectively been designed—and could be designed even better—to enable modal operators to rely on technology to reduce transportation externalities. Other market designs, where the government applies market principles, also help to reduce externalities.

INTRODUCE CAP-AND-TRADE PROGRAMS. Beginning in the 1980s, the federal government introduced cap-and-trade programs in the United States. A cap-and-trade program puts a price on energy emissions by requiring power plants, natural gas utilities, and other energy industry participants to buy permits to pollute. The "price" reduces emissions damage to the environment by encouraging firms and consumers to reduce their use of fossil fuels, and by encouraging firms to develop innovative production technologies and to switch to alternative sources of energy.

Richard Schmalensee and Robert Stavins (2017) surveyed the major experiences with several cap-and-trade programs during the past three decades, including sulfur dioxide allowance trading, nitrogen oxide trading in the eastern United States, the regional greenhouse gas initiative, and other programs, and concluded that cap-and-trade programs were a significant cost-efficiency improvement over traditional command and control regulations and also were more effective at improving the environment.[16] The market-based systems also spurred innovations and technological change by firms that helped improve the environment and that would not have occurred otherwise.

The overall success of cap-and-trade programs merits their consideration and broader application to address environmental problems. However, because the states and the federal government determine whether a cap-and-trade program will be adopted and its design, it is uncertain whether the

United States will expand their use and fully realize the potential benefits of market-based environmental policies.[17]

DEVISE INSTITUTIONAL GUIDELINES TO PROMOTE LOBSTER SUSTAINABILITY. The "tragedy of the commons" or, in the case of lobsters, overfishing, has been avoided by devising institutional guidelines (Ostrom 1990) that identify the lobsters that are allowed to be caught instead of establishing regulatory limits on the *number* of lobsters that can be caught. Lobster catches have remained at high levels because lobstermen and women have been receptive to and complied with specific guidelines that certain lobsters, marked by notches cut in their tails, are off-limits for life. Lobsters must be returned to the ocean if they are too small, too large (because mature lobsters produce the most offspring), or egg-bearing females (Fox 2017).

SUMMARY

Externality taxes based on market principles and government design programs in stylized market settings, such as cap and trade and lobster fishing (using traps), illustrate that government externality policies and market forces can complement each other to reduce externalities efficiently. However, government externality policies to improve the environment and reduce energy consumption, congestion, and airplane noise must be extensively reformed to reduce their inefficiencies, and policymakers must take greater care not to compromise the ability of market participants to help reduce externalities by, for example, instituting regulations that discourage the mobility of people and goods.[18]

In the process of responding to economic incentives and implementing alternative technologies, market participants are gradually increasing their contributions to reducing externalities. During the past ten years, we have witnessed the positive interaction between greater economic efficiency and fewer negative externalities in the energy sector as both the real price of electricity and carbon dioxide emissions have fallen because utilities have substituted natural gas for coal and begun to make use of wind and solar energy.[19] Deregulation of natural gas also spurred technological change that helped reduce the cost of energy and air pollution. And technological advances in electric vehicles, wind and solar energy, and the adoption of new technologies, such as NETs, in conjunction with the concerted efforts of firms and third parties to improve the environment strongly hint at the major externality improvements that markets may yield in the future.[20]

EIGHT

Improving Public Production

A good or service may be socially desirable but it may not be provided by the market because a private firm cannot earn a normal profit due to, for example, large capital requirements. Or, in the case of public goods, they may be undersupplied because the characteristics of nonrivalry and non-excludability provide an incentive for consumers not to pay. Both cases justify government intervention that could increase social welfare by financing socially desirable services, including public goods, which would not be supplied or would be undersupplied by the private sector.

Market forces can complement public provision by offering an alternative private service to consumers that could compete with the government service or substitute entirely for public provision by encouraging private companies to form and compete with each other. The private sector has a strong incentive to invest capital in activities where profit opportunities exist. Because those opportunities may change over time, in large part due to technological change, government should allow the private sector to act on them if the efficiency advantages that arise from operating in a competitive environment can improve on public provision and raise social welfare.

GOVERNMENT PERFORMANCE

The evidence in *Government Failure* indicates that public financing and management of transportation infrastructure and services and public lands have been extremely inefficient and have strained the budgets of all levels of government. Recent evidence is consistent with that finding.

Transportation Infrastructure and Services

I have assessed the efficiency of US transportation infrastructure (highways, airports, and the like) provided by the public sector and transportation services (public transit, taxi, and Amtrak) provided and/or regulated by the public sector (Winston 2013) and concluded that the public sector's extensive involvement in the transportation system has resulted in policies that have generated excessive costs. The public sector's provision and management of infrastructure and urban transit has not been guided by basic economic principles. Instead, government policies subsidize users because prices do not reflect social marginal costs and restrict efficient supply; investments are not based on cost-benefit analysis and have failed to maximize net benefits; and operating costs are inflated by regulations on labor and capital. Economic regulations of transportation operations have not promoted efficiency and, in some cases, they have hurt consumers. I estimated that the total annual welfare costs of inefficient transportation policies and operations exceeded $100 billion (in 2005 dollars), which is an extreme lower bound because it does not include the additional costs of reduced performance in labor, trade, urban, and industrial markets that have been adversely affected by the transportation system's inefficiencies, and the slow rate of innovation and technological advance in several areas of transportation.

Specific well-known examples of highly inefficient transportation services and infrastructure projects include New York City subways (Rosenthal 2017); the construction of Boston's Big Dig highway (Flint 2015); the Federal Aviation Administration's air traffic control modernization program known as NextGen (US Department of Transportation 2018); and California's high-speed rail project (Vartabedian 2018), which reported large increases in its expected costs before it was significantly scaled back to serve only a modest corridor in inland California.

Postal Services

The United States Postal Service (USPS) has incurred consecutive annual multibillion-dollar losses for more than a decade. As an example of financial mismanagement, the USPS provides discounts to customers who sort their own mail that are greater than the cost to the USPS of sorting that mail internally (McCoy 2015). The significant long-run decline in first-class mail, attributable to the growth of information technology, and the intense competition in package delivery from Amazon, UPS, and Federal Express have combined to paint a dismal picture of USPS's financial future.[1]

Public Lands

The federal government is the largest landowner in the United States, controlling more than one-fourth of the nation's land area, and nearly one-half of all land in the West. In some states, including Oregon, Utah, and Nevada, most of the land is owned by the federal government.[2]

The federal government's land management has assumed little fiscal responsibility and incurred large losses, which are borne by taxpayers (Fretwell 2009). For example, compared with private landowners, the federal government has charged lower rents for grazing and mining permits and sold land at prices below market value. And compared with state trust agencies, the federal government often has lost money managing valuable resources, such as timber, grazing, minerals, and recreation (Fretwell and Regan 2015). In recent years, the National Park Service has been burdened by a backlog of $12 billion in deferred maintenance (Evans, Harrison, and Lindquist 2020).

The federal government also has adopted inefficient leasing policies for energy resources. About 40 percent of all the coal mined in the United States is extracted from lands owned by the federal government under leases managed by the US Department of the Interior. Kenneth Gillingham and others (2016) estimated that the prices charged firms for ten-year leases on government land, which include bids set by auction and royalty payments per ton of coal produced, do not reflect the full social costs of mining and burning the coal. Thus, government's poor fiscal performance has also compromised environmental stewardship.

According to the Bureau of Land Management, the Trump administration increased the amount of federal land offered for oil and gas leasing from 4 million acres available under the Obama administration to nearly 13 million acres. Companies pay a 12.5 percent royalty on any oil or gas they extract, and they can hold the leases indefinitely. It appears American taxpayers are not earning a fair return, because the royalty rate of 12.5 percent has not changed since 1920 even though technological advance and changing energy markets have made oil and gas extraction much more lucrative. In comparison, state oil and gas leasing rates are much higher, climbing, for example, to as much as 25 percent in Texas.

Still another land management concern is that, in the 1970s, the Federal Land Policy and Management Act shifted the focus of the Bureau of Land Management from resource extraction to conservation. Rural communities believe that new regulations have undermined their prosperity and have shifted their economic fate into the hands of the federal government. For example, the bureau could cut cattle numbers and threaten the viability of ranching if an endangered species lived on the range.

Excluding public parks, local governments own about a fifth of all the land within many US cities' limits (Klein 2017). However, such land often is used inefficiently. For example, Boston's Logan Airport occupies land on desirable waterfront property close to the urban core, which, if properly valued in its most productive use, would be worth tens of billions of dollars instead of the much lower valuation reported by the Massachusetts Port Authority. Dag Detter and Stefan Folster (2017) estimated that the value of land owned by US cities is worth more than $20 trillion, but they point out that policymakers—and the public—have failed to capture its full asset value because city governments do not know the real value of the land they own, and they have not carefully considered how to maximize its potential value.

MARKET FORCES

Although market forces could help reduce the costs and improve the quality of public production, policymakers have not fully explored market-oriented approaches. Independently, the private sector is developing some innovations that may help improve the efficiency of public production.

Transportation Infrastructure

Creating a market environment to improve the performance of highways, airports, and air traffic control is difficult, but policymakers could explore privatization experiments to determine whether competition among private providers is feasible and likely to increase social welfare. Policymakers also should take notice that the private sector's innovations have the potential to improve public transportation infrastructure performance and may align well with privatized transportation infrastructure.

HIGHWAYS

Privatization potentially could improve the performance of US highways, but the challenges are formidable. To begin, a competitive private highway market would have to be designed. Clifford Winston and Jia Yan (2011) analyzed the economic effects of highway privatization by characterizing a competitive environment on State Route 91 in California consisting of two routes with equal lane capacities that would be operated by two different private highway companies. A third party would represent motorists and negotiate tolls and capacities with the private companies and obtain a contract equilibrium. Winston and Yan found that motorists would gain from highway privatization when the contract equilibrium consisted of differentiated prices and service—that is, motorists were given the choice of paying a high toll to use lanes with little congestion or paying a low toll to use lanes that were highly congested.

In practice, the United States has no experience with highway privatization where the goal of the policy was to generate competition between highway providers that would improve the efficiency of road travel. Instead, the public sector has allowed some privatizations to occur to raise revenue to fund highway projects as part of long-term leases and to build new capacity. The most encouraging public-private partnerships have led to high-occupancy-toll lanes, where the private sector has built, financed, and maintained express lanes that have enhanced travelers' welfare. On the other hand, the first company that leased the Indiana toll road went into bankruptcy; the road is currently operated by IFM Partners.[3]

It is uncertain whether policymakers could design a competitive private highway system effectively and that sufficient managerial talent exists to operate competing highway companies that would remain profitable and would provide highway services that would raise motorists' welfare. The highway privatization option should be explored with carefully designed experiments, which could give policymakers valuable guidance on the potential costs and benefits of the policy and could indicate whether and under what conditions it would be socially desirable to privatize part or all of the US highway system.

The greatest potential for the private sector to improve the performance of the public highway system is to convert the vehicles that use the system from manually driven to driverless or autonomous. Autonomous vehicles (AVs) are operated by computers that obtain information, including the location of pedestrians and other vehicles and the speed and trajectories of those vehicles, from an array of sensors and pulses of infrared light on the surrounding road conditions. By gathering and reacting immediately to real-time traffic information and eliminating risky driver behavior, such as driving under the influence and speeding, AVs have the potential to reduce traffic delays by creating a much smoother traffic flow and eliminating incident delays (because AVs do not "rubberneck" to examine the aftermath of an accident), and would greatly improve safety by significantly reducing the likelihood of an accident. Autonomous trucks are in development and would have the same positive attributes as autonomous cars, and would eventually comprise part of the nation's autonomous vehicle fleet.

However, autonomous vehicles potentially can generate large improvements in the efficiency and safety of highway travel only after the federal government establishes the institutional framework for automobile and technology companies to test their vehicles to ensure they are safe for public adoption. In addition, local and state governments need to upgrade their infrastructure to enable AVs to operate as efficiently and safely as possible. Among the most important improvements are the adoption of new technology to facilitate vehicle-to-network, vehicle-to-infrastructure, and vehicle-to-vehicle communications and to implement pricing policies that apply market principles to efficiently allocate scarce road capacity and durability.[4]

Apps could be used to set real-time prices for road travel that vary with traffic, and set prices for pavement damage inflicted by trucks to encourage truckers to reduce that damage by using vehicles with more axles that do less damage to the pavement (Small, Winston, and Evans 1989). If policymakers fail to address the pricing inefficiencies that have plagued the public highway system, then AV operations are likely to be compromised by potholes and congestion, which would significantly disturb the traffic flow. This failure could motivate exploring the potential of privatized roads to set congestion and pavement wear prices that enhance AV operations by improving the traffic flow.

By significantly reducing congestion, AVs also could generate benefits by improving the efficiency of other sectors of the US economy. Clifford Winston and Quentin Karpilow (2020) argue that AVs' improvement in highway travel speeds and travel-time reliability could increase trade flows, land-use efficiency, the quality of job matching and employment, and industry productivity. Accounting for those benefits, the successful adoption of AVs could increase annual economic growth by at least 1 percentage point.

AVIATION

Privatization of both airports and air traffic control could improve the efficiency of their operations. Multiple public airports already serve several US metropolitan areas, but they have little incentive to compete on pricing and service because their funding is assured by weight-based aircraft landing fees (based on FAA guidelines), charges to airlines for gates and terminal space, and revenues from parking and other concessions. Private airport competition that could generate more efficient pricing and service and spur airports to modernize their operations and expand gate and terminal capacity is potentially feasible in the Washington, DC, New York, Boston, Chicago, San Francisco, Los Angeles, and other US metropolitan areas.[5] In addition, it is possible that new private airports could provide competition in major metropolitan areas currently served by only one airport, such as Atlanta, Las Vegas, Denver, and Minneapolis.

Jia Yan and Clifford Winston (2014) developed a model in which the three major airports in the San Francisco Bay Area (San Francisco, Oakland, and San Jose) were assumed to be sold to different owners and to compete for airline operations as profit-maximizing private airports. The airports' charges reduced travel delays, and by setting charges that varied for different classifications of airport users, scheduled commercial carriers, and general aviation, the authors found the Bay Area airports would be profitable under privatization, airlines would increase their profits, and air travelers' welfare would improve because the travel-time savings from less-congested air travel would offset the higher airport charges to airlines that would be passed on to travelers in higher fares. General aviation would face higher charges than they do when they pay the current weight-based landing fees. However, their losses would be softened if policymakers expanded airport privatization to encourage (smaller) private airports to compete for (smaller) aircraft operations by taking advantage of advances in GPS technology that could improve access to smaller airports, and by upgrading runways and gates and offering ground transfer service to improve travelers' access to the central city and other preferred parts of the metropolitan area.

Countries throughout the world have privatized their airports and obtained successful outcomes, provided the airports were sold to separate owners (Oum, Yan, and Yu 2008). US policymakers should draw on foreign experience with market forces to improve the efficiency of the nation's air-port system by designing careful airport privatization experiments in selected metropolitan areas. Based on the airline deregulation experience, such ex-periments are likely to reveal that public airports have suppressed innova-tions and potential efficiency improvements that policymakers were unable to envision.[6]

Foreign experience also lends support to the case for privatizing the na-tion's air traffic control (ATC) system. Currently, the FAA simultaneously regulates aviation safety and provides ATC services for users of US airspace through the Air Traffic Organization (ATO). In the interest of modernizing and improving the efficiency of their ATC services, more than sixty countries have restructured their providers by granting them managerial and financial authority. Nav Canada, established in 1996 and financed by publicly traded debt, represents an example the US could follow by spinning off the ATO to a self-supporting nonprofit corporation.

Comparisons of the current performance of the US ATO with Nav Can-ada's performance have found that, under privatization, modernization of technology was greatly improved, air travel became safer, and users benefited from improved service quality (Oster 2006; McDougall and Roberts 2008). In addition, the Eno Foundation (2018) compared the ATC fees charged by Nav Canada with the comparable taxes charged to passengers and airlines in the United States and found that Nav Canada's fees were significantly lower, an indication that the Canadian model is more cost effective.

Policymakers, led by former Congressman Bill Shuster, have indicated a strong interest in spinning off ATC from the FAA and running it as a private nonprofit corporation; however, the Trump administration pulled its support for the proposal and Schuster's bill never made it to the floor to be voted on by the House of Representatives. In any event, the case for reforming ATC by exposing it to more of a market environment remains strong.

Urban Transportation Services

The public sector is also responsible for managing and operating urban public bus and rail transit services and regulating fares and entry of taxi companies in most metropolitan areas. The private sector's development of private vans and ride-sharing and the potential development of AVs represent superior transportation alternatives to regulated taxis and public transit. I indicated that taxi companies might improve their competitiveness in this environment if they were deregulated. However, even private transit operators are unlikely to attract sufficient ridership to be profitable because of the growing adoption of ride-sharing and the eventual adoption of AVs.

Private van services exist in a handful of major US cities. The services tend to keep a low profile because, although some are legal, others have not obtained a license to operate. Nonetheless, they exist because they provide a highly-valued, low-cost service, with fares that are usually only a few dollars and with a route network made by working class people for working class people.[7] Annie Correal (2018) provides examples of private vans' service areas and fares in the New York City-New Jersey metropolitan area. Carolyn Said (2019) reports that Via, a private transit operator, will run on-demand vans in Cupertino; these are eagerly awaited because the public bus option run by Santa Clara Valley Transportation Authority is too slow.

The developers of a new app, Dollaride, are hoping to generate more business for private vans in New York City (and possibly elsewhere) and to challenge public bus transit, like Uber has taken on the taxi industry (de Freytas-Tamura 2019). The app allows users to see where licensed vans are operating within a one-mile radius, as well as where they are headed, helping commuters decide whether taking a van might be faster than waiting for a bus. The app allows drivers to spot passengers more easily and plan for demand and possibly future routes. The app also may encourage unlicensed vans to register with the city.

In sum, a revolution in private urban transportation that began with ride-sharing services and will eventually culminate with AVs will benefit the public as well as free government from the responsibility and high cost of providing and subsidizing urban transportation.

Postal Services

Although it has a legal monopoly over the delivery of first-class mail, high labor costs, lack of innovation in its first-class mail operations, and competition from private-sector mail and small package delivery services, including electronic mail, have contributed to the US Postal Service's continuing losses, which are covered by multibillions of dollars in annual taxpayer subsidies.

In the short run, the subsidies could be eliminated and efficiency could be improved if the mail and small package delivery market were privatized. European countries have successfully transitioned to such a privatized market and have licensed new firms to deliver mail to satisfy universal delivery requirements. US policymakers could privatize the postal service and give it the flexibility to compete with ground-based delivery service companies, but they would have to overcome postal unions' opposition.

In the long run, drones, a new technology, represent the future of a privatized mail and small package delivery market. Although they were not initially designed to address the financial problems of the USPS, commercial drones have significant potential to provide more efficient service than any land-based delivery company because of their automated operations and the vast capacity in low-altitude air space.[8]

Wing, an offshoot of Google, is the first drone operator to receive US governmental approval to operate as an airline and to drop products to actual customers. It will provide service in southwest Virginia. UPS has formed a new drone delivery subsidiary, called UPS Flight Forward, and will seek FAA approval to operate commercial flights. UPS is striking agreements with healthcare groups to use drones to deliver medical supplies—for example, to hospital campuses in Utah and elsewhere—and is making an agreement with CVS Health Corp. to evaluate the use of drones for home delivery of prescriptions and other products. Finally, Amazon launched a trial of its Prime Air drone delivery service for select customers in Cambridge, England, in December 2016, and they have recently received approval from the FAA to operate a fleet of delivery drones and begin testing customer deliveries. Other companies, including Microsoft, Uber, and FedEx, have announced plans for drone delivery service trials, as well.

The FAA recently announced that it would allow fully automated commercial drone flights without hands-on piloting or direct observation by human controllers or observers. American Robotics is the first US company to gain this approval. For its part, the US commercial drone industry wants to create a privately funded and operated ATC network separate from the US ATO that would facilitate operations and prevent collisions. By working constructively with the drone industry, law enforcement agencies could address security concerns and enable the private sector to develop a technologically advanced mail and small package delivery industry.

Public Lands and Structures

Federal, state, and local governments own a considerable amount of US land that they rent for grazing and mining, manage for recreational purposes, and sell to private investors. Different levels of government also own land and structures within city limits that are used for various purposes. Those valuable assets could generate much higher rates of return, but, as noted, they generally have underperformed under government ownership and management and have cost taxpayers significant amounts of revenue.

The private sector could help governments increase the returns on public land and structures by managing more efficiently the land and structures governments continue to own for a specific purpose, such as state capital buildings and the White House.[9] The Federal Assets Sale and Transfer Act of 2016, which allows the federal government to consolidate and sell federal buildings and other civilian real property, could generate large benefits if investment firms were hired to estimate accurately the fair market value of public land and structures and determine the assets the public sector should gradually sell to private investors, who could put them to more productive use.[10]

It also would be desirable for policymakers to pass legislation that enables state and local governments to sell their assets to private investors. For example, Washington, DC, Inspector General Daniel W. Lucas found that the city's Department of General Services had essentially lost track of government-owned real estate in the nation's capital and was spending nearly $180 million a year leasing additional buildings (Jamison 2017). Following Dag Detter and Stefan Folster (2017), Washington, DC, clearly could make better choices that enhance real returns by first hiring an objective private budgetary expert to gain a proper understanding of and document the city's balance sheet. The district could then work with a private investment team with experience in real estate and finance to determine the commercial assets it should sell to private investors and to develop an Urban Wealth Fund to maximize the value of the assets it keeps in its portfolio.

SUMMARY

The positive features of market forces stressed here—incentives for efficiency and the ability to create competition—can help the government improve public production by complementing or even substituting for government provision of transportation infrastructure, urban transportation, and postal services. In addition, the private sector's ability to attract talent and its expertise in financial markets could result in private investment teams applying state-of-the-art valuation techniques and investment strategies to generate greater returns on public lands and structures.

Advances in technology offer great potential for the private sector to help even more. Shared and autonomous vehicles could transform highway infrastructure and urban transportation; technologically advanced aviation infrastructure could develop in a competitive market setting; and drones could transform postal and small package delivery services. Congress and administrative agencies should embrace those technologies and make it easier for the private sector to put them into practice.

NINE

Encouraging Innovations by Firms and Individuals

Research and development (R&D) by private firms may generate positive externalities for competitors, thereby resulting in a suboptimal level of innovative activity because firms cannot fully appropriate the benefits of their R&D activities. Government has tried to spur innovative activity by subsidizing firms' R&D and providing patent protection. However, it is not clear that those actions are necessary, because firms and industries are strongly motivated by the pursuit of profits to invest in R&D that could lead to successful innovations and technological advances that spur economic growth and greatly increase social welfare.

GOVERNMENT TECHNOLOGY POLICY

The evidence in *Government Failure* questioned whether federal R&D subsidies have supported socially beneficial programs that would not have been undertaken without federal assistance. The evidence on the performance of the patent system concluded that it has, at best, mixed effects. Patent protection is possibly warranted for firms in a few select industries, but firms in other industries have been given monopoly rents. Overall, it is not clear that the welfare effects of the patent system have been positive.

More recent work continues to question the efficacy of government's technology policy. Josh Lerner (2009) contends that R&D subsidy programs crowd out investment by the private sector and do not efficiently allocate funds to firms. Lerner's 2020 paper finds that the US Department of Energy's recent clean energy initiative to promote entrepreneurial activity, largely by providing financing to firms, ended in disappointment because structural issues make it difficult for the Department to sustain successful entrepreneurship.

Sabrina Howell (2017) analyzed the US Department of Energy's Small Business Innovation Research program and found that its Phase 1 awards of $150,000 to fund nine months of proof-of-concept work increased the likelihood that a firm would receive both subsequent venture capital and increase its (citation-weighted) patents. However, Howell did not find that the Phase 2 grants of $1 million to fund later-stage demonstrations produced similar positive outcomes; thus, she concluded that it may be more effective to stimulate innovation by providing grants to small, young firms on a one-time basis instead of providing larger grants that follow firms through multiple stages of technology development.

Given that considerable innovation occurs outside the US patent system (Sampat 2018), researchers continue to question the system's social value. James Bessen and Michael Meurer (2008) and Michele Boldrin and others (2011) argued that empirical evidence suggests that patent protection has reduced innovation in most industries, while Boldrin and David Levine (2008) called for the complete elimination of patents. Michael Frakes and Melissa Wasserman (2017) followed patent examiners throughout their careers and noted that, as they are promoted, they are given other responsibilities that diminish the time they can devote to patent examinations. The authors found that, as patent examiners are given less time to review patent applications, the average quality of the patents they approve declines.[1] The General Accountability Office concluded in an audit that the patent office "does not have a consistent definition of patent quality that is clearly articulated, and that patent officials have almost no way of knowing whether their examiners are doing a good job" (Rein 2016).

The critical assessments of government's conventional technology policies do not change the fact that government has complemented industry innovations with military expenditures that have supported R&D and led to useful civilian applications. In addition, government support to universities in the late 1960s helped develop the internet; investment in the Human Genome Project in the early 1990s increased our understanding of human disease; and funding in the mid-1990s helped create Google.

MARKET FORCES

A major theme throughout this part of the book has been that private firms and industries have developed many innovations that have helped reduce or eliminate government policy inefficiencies and have increased the nation's welfare by trillions of dollars. Table 9-1 summarizes those innovations. In addition, innovations in one industry have been used to overcome government regulations that suppress innovative activity in another industry. For example, in an interview with Noah Smith (2021), Patrick Collison observes that the avionics in cockpits of commercial planes are primitive because it is so hard, slow, and expensive to get the FAA to approve a new technology. However, commercial airlines have still been able to improve their operations because most pilots fly with an iPad running sophisticated flight planning software.

Although critics of the state of innovation in the United States exist, private markets contain the seeds of well-recognized sources of innovation, and they will continue to generate technological advances that promote economic growth.

Sources of Innovation

Understanding the sources of innovation and technological change is among the most important and challenging topics in economics. One approach recognizes the importance of technological change for economic growth but treats it as exogenous (Solow 1957). The intuitive justification for this approach, as explained by Matt Ridley (2015, 2020), is that innovation is notoriously difficult to dictate; technology changes by inexorable, evolutionary progress—which we probably cannot stop or speed up very much. Technology finds its inventors, rather than vice versa. For example, more than twenty people deserve some credit for inventing some version of the incandescent light bulb before Thomas Edison's contribution, and multiple independent researchers often deserve credit for other major inventions.

An alternative approach seeks to identify endogenous influences on technological change, including but not limited to investments in human capital and in R&D (Romer 1990). This approach stresses ideas and the dissemina-

TABLE 9-1. Innovations Addressing Policy Inefficiencies
and Improving Market Performance

Policy Inefficiency	Market Innovation
Economic regulation	New communications services
	Improved transport logistics and distribution
	Horizontal drilling and hydraulic fracturing
	Digital ride-sharing platforms
Antitrust enforcement	Using new technologies in one industry to challenge industry leaders in other industries
	Using the internet and social media to obtain and disseminate information that increases competition
Imperfect information	New technologies that facilitate new sources of information about products and services
Negative externalities	Technological innovations that increase the availability of nonfossil fuel sources of energy for households and firms
	Technologies to reduce carbon dioxide emissions in the air
Public production	Technological advances have the potential to improve infrastructure, urban transport, postal delivery, and returns on public assets in a competitive environment

tion of knowledge; research that helps develop innovative ideas merits public and private support.

Market forces continue to provide favorable conditions for important sources of innovation. Certainly, R&D plays a critical role, and aggregate data indicate that the private sector has surpassed the federal government in funding it. According to the National Science Foundation, support for R&D from the federal government has declined from nearly 2 percent of GDP during the 1960s to about 0.6 percent in recent years. In the same time period, corporate

R&D has grown to nearly 2 percent of GDP, from less than 0.6 percent of GDP during the 1960s.

Human capital also is essential if R&D is to produce fruitful outcomes. As discussed later, the private sector tends to attract higher-caliber human capital than the government attracts for a given occupation, which gives it an advantage in managing and performing R&D. In addition, innovation and growth are positively affected if educated engineers comprise a notable component of a society's human capital (Murphy, Shleifer, and Vishny 1991; Maloney and Caicedo 2017).

Future Innovative Activity

Notwithstanding the capital and labor that the private sector can draw on to perform R&D, some have doubts about the state of innovation in the United States. Eric Posner and Glen Weyl (2014) raise concerns that a dramatic shift has occurred in the types of careers that highly talented individuals are pursuing in the United States—away from modestly paying, public-spirited research, education, and engineering jobs and toward more lucrative careers in business and finance. Anne Marie Knott (2017) argues that the money companies have been spending on R&D is producing fewer and fewer results and its returns have been declining over the past three decades either because it has become much harder for R&D to lead to major innovations, which is consistent with the views of Nicholas Bloom and others (2018), Robert Gordon (2016), and Tyler Cowen (2011), or because companies have gotten worse at performing R&D, which is consistent with Posner and Weyl's concern about the effects of career shifts by talented individuals.

Knott, however, takes the somewhat optimistic view that although the opportunities for R&D that led to important innovations and technological advance decline within industries over time, the best companies and entrepreneurs respond by creating new industries with greater technological opportunities. In other words, certain industries may be doomed but companies do not have to be. Bill Gates is even more optimistic, claiming in an article by Uri Friedman (2014) that "the idea that innovation is slowing down is stupid." Gates supports his claim by pointing to the potential advances in how American society produces energy, designs materials, creates medicines, educates people, uses virtual reality, and other exciting possibilities.

I would add travel within and between cities and between countries. I have mentioned the potential for automobile travel to be revolutionized by electric and autonomous vehicles. Air travel could be revolutionized by new supersonic commercial airliners that travel at nearly 4,000 miles per hour. Aerion has developed such an airliner and expects it to make its first commercial flight before the end of the decade. It also expects it to overcome emissions problems by using direct air capture to lessen carbon dioxide output in the synthetic fuel that its jets use and to overcome noise problems by developing a technology that will do away with sonic booms over land. The vitality and dynamism of the private sector suggest that the United States can look forward to many advances that may seem unimaginable today.

The new COVID-19 vaccines are an extraordinary achievement and are likely to be worth trillions of dollars to the world but only billions of dollars to the creator.[2] William Nordhaus (2004) estimated that only 2.2 percent of the value of an innovation was captured by innovators, while Benjamin Jones and Lawrence Summers (2020) find that the average social returns from innovation are large and produce social benefits that are a multiple, perhaps as high as ten or possibly twenty times, the investment costs.

Additional Sources of Innovation

Two avenues are worth pursuing that have the potential to significantly enhance the nation's culture for innovation. First, more than a century ago, leading industrialists, including Leland Stanford, Andrew Carnegie, and John D. Rockefeller, used their fortunes to found some of the nation's greatest research universities, which have contributed greatly to advances in knowledge that have spurred innovation and technological advance. It is time for the leading technology company industrialists to found another great US university. Government, specifically the California state government, also could add to the research strength of our universities by allowing and facilitating Berkeley and Los Angeles to become private institutions, freeing them of the state's uncertain funding streams and operating restrictions.[3]

Second, Alexander Bell and others (2017) point to the existence of "lost Einsteins," who could have contributed to innovative activity if they had been encouraged when they were students and if they had the opportunity throughout their lives to pursue such work. Socioeconomic background is the binding constraint, as the authors find that highly able students from low-income households have very little likelihood of becoming inventors. Students who are exposed to a particular invention or who grow up close to an inventor, especially a patent holder, are more likely to follow that career path; African-Americans, Latinos, women, and Southerners do not tend to have that exposure.

The existence of many lost Einsteins in the US population can partly be interpreted as a shortcoming of our education system to provide less advantaged children with the opportunity to overcome their socioeconomic backgrounds and develop their full potential. In the spirit of this book, this signals an opportunity for and potential example of market forces producing large benefits by engaging less-affluent members of society to increase innovative activity and economic growth.

Could markets play that role successfully? Pioneer, an independently funded small team of individuals, is attempting to address the problem of lost Einsteins, or the opportunity gap, by setting up an experimental fund to select promising candidates from all over the world who may make important scientific discoveries.[4] Emergent Ventures, a fellowship and grant program from the Mercatus Center at George Mason University, has a similar objective.[5] The next part of this book broadly explores the issue through the interaction between market forces and social goals.

PART II

How Markets
Can Help Government
Accomplish Social Goals

TEN

Why Markets Could Help
Government Achieve Social Goals

American society, like any society, seeks to address other social problems besides economic efficiency. The primary social goals that US policymakers have attempted to accomplish are to reduce poverty, ensure fairness in labor markets, and provide merit goods. Even if markets are efficient, people could live in poverty, job applicants and workers could be treated unfairly, and merit goods could be underprovided. Government has, therefore, played an active role to accomplish social goals by redistributing resources from taxpayers to certain individuals and groups and by passing regulations and other legislation that attempt to benefit certain groups.

Government's weaknesses, mentioned in chapter 3, suggest its efforts could be compromised if it fails to account for individuals' incentives and unanticipated behavioral responses. In *Government Failure*, I concluded that those failures caused social goals policies to make modest progress, at best, in achieving its goals, while wasting considerable resources in the process.

Generally, markets' strengths seem to be better suited to accomplishing economic goals rather than social goals. However, markets have the potential to help government by providing opportunities for households and firms to respond to incentives to improve their economic circumstances and by producing innovations that particularly benefit people who social goals policies are attempting to target. Specifically, market forces could enable lower-income workers to improve their productivity and earnings while enabling firms to become more profitable; penalize firms that continue to discriminate against hiring certain workers and reward firms that hire those workers; and lead to technological advances that, for example, simultaneously improve the environment and the health and lifetime earnings of lower-income households that are less able than higher-income households to avoid living in polluted neighborhoods.

The assistance of market forces has been questioned because a firm's objective should be to maximize profit or shareholder value (Friedman 1970) and because it is not clear that executives have any particular skills to address broad social issues (Mankiw 2020). However, the inefficiencies of social goals policies are so large and the issues so important that I consider at the end of this part of the book whether firms could be incentivized to expand their role to help the nation accomplish social goals more efficiently. An encouraging starting point is that private firms are increasingly expressing an interest in helping solve social problems and, as discussed in this part of the book, some have taken modest steps to do so.[1]

ELEVEN

Reducing Poverty

Richard Burkhauser and others (2020) conclude that Lyndon B. Johnson's War on Poverty is largely over and has turned out to be a success. However, policymakers continue to redistribute enormous sums of money to maintain this success. The specific policies currently used to reduce poverty, summarized in table 11-1, have taken three approaches: direct financial assistance, labor market interventions, and in-kind benefits.

Markets can help disadvantaged people achieve a material quality of life that exceeds the poverty level by helping children who must grow up in poor households get a better start in life, improving adults' employment prospects, and initiating programs that increase low-wage workers' earnings and non-wage benefits. In chapter 2, I acknowledged that, although the examples that illustrate markets' help to reduce poverty are not necessarily durable, they offer possibilities that may evolve in their importance.

GOVERNMENT POVERTY POLICIES

Based on the US Census Bureau's measure known as the Official Poverty Rate, the poverty rate in the United States has hovered between 11 and 15 percent since the 1960s.[1] The OECD provides international comparisons, and its measure put the US poverty rate at slightly above 15 percent in 2015, which exceeds the poverty rates of most other OECD member countries.[2] David Brady, Ryan Finnigan, and Sabine Hubgen (2017) argued that single-mother families do not explain the comparatively higher poverty rate in the United States, because those families are only a small share of the US population: among households headed by working-age adults, 8.8 percent of people lived in single-mother households in 2013, only a modest increase over the 7.4 percent share in 1970. The authors' thesis was that the comparatively high poverty rate in the United States was attributable to the higher "penalty" attached to un-employment, low levels of education, household formation by young people, and single motherhood. Evidence also exists that some Americans are forced to live in extreme poverty, although the actual number is strongly disputed.[3]

Policymakers seek to enable all US citizens to have a decent material quality of life by redistributing more than $1 trillion a year by taxing higher-income households and transferring the proceeds to lower-income house-holds to reduce poverty in the United States (Congressional Budget Office 2018).[4] In fact, contrary to the official poverty statistics just noted, when those annual transfer payments are included in the construction of the poverty rate, the actual poverty rate in the United States appears to be low. For example, Burkhauser and others (2020) assess the change in the US poverty rate by developing a full-income poverty measure that includes cash income, taxes, and in-kind transfers and comparing it with the Official Poverty Rate when President Johnson declared war on poverty in 1964. The authors find that, while the Official Poverty Rate fell from 19.5 percent in 1963 to 12.3 percent in 2017, their measure showed the rate actually fell from 19.5 percent to 2.3 percent during that period, with the difference by 2017 between 12.3 percent and 2.3 percent due to the creation and expansion of major safety net pro-grams. Other studies also conclude that the poverty rate is less than 3 percent (Gramm and Early 2018; Meyer and Sullivan 2016). Bruce Meyer and Nikolas Mittag (2019) argue that consumption is a better measure for identifying low-income households in America because income, including transfers, may be underreported, but they also find that the poverty rate is less than 3 percent.

Because poverty may be an economic condition that begins at birth, may continue throughout an individual's entire life, and may be transmitted to subsequent generations of the individual's family, an efficient policy to reduce poverty would strive to improve a poor child's early life conditions, especially the child's health and education. Janet Currie and Maya Rossin-Slater (2015) point out that those improvements would have implications throughout the individual's life for educational attainment, labor market experience, adult health, and other indicators of socioeconomic status, and they would possibly break the transmission of poverty from one family generation to another. Importantly, the costs to the nation of providing certain merit goods, such as healthcare and safety and security, also would be significantly reduced because people who are in poor health and those who commit crimes, especially violent ones, tend to have lower incomes. Michael McLaughlin and Mark Rank (2018) put the cost of childhood poverty, including productivity losses, greater healthcare problems, and the higher likelihood of engaging in crime, at roughly $1 trillion in 2015. The authors also find that increasing spending to reduce childhood poverty would provide large returns, but they do not assess the efficiency of Special Supplemental Nutrition Programs or analyze how the returns could be obtained at lower cost.

As indicated in table 11-1, anti-poverty programs take a patchwork approach, which to some extent attempts to address the costs associated with unemployment and low levels of education but does not attempt to address the costs to individuals and to society of early childbirth and household formation. Specifically, the Child Care and Development Block Grant and WIC are intended to help children born into poor families, while Temporary Assistance to Needy Families (TANF) grants, food stamps (SNAP), Medicaid, and so on, may assist individuals who remain poor throughout their lives; thus, those programs have been criticized for discouraging work that could help those individuals escape poverty (Glaeser 2017b).[5]

To be fair, work disincentives should account for taxes and transfers. For example, the effective federal marginal tax rate when a person moves from the bottom quintile to the middle quintile in the distribution of income is 76 percent.[6] Thus, a constructive assessment of the work disincentives of poverty programs should be conducted in the broader context of the US tax system. In any case, social goals programs and policies may conflict because policies that discourage work may, for example, reduce the potential social value of job training and employment programs.[7]

R. Anton Braun, Karen Kopecky, and Tatyana Koreshkova (2017) caution that collectively removing means-tested programs for retirees, including SSI, Medicaid, food stamps, and housing programs, would, based on their evidence, reduce overall social welfare. But the performance of individual programs appears to vary greatly, and it is possible to raise serious concerns about the efficiency of even the most effective programs and policies.

TABLE 11-1. Policies to Reduce Poverty

Direct Financial Assistance
Temporary Assistance to Needy Families (TANF) grants
Earned Income Tax Credit (EITC)
The Supplementary Security Income (SSI) program
Child Care and Development block grant
Labor Market Interventions
Minimum legal wage for full-time workers
Comprehensive Employment and Training Act (CETA)
Job Training and Partnership Act (JTPA)
Workforce Investment Act (WIA)
Early education (Head Start and other programs)
In-Kind Benefits
Child care tax credits
Food stamps (SNAP, Supplemental Nutrition Assistance Program)
Special Supplemental Nutrition Program for Women, Infants, and Children (WIC)
National school lunch program
Building public housing
Subsidies for private rental housing (Section 8 program)
Low-income housing tax credits
Medicaid

EITC AND TANF

Robert Moffitt (2012, 2014) credited EITC for transferring money to less-affluent individuals and for providing work incentives for those at the bottom of the income distribution. Amanda Agan and Michael Milosky (2018) found that the availability of state EITCs also reduced recidivism, but only for women. Given that state EITCs are predominantly available to custodial parents of minor children, this asymmetry is not surprising.

Households must file a tax return to receive benefits from EITC; thus, some low-income households do not receive tax-based benefits because they fail to file tax returns (Ramnath and Tong 2017). Similarly, Aparna Mathur (2015) suggested that the nonworking poor have not been helped by TANF because many poor families are unaware that they are eligible for assistance from the TANF program. Other families know about TANF but choose not to apply for benefits because they envision the process as too complicated or believe they will likely be rejected despite having hardly any cash income. In addition, the average monthly benefit amounts are modest, ranging from $300 to $400 for a family of three.

Moffitt (2015) concluded that, although aggregate welfare spending has increased over time, it has evolved very differently for different demographic and economic groups, with the disabled and aged experiencing much greater increases in support than the rest of the population, and with much slower rates of increase, if not decreases, for single mothers and their children—that is, a penalty for single-mother households. Zachary Parolin (2018) identified a disturbing feature of the distributional effects of TANF funds by finding that states with larger percentages of Black residents are less likely to prioritize the provision of cash assistance. He estimated that neutralizing the inequality in TANF spending would reduce the Black-white child poverty gap by approximately 13 percent.

EITC is an anti-poverty program with the attractive feature that individuals can benefit from it only if they work. Accordingly, it also could be attractive because it increases employment. However, Hendrik Kleven (2019) has recently questioned the extent that EITC incentivizes work by investigating every EITC program at the state and federal level since the inception of the policy in 1975. He shows that the only EITC reform associated with clear employment increases is the expansion enacted in 1993, which was aided by a favorable business cycle. He concludes that, overall, the case for sizable EITC employment-enhancing effects of single mothers relative to single women without children is fragile.

Child Care and Development Block Grant

The Child Care and Development block grant is the primary source of federal funding for child care subsidies (tax credits) for low-income working families and for funds to improve child care quality. The block grant is not solely an anti-poverty program because it is broadly available, but it could make an important contribution to reducing poverty by relieving the financial burden of child care. Luke Rodgers (2018) documents a classic case of "unintentional consequences" from the policy as he finds that over half of every dollar in tax credits is passed through to child care providers in the form of higher prices and wages, making child care less affordable for low-income families.

Martha Bailey and others (2019) assess the effects of California's 2004 Paid Family Leave Act (PFLA) on women's careers and finds that it did not improve their short- or long-term careers. To be sure, one could assess the PFLA in terms of the additional time it enabled women to be with their children. However, taking the perspective of the PFLA as an anti-poverty tool, the authors find little evidence that it increased women's employment, wage earnings, or attachment to employers. For new mothers, taking paid family leave reduced employment by 7 percent and lowered annual wages by 8 percent six to ten years after giving birth. Overall, paid family leave tended to reduce the number of children being born and, by decreasing mothers' time at work, increase the time they spent with their children.

Minimum Wage

According to the US Department of Labor, only a tiny share, just 0.28 percent of the 156 million civilian workers, earned the federal minimum wage in 2018.[8] Most of the workers were younger than twenty-five. So, the federal minimum wage of $7.25 per hour, which has not been adjusted for a decade, has become somewhat irrelevant, as states' minimum wages are higher and, as discussed below, dozens of large employers have pledged to pay employees much more than $7.25 per hour.

Yet, the effects of the minimum wage on employment and the distribution of income still attract considerable attention and apparently generate never-ending controversy among economists. There are many studies on each side of the employment/disemployment effect and the overall net benefits to low-income workers. Recent supportive findings of increasing the federal minimum wage include Doruk Cengiz and others (2019), who examine 138 prominent state-level minimum wage changes between 1979 and 2016 and find that the overall number of low-wage jobs remained essentially unchanged over five years following an increase. The authors also find no evidence of disemployment when they consider higher levels of minimum wage. However, they do find some evidence of reduced employment in tradable sectors.

Jose Azar and others (2019) take a more nuanced approach and study the effects of the minimum wage in labor markets that vary in concentration. They find that raising the minimum wage reduces employment when labor market concentration is low and gradually increases it as concentration increases, implying that raising the minimum wage would increase employment in monopsony labor markets, but it is likely to reduce employment in most other labor markets. Alan Krueger (2015) cautions that the amount of increase in the minimum wage is critical to its effects: raising the federal minimum wage from $7.25 per hour to $12 per hour would do more good than harm for low-wage workers, but raising it to $15 per hour would risk undesirable and unintended consequences.[9] As of this writing, President Biden proposed a $1.9 trillion relief package that calls for gradually increasing the minimum hourly wage until it hits $15 in 2025.

On the other side, recent critical findings of increasing the minimum wage include: (1) long-run employment disincentives in the restaurant industry as labor-intensive incumbent restaurants are replaced by more capital-intensive restaurants with fewer employees subject to the minimum wage (Aaronson and others 2018); (2) a lower likelihood that individuals would have employer-sponsored health insurance, with the largest offset effects occurring among workers in very low-paying occupations (Clemens, Kahn, and Meer 2018); and (3) updates from Seattle's experience where raising the minimum wage had a negative effect on overall pay, harmed people who were not working but looking for a job, and helped people who were already working at low-wage jobs (Jardim and others 2018). David Neumark and Peter Shirley (2021) attempt to distill what the vast body of research literature says about the employment effects of the minimum wage and reach conclusions that point to only its negative effects.

As we await for minimum wage proponents to respond, little doubt exists that increasing the minimum wage would primarily benefit workers who do not come from poor households (Sabia and Burkhauser 2010) and would harm poor households by raising the prices of goods that they consume (MaCurdy 2015).

Job Training and Assistance

Individuals have to be employed if they are to gain any benefits from EITC and a higher minimum wage, so job training and assistance to enhance individuals' productive skills and to promote employment is potentially important. Robert LaLonde (1995) synthesized findings on the efficacy of the training programs and found that the investments in them were too small to have much effect on poverty rates. The Comprehensive Employment and Training Act (CETA) programs were found to yield modest gains for adult women (generally less than $2,000 per year) and smaller gains for adult men and youths. Thus, the increase in the earnings of program participants may be entirely offset by the programs' cost in public assistance funding. More expensive programs appear to be necessary to have any hope of achieving large post-program earning gains, especially because case workers at training centers have shown a marked preference for accepting the most disadvantaged and least employable applicants into their programs (Heckman, Smith, and Taber 1996).

Job Corps is the largest free job training program for young adults. Recently, the inspector general of the Department of Labor concluded that "Job Corps could not demonstrate beneficial job training outcomes." Graduates at most Job Corps' centers were placed in jobs, but many of the placements were in low-wage jobs that the graduates could have obtained without a program that cost from $15,000 to $45,000 per student (Thrush 2018).

Benjamin Hyman (2018) compared the earnings over a twenty-year period of people who received trade adjustment assistance with the earnings of similar workers who did not receive that assistance, and he found that TAA-trained workers lost out on $10,000 in income while in training compared with others who were not in training. TAA recipients earned $50,000 more than their peers over a ten-year period, but a decade later, the average annual income for those who did and who did not receive training converged.

Early and Secondary Education

David Freedman (2016) pointed out that high-quality early education programs that improved learning for children from poor households seemed to largely overcome whatever cognitive and emotional deficits poverty and other environmental circumstances imparted in the first years of their lives. Early education programs can succeed in significantly improving the lives of children and their lives as adults. The best ones, including the Perry Preschool Project in Ypsilanti, Michigan, in the 1960s, which benefited participants and their children (Heckman and Karapakula 2019); the Carolina Abecedarian Project and the Carolina Approach to Responsive Education, two closely related early-childhood programs that engaged participants, predominantly African American children, in the 1970s (Garcia and others 2020); and, more recently, the Educare program in Chicago, were developed for children at the age of five or earlier, with teachers who were well trained in the particular demands of early education.

However, Head Start and other public early education programs rarely come close to this level of quality and are nowhere near universal in their effect. Patrick Klein and Christopher Walters (2016) cast a favorable light on Head Start when it was compared with home care and competing preschools. But the authors did not attempt to make the case that Head Start was an exceptional program that could notably improve the life cycle of poor children nationwide.[10] Expenditures to reform primary and secondary schools cannot overcome cognitive and noncognitive disadvantages acquired in the early years of life.[11]

Title I of the Elementary and Secondary Education Act was created to provide extra funding to schools and school districts with a high percentage of students from low-income families. It was hoped that the additional funding would help reduce the academic achievement skills gap for students with high and low socioeconomic status and help increase the lifetime earnings of the latter. Eric Hanushek and others (2019) reviewed test scores for Americans born between 1954 and 2001 and found that the skills gap hardly had closed at all. The central problem appeared to occur in high schools, as any improvements before then were reversed. High schools were not capable of overcoming the competitive disadvantages caused by the family life that students of low socioeconomic status may endure.

In-Kind Benefits

Food stamps (SNAP) have become a mainstay for low-income households during hard economic times, and more people have been using them in recent decades. Marianne Bitler and Hilary Hoynes (2016) found that, in 2010, the share of people under sixty-five living below the poverty line and in extreme poverty would have been greater had food stamps not been available. But Charles Lane (2017) reported that 20 percent of food stamp dollars were spent on items that utterly lacked nutritional value and that may contribute to poor health.

Medicaid benefits are provided by the states for some low-income people, families and children, pregnant women, the elderly, and people with disabilities. Broadly speaking, participants value the programs, especially the elderly (De Nardi, French, and Jones 2016). But the programs vary greatly in quality, and reimbursement rates in some states are often so low that many doctors have refused to take Medicaid patients.

Medicaid also appears to be a good investment in children born into low-income families. David Brown, Amanda Kowalski, and Ithai Lurie (2020) measure the long-term impact of expansions of Medicaid in the 1980s and 1990s and find that government investment in Medicaid for children results in them paying more taxes when they become adults. Children whose Medicaid eligibility increased collected less in EITC payments, paid more in cumulative taxes by age twenty-eight, and the women had higher cumulative wages by age twenty-eight. Overall, the government recouped 56 cents of each dollar spent on childhood Medicaid by the time those children reached age sixty. This does not include other benefits, including decreases in mortality and increases in college attendance.

In response to criticisms that in-kind benefits discourage work, the Trump administration proposed a rule to tighten eligibility requirements for low-income households that use SNAP and separate programs, such as TANF. Under the new rule, households would be eligible for nutritional assistance only if they receive cash or other benefits worth at least $50 a month from the TANF program for six months or more. Under that plan, an estimated 3.1 million SNAP participants would lose food assistance benefits. In addition, some states have announced plans to require Medicaid recipients to work, volunteer, or train for a job, and impose time limits on coverage. Although the Biden administration is likely to eventually reverse Trump's actions, even if it takes a long time to do so, future research can assess whether reducing the in-kind benefits had their intended effects on individuals' labor market participation and on reducing the social costs of the programs.

Summary

The preceding assortment of policies has alleviated poverty in the United States over time to some extent or, more appropriately, improved the quality of life for those with low incomes, and has affirmed the importance of government involvement in this area of policy. Using a consumption-based measure of poverty instead of a traditional, income-based measure and adjusting biases in price indexes, Bruce Meyer and James Sullivan (2013) found that the poverty rate declined by 26.4 percentage points between 1960 and 2010.

Scott Winship (2016) concluded that, as a result of TANF being enacted, child poverty fell 5 percentage points from 1996 to 2014.

Nathaniel Hendren and Ben Sprung-Keyser (2019) provide a unified welfare analysis that reinforces the findings that direct investments in low-income children's health and education have historically generated benefits that exceed government costs as children pay back the initial cost as adult earners through additional tax revenue and reduced transfer payments. James Heckman (2006) also argued that the benefits of expenditures on children in their early lives substantially exceed the costs.[12]

Overall, however, anti-poverty policies are characterized by significant inefficiencies, and constructive reform could yield large cost savings. Unfortunately, reform appears to be difficult, as Janet Currie and Maya Rossin-Slater (2015) and Douglas Almond, Janet Currie, and Valentina Duque (2018) point out, because comparisons of the policies suffer from a lack of consistent cost-benefit analysis. Unless policymakers follow a more systematic approach, the cost of anti-poverty policies will continue to be inflated by waste and fraud, and some recipients who could have taken steps to improve their own lives will continue to have little incentive to do so. Importantly, inefficiencies persist because poor families with children work less than half as many hours as their nonpoor counterparts (Schuck 2017). If the poor worked full time, the poverty rate would drop 40 percent. Even a less dramatic improvement in the poor's labor force participation still would have a notable effect on the poverty rate.

MARKET FORCES

Individuals find it difficult to escape a life of poverty because of the bad luck of premature household formation early in life and because the lack of a quality education prevents them from developing cognitive and noncognitive skills valued by the labor market. The evidence presented here on market-generated outcomes that reduce poverty in the United States should be qualified as largely anecdotal. But, as noted, they suggest possibilities that may evolve into actions that have a measurable effect on the poverty rate in the future.

Market Opportunities to Help Children Overcome Bad Luck
Individuals who are born into households headed by young parents or by a single mother are more likely than other individuals to begin life in poverty, and the likelihood that those individuals' lives in poverty will persist is

greater if they are poorly educated and if they spend long spells in unemployment. Markets can reduce the likelihood of those possibilities by discouraging premature household formations and helping children who are born into premature household formations to develop noncognitive and cognitive skills to increase their chances for a more productive life.

Markets can discourage potentially premature household formations by providing information to young people and would-be single mothers about the consequences of poor life choices. For example, the MTV reality television show *16 and Pregnant* provided such information by documenting several months in the difficult lives of teenagers who dealt with being pregnant. Melissa Kearney and Phillip Levine (2015) found that this show led to a 4.3 percent reduction in teen births and to an increased interest in the use of contraceptives and abortion. Although the study's findings have been debated and, undoubtedly, will continue to be debated, they motivate the possibility that a well-targeted media production could discourage a social outcome that contributes to poverty.[13] If media companies find it in their interest to produce more of those productions, the possibility could be realized.

Although early life conditions are important, children can be resilient, and several interventions can enable them to recover to a significant extent. Marco Francesconi and James Heckman (2016) singled out workplace-based adolescent intervention programs, apprenticeships with mentoring, and surrogate parenting and guidance as demonstrating the potential to turn a child's life around by fostering important character skills, such as increasing self-confidence, the ability to work in teams, and autonomy and discipline. Again, if firms find it in their interest to expand such interventions, they could help to reduce poverty.

In some cases, children from low-income families can improve the cognitive skills they develop from their education by homeschooling, attending charter schools, and using computers to increase learning. Currently, about 2.3 million children receive homeschooling, or parent-led home-based education. Homeschooling—even in low-income families—may be an attractive alternative to overcome the potentially toxic environment of the local institutional schools, because it enables students to focus more closely on their studies in a safer environment and to reduce their exposure to physical violence, drugs and alcohol, psychological abuse, racism, and unhealthy sexual behavior. While not causal, descriptive evidence shows that homeschooled students score above average on standardized academic achievement tests, regardless of their parents' level of formal education or their family's household income, and that Black homeschooled students score notably higher than Black public school students on those tests.[14]

Sesame Street, the well-known television show for children, can be considered a component of homeschooling.[15] Kearney and Levine (2019) studied its effects and found that children's exposure to *Sesame Street* improved their performance at school, especially for boys. In addition, exposed cohorts of students were more likely to become employed and to have somewhat higher wages as adults, but those outcomes were not precisely estimated.

David Leonhardt (2016) took a close look at charter schools in Massachusetts, which are privately managed but receive public and private funding. His examination indicated that those schools serve underprivileged children effectively. And, they have produced benefits that have been quantified, such as reducing the Black-white wage gap. Some of Boston's charter schools, despite enrolling mostly lower-income students, report test scores that resemble those of upper middle-class public schools. Boston's experience shows that competition among schools can force them to improve and help address government objectives in education.

Sesame Street is an example of corporations and foundations supporting education initiatives that have beneficial effects. Corporations and foundations also have provided resources to improve the quality of education in the United States. Google has contributed low-cost Chromebooks, free apps, and the like to public schools to help students develop skills such as problem solving and teamwork. The On It Foundation has provided free computers, computer training, and internet service to low-income families with students in grades K–12. And JP Morgan Chase's *New Skills for Youth* initiative is expanding career-focused education programs for minority and inner-city populations in secondary schools, with investments that attempt to lay the foundation for a life free of poverty. Finally, the Bill and Melinda Gates Foundation has recently pledged roughly $500 million over the next five years to fund networks of school programs that would help low-income and minority students get to college, and Jeff Bezos has committed an initial $2 billion to fund a new charitable organization to help the homeless and educate preschoolers. The value of those initiatives is that they may encourage and facilitate important trial-and-error experiments that eventually lead to a new, more effective approach to addressing a significant social problem.

Improving Adults' Employment Opportunities

The most comprehensive and potentially effective approach to reducing poverty is a strong labor market that addresses long-term joblessness and lifts households above the poverty level by enabling the adult members to find work that pays a "living wage," which, in turn, will increase the likelihood that the child members will be employed later in life (Aaronson and others 2019; Chetty and others 2016). Aaron Renn (2018) suggests that the macroeconomic expansion that began in 2009 appeared to be having those effects as firms increasingly adopted a "no experience required" policy to try to fill some jobs and, in some cases, eliminated the requirement for a college degree. Importantly, adults with a sizable employment gap, which rendered them unemployable, were in a pool of potential workers that employers were tapping. However, the recession recently caused by COVID-19 has significantly diminished the efficacy of the labor market overall. The type of recovery the United States experiences will determine how much time it takes before the labor market can resume its important role of reducing poverty.

Markets also have occasionally helped the nearly one-third of the adult working-age population with a criminal conviction become employed. For example, manufacturers in Dane County, Wisconsin, are hiring inmates at full wages to work in factories while they serve the remainder of their prison sentences. Nationwide, Honest Jobs is a website where formerly incarcerated people can find work from job openings posted by "felon-friendly employers" around the country who will consider hiring candidates with criminal convictions.[16] Honest Jobs is free to view, and employers can post up to three jobs for no charge; a monthly fee is required for additional job listings.

The effectiveness of a strong job market is enhanced by a good transportation system that enables people seeking work to have wide access to potential job opportunities. Nationwide, roughly 20 percent of households at or below the poverty level do not have access to a car (DeGood and Schwartz 2016), while public transit enables commuters to reach less than one-third of metrowide jobs within ninety minutes (Tomer 2012). Fortunately, the private sector has developed alternatives to enable people to have greater access to jobs, including low-cost van service in major urban areas and ride-sharing services. In the future, US society's successful adoption of autonomous vehicles could enhance job access even further and address Chetty and others' (2014) finding that lengthy commute times are a significant factor in people's inability to improve job matching, raise earnings, and leave poverty.

Actions by Firms to Reduce Poverty

Historically, the actions of the leading US firms have contributed significantly to raising households' living standards. For example, beginning in 1914, Henry Ford gave hundreds of thousands of Americans without college degrees a good living by hiring them to assemble automobiles. Today, technology firms in Silicon Valley hire thousands of highly educated, talented programmers. Some firms have recently initiated specific policies that have helped alleviate poverty by increasing low-wage workers' earnings, providing paid leave, and improving training and workers' skills, while other firms have directly improved public assistance programs for people who depend on them. An important question is whether the examples I present will evolve into permanent and widespread actions that have a measurable effect on the poverty rate or whether they will appear periodically, only during favorable stages of the business cycle.

INCREASING EARNINGS. Although it has long been argued that the primary responsibility of a firm's CEO is to maximize stockholders' returns, some executives appear to believe that leading firms have social responsibilities, which include enabling their full-time workers to be able to live on what they earn without depending on a government poverty program. At the same time, a firm's "investments" in its lowest-paid workers may improve efficiency and profitability. To take some recent examples:

- Bank of America announced it would be raising its minimum wage to $20 per hour by 2021. The pay increase would affect all of the bank's more than 200,000 employees. If you get a job at Bank of America, you will make at least $41,000 a year.

- Amazon raised its minimum wage in the fall of 2018 for all of its workers, including full-time, part-time, and seasonal, to $15 per hour. Some employees who already made that amount also received a pay increase.

- In early 2015, Walmart announced it would pay its workers more, with the idea that employees also would work more efficiently. Specifically, Walmart raised minimum hourly pay to $10 for workers who completed a training course. As of 2016, Walmart's average hourly pay for a full-time nonmanagerial employee rose 16 percent since 2014 to $13.69 (Irwin 2016). In addition, Walmart clarified the path from entry-level to managerial positions.

- Costco has been known to pay its workers a living wage beyond any level mandated by the government despite being in a very low-margin sector, low-price retailing. In early 2016, Costco raised its minimum hourly pay to $13, with its average pay rising to about $21 per hour. Costco has historically paid its workers more than Walmart has paid its workers and has a lower turnover rate. In late 2017, Target raised its starting pay to $11 an hour and increased it to $15 an hour by July 2020.

- Following Walmart's and Costco's actions, several large US employers announced they were giving raises to their lowest-paid workers, including but not limited to McDonald's, Nationwide Mutual Insurance, JP Morgan Chase, Starbucks, and The Gap. Company executives publicly announced the raises through op-eds and letters to their employees posted on their websites to set a public example, pressure their competitors to follow suit, and reap ancillary benefits in the form of good will from employees, customers, and investors (Morath and Jargon 2016).

- In response to the Tax Cuts and Jobs Act of 2017, which cut federal corporate taxes, many companies gave $1,000 bonuses to their nonexecutive workers, including but not limited to AT&T, Comcast, Walt Disney Company, and various banks. In addition, Disney initiated a $50 million investment in a tuition reimbursement program. Finally, Apple promised to add 20,000 domestic jobs over the next five years, and it is on track to do so.

The efforts by large employers to raise their less-affluent employees' wages illustrate that markets can provide a minimum wage that significantly exceeds the federal minimum wage. In addition, when market forces increase the minimum wage it may result in fewer unintended consequences than when the government hikes the minimum wage.

PAID LEAVE. Hourly employees, who generally constitute lower-wage workers, are least likely to be able to afford unpaid leave or newborn child care. They are also more likely to drop out of the labor force, which increases their chance of entering poverty, because they cannot balance employment with family responsibilities. In addition to raising wages for lower-wage workers, companies are increasing employees' paid time off to care for sick family members and for paternity leave. Extending paid leave also helps reduce poverty in a child's later life by increasing parental interaction and guidance.

In an extreme case, Lowe's, which had been the only one of the largest twenty employers in the United States that did not give women who gave birth paid time off, recently announced a new leave policy where all employed women who gave birth would have ten weeks of paid leave, and all other parents would have two weeks of paid leave (Cain Miller 2018). Other companies increasing their paid leave include Google, which gives new parents eighteen weeks, and Etsy, which gives new parents a full six months. Deloitte introduced a flexible policy benefiting all their employees by giving them access to sixteen weeks of paid "family leave" a year, covering, in addition to the birth or adoption of a child, elder care responsibilities and caring for a spouse or family member who is seriously ill.[17]

JOB TRAINING. Public job training programs have been criticized as being poorly coordinated with employers' labor requirements; thus, workers who complete such programs generally have not improved their employment prospects and earnings. A direct and potentially more effective approach is for firms to develop major training programs, which could raise the skills and wages of low-skilled workers.

For example, Amazon plans to spend $700 million to retrain about one-third of its American workers to do more high-tech tasks (Casselman and Satariano 2019). The plan applies across the company, from corporate employees to warehouse workers, retraining about 100,000 people by 2025 and moving a large swath of workers up one or two rungs on the skills ladder. For example, warehouse floor workers are turned into IT technicians, and low-level coders are turned into data scientists. Other companies that have started training programs include Walmart and AT&T. In addition, Google has donated $1 billion over the next five years to nonprofit companies with the goal to allow anyone with an internet connection to become proficient with the technology and prepare for a job in information technology support and app development.

Per Scholas is a nonprofit company that offers training programs and engages with many potential employers. Per Scholas is funded by a diverse group of leading corporations and foundations and provides tuition-free technology training to unemployed or underemployed adults for careers as information technology professionals. It links up with employers in the areas they serve to determine the kinds of skills that are in demand and that might lead to a well-paying career path. Per Scholas offers a targeted range of tuition-free technology and professional development training, which includes individualized support for job placement and personal and career advancement. By identifying the particular skills employers were looking for, Per Scholas's IT training has increased workers' wages nearly $4,000 per year (Porter 2016).

Pursuit is another example of a private nonprofit firm developing new models of workforce technology training for low-income workers without a four-year college degree (Lohr 2019). Pursuit's program is free, but it is selective given that only 10 percent of applicants are accepted. It receives money from philanthropies, and it has a financing bond, where graduates who make more than $60,000 a year agree to pay 12 percent of their income to the investors for three years. Pursuit has graduated 300 students, and 85 percent of them landed well-paying tech jobs within a year.

In comparison with public programs, private firms and third parties who regularly engage with employers have considerable potential to lift many workers out of poverty by expanding targeted training programs.[18] As discussed later, private firms also have contributed to job training by providing vocational training in public secondary schools.

IMPROVING THE QUALITY OF LIFE FOR PEOPLE IN POVERTY. Firms have taken it upon themselves to take actions that, while not reducing poverty, have increased the availability of food and shelter to make an individual's life in poverty more bearable. Walmart and many other firms donate excess food to a nonprofit organization, Feeding America, which distributes the food to its nationwide network of 210 regional food banks that feed more than 46 million people through food pantries, soup kitchens, shelters, and other community-based agencies.[19] Propel, a startup, developed software for low-income Americans that enables food stamp recipients to manage their accounts more easily and to obtain coupon discounts.[20] Finally, Amazon has tried to be a "good neighbor" by partnering with a nonprofit group called Mary's Place to transform a hotel it purchased into one of the largest homeless shelters in Seattle.

SUMMARY

Reducing poverty is a major social goal taken on by the federal government at a cost of more than a trillion dollars per year. Although it is difficult to quantify the extent to which markets have assisted government's efforts, some of their activities can be interpreted as efficiency improvements to help improve the lives of people in poverty. Market forces have helped children overcome the bad luck of an adverse home environment, improved adults' employment opportunities, and initiated programs to raise low-wage workers' earnings and keep them on the job. The increasing number of firms that believe they have a social obligation to help reduce poverty and the constructive actions that have been taken to date suggest that markets have the potential to play a significant role in helping government accomplish this social goal in the future. The question is whether markets will make a long-term commitment to this effort.

TWELVE

Fairness in Labor Markets

Competitive markets generally enhance economic efficiency by fully reflecting the preferences of buyers and sellers. However, an important exception occurs when labor markets reflect bias and the preferences of employers not to hire or, if they do hire, pay lower wages to workers based on their race, religion, sex, color, or other nonpecuniary characteristics. Such behavior is prohibited by laws, summarized in table 12-1, that attempt to eliminate discrimination against potential new hires and to ensure that all employees are compensated fairly and treated fairly when they may not be able to remain employed at their current job.

Market forces may not be able to change people's inherent prejudices and biases. However, they can play an important role in discouraging discrimination by imposing costs on employers who discriminate against groups of people who may be more efficient and competent than the people they prefer to hire (Becker 1957). Employers are then faced with a tradeoff of lower profits in return for acting on their bigotry. Unfortunately, antidiscrimination laws and market forces have not been sufficient to eliminate discrimination in the United States. However, as in the case of reducing poverty, some market participants have recently expressed an opposition to discrimination followed by constructive actions, and they could take stronger and more extensive actions in the years to come.

TABLE 12-1. Policies to Promote Fairness in Labor Markets

Fair Hiring
Title VII of the 1964 Civil Rights Act
Civil Rights Act of 1991
Americans with Disabilities Act (ADA)
Fair Treatment at the Workplace
Equal Pay Act of 1963
Overtime Pay Requirements (Federal Labor Standards Act)
Worker Adjustment and Retraining Notification Act (WARN)
Family and Medical Leave Act of 1993

LAWS TO ENSURE FAIRNESS IN LABOR MARKETS

Government Failure summarized evidence indicating that policymakers could not legislate the end of discrimination; instead, they could only change the way discrimination manifested itself because it was difficult to prevent firms from offsetting policies that attempted to promote fair hiring and improve the terms of employment. For example, faced with costly lawsuits for terminating female and disabled employees, firms have hired fewer of those workers; forced to pay overtime wages and to warn workers of impending plant closings, firms have reduced straight-time wages and found ways to close plants without providing advance notice; and so on. Recent research on discrimination continues to find offsetting behavior by employers affecting job applicants; some, who the policy attempts to help, have criminal records and others have children.

Equal employment opportunity (EEO) statements intend to influence labor market flows by encouraging more racial minorities to apply for job openings. Andreas Leibbrandt and John List (2018) analyzed data from nearly 2,500 job seekers across ten US cities and found that the presence of an EEO job advertisement statement dampened racial minorities' willingness to apply for jobs because racial minorities perceived that environments with such statements would tend to treat them as token hires instead of employing them on their own merits. EEO statements could, then, backfire by discouraging the very population they intend to help.

Amanda Agan and Sonja Starr (2018) studied the effect of ban-the-box (BTB) policies that restrict employers from asking about applicants' criminal histories on job applications because those questions could reduce employment among Black men, who disproportionately have criminal records. Absent these direct questions, firms could make assumptions about whether applicants have a criminal record based on their race, thereby offsetting the intent of prohibiting questions on criminal histories. The authors found that BTB policies have strongly encouraged racial discrimination, as indicated by the Black-white gap in job application callbacks: before BTB, white applicants to employers with application forms that included the box received 7 percent more callbacks than similar Black applicants, but enacting BTB increased this gap to 43 percent.

Jennifer Doleac and Benjamin Hansen (2016) also investigated whether employers statistically discriminate against demographic groups that are likely to have a criminal record when an applicant's criminal history is unavailable. They relied on variation in the details and timing of state and local BTB policies and found that those policies reduced the probability of young, low-skilled Black men and young, low-skilled Hispanic men being employed, by 5.1 percent and 2.9 percent, respectively.

The growing number of women moving into professional occupations, such as the legal profession and academia, characterized by an initial period of skill development and career accomplishment followed by an evaluation that could lead to a promotion or termination, has led some institutions to preempt possible claims of discrimination against women who bear and raise children during this stressful period. Gender-neutral family policies have been adopted that apply equally to new mothers and fathers. In this case, the institutions are not attempting to circumvent any antidiscrimination laws per se; nonetheless, their well-meaning intention to "level the playing field" could have unintended consequences.

Heather Antecol, Kelly Bedard, and Jenna Stearns (2018) studied the effect of gender-neutral policies adopted by the top fifty research universities in the United States that allow untenured professors to stop their tenure clock for, typically, one year after childbirth or an adoption before they must be evaluated for tenure. The authors confined their analysis to economics departments and found that the probability that a man gets tenure at his first job increases by 19 percentage points after a gender-neutral tenure policy is adopted, while the probability that a female gets tenure at her first job decreases by 22 percentage points after such a policy is adopted. Their explanation for the different outcomes is that men can use the extra time to publish more "top-5" journal articles; however, women are unable to publish more of those articles. The gender-neutral policy effectively raises the standards for tenure by influencing tenure committees to expect a given tenure candidate to have more "top-5" journal publications, which harms women's tenure prospects because it does not adequately reflect the true gender-specific loss in productivity from having children.[1]

Firms also may find ways to offset affirmative action that attempts to correct past discriminatory actions that have disadvantaged certain groups, but it also appears that temporary affirmative action may have persistent effects. Executive Order 11246, the primary affirmative action regulation for employment in the United States, mandates that firms with sizable contracts or subcontracts with the federal government must make a good faith effort to employ minorities at rates that are at least proportional to their shares of the local and qualified workforce. Conrad Miller (2017) found that the order increased the share of Black employees over time even after an establishment was no longer subject to the regulations—that is, when the company was no longer a government contractor. Miller argued that, in this case, the regulation effectively provided information to the firms by inducing them to improve their methods for screening potential hires. Fidan Ana Kurtulus (2016), however, found that the positive impact of the regulation on the combined shares of women and Black men persisted for only a few years.

MARKET FORCES

Market forces rely on firms' incentives to maximize profits to discourage them from engaging in costly discrimination. A common strategy firms have used to avoid antidiscrimination laws is to locate where the people they want to discriminate against do not tend to live. However, that decision would narrow the firms' potential pool of employees, raising labor and other costs, and would have to be balanced against the perceived benefits of discrimination. Market forces also have discouraged discrimination in product markets. For example, Sears was a pioneer in fighting discrimination by allowing rural Black Southerners to avoid the blatant racism they faced at small county stores, where they were charged inflated prices, received humiliating treatment, and were offered lower-quality or no products, by making purchases from the Sears catalogue by mail or over the phone.

Market forces continue to impose costs on employers who discriminate by enabling groups who are discriminated against to invest in their human capital, which makes the cost of discrimination even greater, thereby discouraging it. The success of Asian Americans may illustrate that possibility because, despite experiencing race-based discrimination in labor markets, educational institutions, and the like for many decades, they have achieved strong upward mobility relative to both Blacks and whites for every cohort born in California since 1920 (Hilger 2006). Asian Americans tend to value academic achievement, but Nathaniel Hilger claims their earnings gains are conditional on education; thus, their upward mobility could be due to other legacy advantages that reflect skills, or it could be due primarily to antidiscrimination laws that have enabled their skills to be rewarded by the labor market. The latter explanation, providing a minor role for Asian Americans' investment in human capital, seems dubious because, historically, Asian Americans were intensely discriminated against and firms have continued to find ways to avoid antidiscrimination laws. In contrast, it is difficult for firms not to incur costs from discriminating against Asian Americans, who have developed a high level of human capital.

Information technology and social media also may have helped strengthen the ability of market forces to counteract all forms of discrimination. For example, Legal Services Link is an online service that, among other things, connects people needing legal services to address some form of discrimination with lawyers willing to supply that service. Clients post summaries of their legal problem, geographic location, and payment preference. Lawyers then respond, and a potential client compares responses and follows up with a request for more specific information. Given that clients, at best, tend to be of modest means and wary of the sometimes arduous process of receiving pro bono services, such a service increases the likelihood that clients will find a lawyer willing to take their case (Olson 2016).

Discrimination also may be reduced when a party or person who is being discriminated against provides more (positive) information. For example, Ruomeng Cui, Jun Li, and Dennis Zhang (2018) explore ways to use reputation systems to reduce discrimination in online markets. They find that requests from guests with African American-sounding names are 19.2 percentage points less likely to be accepted by hosts on Airbnb than requests from guests with white-sounding names. However, when the guests who are discriminated against receive a positive review from a previous host, the acceptance rates of guest accounts with white-sounding and African American-sounding names are statistically indistinguishable.

Leading executives at major firms have indicated they believe it is their social responsibility and part of their mission to step up and try to solve a variety of social problems, including discrimination, because government has become much less effective at doing so. For example, Apple, Disney, and Xerox pioneered extending healthcare benefits to gay and lesbian couples (Gelles 2018). In addition, corporations have opposed discrimination that has been legislated by states and promoted by hate groups. Legislators in more than two dozen states have proposed more than 100 bills limiting the rights of lesbian, gay, bisexual, and transgender people, often under the guise of protecting religious freedom (Surowiecki 2016). Executives at leading corporations have signed letters urging governors to repeal such laws; have moved operations out of states that have passed anti-LGBT legislation; and have threatened to cancel projects planned for a state if it passed anti-LGBT legislation. The corporate pressure has yielded some positive results, as Georgia, South Dakota, Indiana, and Arkansas have withdrawn or significantly amended bills that discriminate against LGBT people.

In response to the August 2017 "Unite the Right" rally in Charlottesville, Virginia, major companies, including J.P. Morgan Chase and Apple, have made large donations to organizations that fight against hate groups, such as the Southern Poverty Law Center and the Anti-Defamation League, and that protect communities so that all people are free to live and work anywhere in the United States without being subject to hatred. Again, it is likely that executives who indicate their opposition to discrimination are motivated by their (self-imposed) social obligations and by market forces that reward firms with a good reputation for their concern about the public.[2]

As discussed, private investors have taken actions to improve the environment by telling the most egregious polluters that they might withdraw their investments unless their companies made a greater effort to adopt more "sustainable" production practices. Similarly, Yale's David Swensen, the nation's most prominent endowment chief, has told the seventy managers of the school's money that their firms could lose the university's investments if they do not hire more women and minorities. Swensen indicated he would initially measure the firms' progress in increasing the diversity of their investment staffs (Chung and Lim 2020). Many of Swensen's protégés have gone on to run schools' and foundations' endowments and could follow his lead.

Finally, general counsel and corporate legal officers have indicated that the corporations they represent will prioritize their spending on law firms that are clearly committed to diversity and inclusion in their hiring and partnership decisions. For example, Coca Cola's legal department told outside law firms that diverse lawyers' billings must account for at least 30 percent of new legal matters. In addition, companies including Microsoft, Intel, and U.S. Bancorp are asking the law firms they hire to indicate the diversity of their lawyers and assignments. Law firms may lose business if they do not provide satisfactory responses.

SUMMARY

Despite the existence of antidiscrimination laws and the effects of market forces, David Neumark (2018) concluded from an exhaustive review of the evidence that, unfortunately, hiring discrimination in the United States is still pervasive. The discussion in this chapter indicates that government should reform its antidiscrimination laws to avoid unintentional consequences. In addition, it would help if policymakers could draw on research that provided a greater understanding of the causes of discrimination that could guide more effective antidiscrimination policy.

Market forces also could be more effective in addressing the problem if: (1) corporate executives' recent opposition to discrimination by legislatures and hate groups; (2) endowment managers' pressure on investment firms to increase the diversity of their employees; and (3) corporations' demands that law firms increase the diversity of their lawyers attracted a large private-sector following. Developing and publicizing evidence that shows the cost to firms that treat current and prospective employees with prejudice would also be useful.

THIRTEEN

Merit Goods

Temporary Assistance for Needy Families, food stamps, Medicaid, and the like are means-tested aid programs that provide benefits only to poor and lower-income individuals.[1] In contrast, merit goods programs are universal programs that cover a broad range of goods and services that policymakers believe should be available to all US citizens regardless of income. The specific policies summarized in table 13-1 indicate that direct financial assistance and tax-based subsidies have been provided for education, homeownership, social insurance, crime prevention, national defense, and homeland security.[2] Society has decided through the democratic political process that government should help provide citizens with those merit goods.

If firms believe profit opportunities exist from providing merit goods, they can contribute to their provision unless they are prevented from doing so by the government. As in the case of helping reduce poverty and discrimination, some firms believe they have a social obligation to help provide certain merit goods, which also could enhance their reputation with the public.

GOVERNMENT POLICIES

Researchers have not questioned the choice of any merit goods per se; instead, available research has provided evidence that the policies that have governed their provision have imposed excessive costs on taxpayers. Stylized facts also raise concerns, including the enormous amount of US student loan debt, currently exceeding $1 trillion; the significant tax breaks to affluent consumers of housing; and the large and growing share of the federal budget accounted for by entitlements such as Social Security and Medicare, and by national defense.

TABLE 13-1. Policies to Provide Merit Goods (Education, Food, Housing, Social Insurance, Health, Safety)

Education and Home Ownership
Subsidies to public elementary and secondary schools
Federal tax incentives and subsidies for college education (Hope Scholarships, tax credits for lifelong learning, education IRAs, Pell grants, tax deductibility of interest on student loans)
Amending the tax code to encourage home ownership (mortgage interest deductibility, tax exempt rental income from home that is occupied)
Fannie Mae and Freddie Mac mortgage funds
Social Insurance
Workers' Compensation
Unemployment Insurance
Social Security
Social Security Disability Insurance Program (SSDI)
Medicare
Crime Prevention, National Defense, and Homeland Security
Public expenditures to reduce crime (police and prisons)
Prison sentencing
Military spending
Transportation Security Administration
Immigration policies

Education and Homeownership

The 2018 Tax Cut and Jobs Act took a step toward providing merit goods at lower social cost by reducing the tax break for homeownership, limiting the mortgage interest deduction to the first $750,000 in principal value, and limiting the state and local tax deduction to a combined $10,000 for income, sales, and property taxes. In addition, for universities with more than 500 students, the act levied a 1.4 percent excise tax on the returns of university endowments that amounted to more than $500,000 per student. Early versions of the act also eliminated the deduction of interest on student loan debt, but that change did not survive the act's passage by Congress. In any case, policymakers clearly set their sights on reducing the total cost to the public sector of providing education and housing.[3] The Biden administration may have different priorities.

Social Insurance

The cost of social insurance programs is projected to grow much faster than the national income, and the revenue needed to fund them and their unfunded liabilities exceeds the national debt. Because more than 40 percent of working-age households receive benefits from at least one federal welfare entitlement program, reducing program costs to strengthen long-term financial viability has encountered strong political resistance.

Economists have assessed the efficiency of social insurance programs by comparing the cost of their disincentives to save and work with the benefits of providing insurance. For example, a long line of literature, beginning with Alan Auerbach and Laurence Kotlikoff (1987) has found that the Social Security program reduces steady-state welfare in dynamically efficient economies. Similarly, the growth of the Social Security Disability Insurance (SSDI) program has decreased labor force participation, although the magnitude of the effect continues to be debated (Autor and Duggan 2003; Gelber, Moore, and Strand 2017). It has long been argued that means-testing of social insurance programs would save large amounts of money, but doing so could have unintended consequences, such as depressing economic activity because the most productive people would be harmed the most, and it also would encounter political opposition from most of the population.

Meanwhile, empirical research has identified substantial inefficiencies in specific social insurance programs. For example, Liran Einav, Amy Finkelstein, and Neale Mahoney (2018) estimated the waste in healthcare attributable to Medicare spending on long-term care hospitals (LTCHs). The authors concluded that most LTCH patients would have received comparable and less-costly care at skilled nursing facilities. Medicare could have saved nearly $5 billion annually, with no harm to patients, by not allowing discharges to LTCHs.

Crime

The amount of violent crime in the United States peaked in the early 1990s; shortly thereafter, states hired more police officers, built more prisons, and incarcerated more criminal offenders, among other actions. The sharp decline in violent crime during the quarter century that followed was certainly welcome news for all members of society, especially the poorest and most vulnerable. Unfortunately, researchers have not offered dispositive empirical explanations about the underlying factors that caused the decline, which could be replicated in areas of the country with high crime rates. Efforts to assess the effects of government interventions are impeded by inaccurate measures of crime due to underreporting and misreporting.

Among the positive evidence, Aaron Chalfin and Justin McCrary (2018) found that efforts to hire more police officers strongly deterred violent crime, especially murder, and that, in fact, US cities were under-policed because $1 invested in policing yielded a social return of $1.63. Patrick Sharkey (2018) added that incarceration and technology (more surveillance cameras and LoJack systems) also played a role. Researchers have found that police enforcement has been aided in a cost-effective manner by the Law Enforcement Support Program (the 1033 Program), which has transferred more than $4 billion worth of surplus military and tactical equipment from the Department of Defense to domestic police agencies across the United States (Bove and Gavrilova 2017; Harris and others 2017).[4]

What remains to be addressed is whether further declines in crime can be accomplished by more efficient means than the high social costs of mass incarceration, whether managed by the public or the private sector. Adam Gopnik (2018) concluded that the United States has curbed crime without really knowing how it did it, other than by doing it several ways simultaneously.

National Defense

K. K. Rebecca Lai and others (2017) provided a detailed breakdown of the major elements of US military annual expenditures, including troops, air power, naval power, and nuclear weapons, and pointed out that the United States has higher military spending, roughly $600 billion, than any other country partly because its ambitious foreign policy goals seek to uphold international order and promote American interests abroad, as well as to defend its own borders. Economists have produced few, if any, analyses of the benefits of the expenditures. However, economists and others have argued that recent exorbitant military expenditures have entailed considerable waste, including the Pentagon's enormous administrative inefficiencies (Whitlock and Woodward (2016); nearly a trillion dollars appropriated for military operations in Afghanistan that achieved very little (Aikins 2016); even greater expenditures on the Iraq war that the US initiated on a false premise (Wallsten and Kosec 2005; Stiglitz and Bilimes 2006); and billions of dollars in arms and training that have flowed to the Iraqi army, which has struggled mightily (Morris and Ryan 2016). President Trump called on America's allies to contribute more to their defense, but that policy did not address the extensive waste associated with US military expenditures.

Homeland Security

The FBI and CIA represent the frontline of defense against terrorist threats to the US homeland. Such threats also include cybersecurity attacks from foreign countries that inject malware into our computer network. Einstein is a multibillion-dollar detecting system operated by the Department of Homeland Security's Cybersecurity and Infrastructure Security Agency that finds new uses of known malware and detects connections to parts of the internet used in previous computer hacks (Timberg and Nakashima 2020). However, Russian hackers were able to evade the system and hack federal networks for months. The scope and extent of the cyberattack is currently unknown.

The Transportation Security Administration (TSA) is responsible for protecting aviation from terrorist threats, while the Trump administration refocused immigration policy on combating terrorism. The TSA has elected to trade off manpower for enhanced technology and targeted screening. In 2015, the TSA spent roughly $7.5 billion on passenger prescreening, checkpoint screening, checked baggage screening, canines, behavior detection, and the Federal Air Marshals Service. The General Accountability Office (2017) determined that the TSA has little knowledge of the cost-effectiveness of its programs and has no basis for making efficient reforms. To make matters worse, the TSA has failed to consider the disutility of travelers' time spent waiting in line to get through security checkpoints; thus, its decision to operate with an undersized workforce during heavy periods of air travel has inflated the time costs that travelers incur.

In recent decades, US immigration policy has put a lower priority on reuniting families and greater emphasis on allowing only those immigrants who will enhance US economic welfare to enter the country; in 2019, the US began to deny entry to those the government believes will not improve the economy.[5] The Trump administration did not place a priority on providing asylum to oppressed people from other countries; instead, it wanted to prevent immigrants from taking jobs from current American workers and from providing cover for eventual terrorist attacks. The Biden administration's immigration priorities are different and it will likely provide asylum to more oppressed people from other countries.

Immigration broadly benefits the economy by enabling highly educated and intelligent workers and entrepreneurs to advance our most important industries and by enabling low-skilled migrant workers to perform important tasks that many American workers are unwilling to perform at market wages (Posner and Weyl 2018). In addition, Figlio et al. (2021) find that immigrants have a positive effect on the performance of US-born students, especially those with disadvantaged backgrounds. At the same time, the presence of immigrants does not adversely affect the performance of affluent US-born students, who generally perform at a higher level compared with immigrant students. The relative performance and behavior of immigrants appear overall to have a constructive effect on US-born students. The preceding benefits must be balanced against job losses to US workers, and additional crime and terrorism.[6]

Given those considerations, immigration policy under the Trump administration appeared to have become too restrictive, because the substitutability between foreign-born individuals who are allowed to work in the United States on the H-1B visa program and native workers is low (Mayda and others 2017), and because the incidence of crimes committed by immigrants is much lower than that committed by native counterparts (Butcher and Piehl 2007). The effects that a more aggressive policy toward illegal immigrants and a more restrictive legal immigration policy have had on deterring terrorism is not clear.

MARKET FORCES

Private markets provide merit goods and have complemented government efforts by reducing the social costs of homeownership, education, social insurance, and protection against criminals, and they could reduce the cost further if they were not prevented by government policies from expanding their provision.

Homeownership

Commercial banks, investment companies, and traditional firms help expand homeownership, especially when they are not constrained by regulations. For much of their history, commercial banks were subject to geographic restrictions that prevented them from opening branches within or across state borders. Ishani Tewari (2014) focused on intrastate branch bank deregulation from the late 1970s to the early 1990s and found it caused mortgage access to increase for lower-middle-income, young, and Black households. Over five years, homeownership rates rose 4.1 percent for households with incomes below the median of the income distribution, 3.7 percent for younger borrowers, and 11 percent for Black households.

Consistent with deregulation in other industries, the removal of geographic restrictions intensified competition and consolidation and encouraged banks to invest in new technologies, including electronic links to credit bureaus, automated underwriting, artificial intelligence software, automated appraisals of homes, and credit scoring. The new technologies enabled lenders to assess borrower credit risk faster and more accurately and to increase mortgage access, particularly among borrowers constrained by initial wealth.[7]

Despite obstacles created by government tax policies, the private sector has begun to increase homeownership by offering shared equity, where a company provides at least half of a consumer's down payment in exchange for a piece of any appreciation in the home's value when it is sold. The company also would absorb a share of any loss when the home is sold. Andrew Caplin and others (2007) presented computations that showed that shared equity markets could benefit consumers and increase the US homeownership rate. Those markets also could diversify homebuyers' risk and could have prevented the 2008 financial crisis from inflicting as much pain as it did.

However, Caplin, Noel Cunningham, and Mitchell Engler (2009) argued that tax rules made it difficult for shared appreciation mortgage markets to develop quickly in the United States because, in 1983, the Treasury Department made it impossible to get an advance ruling on the ownership implications and the tax status of borrowers and lenders using those markets. Beginning in high-price markets like California, Unison began to invest with high-income homebuyers. Today, Unison operates in twenty-two states and has become the nation's largest shared equity company. It was expected to invest with roughly 3,000 homebuyers in 2018 (Bernard 2018).

Although shared equity deals currently account for only a tiny fraction of new mortgages, their share could expand if policymakers curb the dominance of Fannie Mae and Freddie Mac—the home mortgage companies created by the US Congress to make the mortgage market more liquid and affordable by buying and guaranteeing mortgages through the secondary mortgage market. Such actions could spur additional competition in the mortgage market and lead to mortgage companies working more often with shared equity companies and with more home buyers of all income levels. Shared equity could be especially attractive to households who can afford only to rent, because it would give those households an opportunity to build equity and improve their material existence and financial security.

The notion of a company town—there are both good and bad historic examples in the United States (Streitfeld 2018)—is still another way the private sector has promoted homeownership. Certain private universities continue in that tradition by acquiring and building housing for their faculty. Recently, technology companies, including Facebook and Google, have been reviving elements of a company town by building new housing developments and offering below-market rental units for their employees.

The benefits of the federal government's tax subsidies and sponsored enterprises to encourage homeownership have been accrued by households that earn enough money to make a down payment and monthly mortgage payments, but they have not benefited less-affluent households that cannot qualify for a mortgage. The federal government may be crowding out firms, banks, and investment companies from encouraging homeownership to the broader population by, for example, offering shared equity mortgages and including housing as part of nonwage compensation. If so, eliminating or significantly curbing government housing-related tax subsidies could spur greater activity by private markets to promote homeownership, and could increase efficiency by reducing the distortions created by relying on the tax system. The Trump administration's limits on housing-related deductions may be a start at shedding light on the efficiency gains from reducing the role of government and expanding the role of markets to increase homeownership.

Certain major firms, especially in the San Francisco Bay Area, are stepping up to help less-affluent individuals obtain housing. Apple has announced a $2.5 billion housing finance package that includes $1 billion for an affordable housing investment fund, $1 billion in mortgage assistance for first-time home buyers, and opening some Apple-owned land valued at $300 million for development. The remaining $200 million will go toward a San Francisco housing fund and to support vulnerable populations. In addition, Stanford University has proposed to invest $3.4 billion to mitigate the impact of its expansion on the tight housing market in the Bay Area; The Chan Zuckerberg

Initiative, Facebook, Genentech, and other firms plan to create a $500 million investment fund to help build affordable housing; Facebook has committed $1 billion to help address the East Bay housing crisis; and Google has pledged to invest $1 billion by repurposing $750 million of commercially zoned land that it owns to allow developers to lease the land to build homes, and by creating a $250 million investment fund to provide incentives for developers to create more affordable homes in the area. In January 2019, Microsoft pledged to contribute $500 million to help build affordable housing in Seattle.

Finally, as reported by Pamela Babcock (2019), new companies are using technology to create more affordable housing, including:

- Module, which allows buyers to start small but easily add on to their homes as needed. Households purchase less expensive, smaller homes initially and, over time, expand them by adding another story or another bedroom on the ground floor.

- Rentlogic, which analyzes data to give grades of A, B, C, or F for 1.1 million multifamily buildings across New York City to give tenants more bargaining power and to put market pressure on landlords to increase the quality of their rentals. Tenants are not charged, but landlords are charged to have their property listed, inspected, and certified.

- PadSplit, which takes existing single-family homes and apartments and subdivides them to accommodate more bedrooms, with shared common spaces and bathrooms. Other co-living startups, such as WeLive, are targeting millennial professionals. The average PadSplit resident makes $21,000 a year.

- Point, which offers homeowners the ability to sell fractional interests in their homes in exchange for a share in the property's future appreciation. Point can underwrite to more forgiving standards and to people with lower credit scores than lenders issuing HELOCs (home equity line of credit) because there is no monthly payment and no interest rate. Point offers ten- and thirty-year agreements. A homeowner can buy out Point or sell the home at any time.

Education

Market forces have attempted to address concerns about the cost and quality of public elementary and secondary school education and the cost and relevance to employers of a college education by providing alternative educational programs, reducing the cost of an individual's education, and improving the quality of public-school education. Although there is resistance in certain quarters, for example, from teachers' unions, to allowing private market forces to influence the education system, especially in elementary and secondary schools, private markets have made some constructive contributions. The available evidence suggests that society is likely to benefit if the role of markets in education were expanded.

ALTERNATIVES TO PUBLIC EDUCATION

Market forces have resulted in alternatives to public education at all grade levels. For PK–12, alternatives include traditional private schools with and without vouchers, homeschooling, and vocational schools. Alternative providers of post-secondary education include private and vocational schools, as well as online schools, for-profit colleges, and, possibly, "corporate" schools.

PK–12 PRIVATE SCHOOLS AND HOMESCHOOLING. Nearly 6 million students, or roughly 10 percent of all PK–12 US students, are enrolled at a private school.[8] Assuming it costs, on average, at least $10,000 a year to send a child to public school, including federal, state, and local government spending,[9] then enrollment at private schools is reducing government expenditures on public education by some $60 billion annually.[10] The benefits of homeschooling for children born into poor households were previously discussed. Evidence also indicates that, compared with public school students, homeschooled students perform better on standardized tests, have higher college GPAs and completion rates, and even may be better adjusted socially. Homeschooling, which accounts for 3 to 4 percent of all PK–12 US students, saves taxpayers more than $20 billion annually.[11]

PK–12 VOUCHERS. The most significant and controversial alternative to public schools has been school choice, where families can use a voucher or a coupon to offset tuition at a private school they wish their children to attend, or they can send their children to a charter school, an independent public school that has some freedom from the rules followed by public schools. In either case, the market principle of choice is used to incentivize the education system to improve.

Choice has been controversial for two reasons. First, there is disagreement on whether it creates a more efficient educational system by reducing government's role in schooling and by allowing market forces to reward or punish schools for the quality of their education programs. Second, regardless of its effects on efficiency, choice could be used by those who want to resist desegregation (Rotherham 2017).

Who is eligible to receive vouchers varies according to the US program (all students or only low-income students), their source of funding (private or tax proceeds), and the criteria for private school participation (all schools or only nonreligious schools). The academic literature has attempted to determine whether introducing school vouchers is a systematically reliable way to improve educational outcomes. Dennis Epple, Richard Romano, and Miguel Urquiola (2017) concluded from their comprehensive synthesis of the evidence that it is premature to recommend vouchers be adopted on a widespread basis, in part because of the adverse effects on the achievement of students who remain in the public sector when higher-quality students (and possibly teachers) exit public schools to join private ones. However, evidence on both small-scale programs, which place significant restrictions on who can receive vouchers, and on large-scale programs, which are outside of the United States and place minimal restrictions on who can receive vouchers, suggests the competition induced by vouchers can cause public schools to improve in some circumstances.[12]

Given the various authors' conclusions, it would be desirable to gain a better understanding of how vouchers could be more effective for students from all types of socioeconomic backgrounds. On the supply side, improvements in the design of voucher programs to limit the adverse effects of sorting and to give greater incentives for public schools to improve would be helpful.[13] On the demand side, Atila Abdulkadiroglu and others (2017b) raise the important issue of whether parents value school effectiveness, as indicated by causal improvements in students' short-run achievement test scores and in longer-run postsecondary school outcomes. In their study of New York City high schools, the authors found that parents placed a large weight on sending their children to schools that enrolled high-achieving peers; that is, the schools were effective at recruiting higher-achieving students and devoted resources to screening and selection. But, controlling for peer quality, the authors also found that school effectiveness did not affect parents' preferences for which school their children attended, suggesting that schools have little incentive to devote resources to better instruction that may improve student outcomes. In sum, competition created by vouchers potentially could result in improvements in public schools, but it is not clear that those improvements are valued sufficiently by parents to cause public schools to notably improve.

For perspective, competition from the private automobile has been unsuccessful at encouraging public bus and rail urban transit to improve quality of service and efficiency of operations. Public transit agencies face too many organizational and political constraints, while tens of billions of dollars in annual taxpayer subsidies destroy any incentive the agencies may have to respond more effectively to travelers' preferences and to increase their market share. As noted, autonomous vehicles may eventually offer a viable alternative to public transit for most travelers. Policymakers would, then, find it more difficult to use subsidies to protect urban transit from the consequences of competition, and they may decide to close those socially undesirable operations (Winston 2013).

Similarly, choice created by vouchers in education may not generate sufficient competition to bring about fundamental changes in the effectiveness of public schools PK–12 because school systems lack the opportunity and incentives to respond to competition in the same way private-sector firms do (Hess 2010).[14] School systems lack the opportunity because they are choked by politics, bureaucracy, collective-bargaining agreements, and institutional timidity, and they lack the incentives because their per-pupil funding is twice the level of funding given to voucher programs in, for example, Washington, DC, and Milwaukee. Indeed, as a result of the Milwaukee public school system's loss of some 20,000 students to the Milwaukee Parental Choice Program, their teacher workforce actually increased slightly, and per-pupil spending increased by more than 80 percent (Hess 2010).

A promising model discussed by Sarah Cohodes, Elizabeth Setren, and Christopher Walters (2021) that shows the benefits of applying the market principle of choice among public schools is No Excuses charter schools. As indicated by the name, the schools have high expectations for and strict discipline of students, frequent teacher feedback and intense tutoring, and data-driven instruction. The results speak for themselves, as No Excuses charter schools have generated test score gains for students large enough to close racial and socioeconomic achievement gaps, and those large achievement gains are not confined to a few campuses, but have been replicated in general by charter schools that use the No Excuses model. Similarly, Success Academy, the largest charter school network in New York City, requires intense parental engagement, and its students outperform students in more-affluent communities.

Market forces are likely to become more effective in education if, in addition to families exercising school choice, schools must bear the responsibility for their success or failure in a competitive environment. Private schools would then expand their presence throughout the country, and would compete more intensely with each other and with public schools for students from affluent as well as poor economic backgrounds, while public schools would either meet the competition without their current funding advantages or exit the market. Any financial assistance provided to students from low-income households would follow those students when they change schools.

Some suggestive evidence of the positive effects of competition provided by private schools is reported by David Figlio, Cassandra Hart, and Krzysztof Karbownik (2020), who explore how the massive expansion of a Florida private school choice program affected public school students' outcomes. The authors find that by generating competitive pressure from increased voucher utilization, the expansion led to higher standardized test scores and lower absenteeism and suspension rates for students attending public schools who had a larger initial degree of private school options. The authors also find that the public school students most positively affected come from comparatively lower socioeconomic backgrounds.

Some people may believe that allowing intense market forces to work in PK–12 education may cross the line because students would be among the victims when a school fails the market test. But large-scale firm exits have occurred in formerly regulated industries that were subjected to market forces, and consumers were the ultimate beneficiaries. Careful privatization experiments should be designed with the goal of determining whether that outcome would occur in education and how to soften the effects of school failure on students.

VOCATIONAL EDUCATION. The private sector has helped create other alternative educational programs that seek to enable students to develop skills that can increase their employment prospects. Private companies are increasing their ties with local high schools to develop programs so they can recruit employees upon graduation instead of having to wait to recruit them out of college in a tight labor market. Nationally, the number of high school students concentrating in so-called career education has risen 22 percent during the past decade to 3.6 million, with participating companies such as Tesla; Volkswagen; CVS; Electric Boat, a submarine manufacturer with headquarters in Groton, Connecticut; and fisheries in Louisiana (Hackman 2018). Students partaking in career education programs can receive industry certificates to help them obtain jobs with other firms in the future.

Vocational schools have long been an option for high school students who do not plan to attend college. Private companies have begun to develop alternatives to traditional vocational schools that provide stronger guarantees of employment and no risk of going into debt by attending their program. For example, MissionU is a tuition-free, year-long program of learning by doing, where companies participate in designing a curriculum of data analytics, financial management, and the like that is relevant to potential employers (Hardman 2018). Students repay the program through their wages after obtaining a job that pays at least $50,000 annually. MissionU is educating only small cohorts of students; but if the program were successful, it could expand quickly because much of it is delivered online, and new companies are likely to compete with MissionU by offering a similar program. The Lambda School has begun to train people to become software engineers with an online educational program designed by private companies with the preferences of potential employers in mind. As in the case of MissionU, students do not begin to repay the program until they have a job that pays at least $50,000 annually.[15]

Pathways in Technology Early College High School, or P-Tech, offers a high school education, college degree, and entrée into the labor force (Ellin 2018). It is a six-year program that gives students with lower-income backgrounds the chance to earn a high school diploma and a cost-free associate degree in a STEM (science, technology, engineering, and mathematics) field. Upon graduation, many students go on to four-year colleges; others take full-time jobs at IBM, one of the founders of the program, or another IT company. The P-Tech umbrella includes 110 schools in eight states, and schools in several countries, while more than 500 industry partners and seventy-seven community colleges also participate.

ONLINE EDUCATION. Lawrence Summers, the former president of Harvard University, has observed that not enough people are innovating in higher education.[16] For example, although General Electric looks nothing like it looked in 1975, Harvard, Yale, Princeton, and Stanford look a lot like they looked in 1975. Summers sees significant potential in online education because it has the benefits of huge economies of scale—thousands of people can watch a lecture once it is filmed at the same cost as the small number of people who initially watched it—and of much more personalization, because students can re-listen to the parts they did not understand and test their understanding with diagnostic questions that are inserted as part of the lecture.

Even before the global pandemic, online education was making its presence felt for people of all ages. Waterfront Upstart is a kindergarten readiness program for four-year-olds that takes place almost entirely online (Bowles 2019). About 16,000 children in fifteen states graduated from the program in 2019; 22,000 students are projected to graduate in 2020. The program is geared to lower-income families with fewer pre-kindergarten options.

Before the pandemic, more than 3 million students were pursuing higher education fully online. Online courses also have become an integral part of the vocational programs discussed previously. Southern New Hampshire University is a nonprofit private university with an expanding online program that has enabled it to become one of the fastest-growing universities in the United States. Its current enrollment of more than 90,000 students has put it in the category of a mega-university. Other mega-universities include Liberty, Western Governors, and Grand Canyon. Schools with online programs are pursuing the more than 30 million Americans who have some college credit but have never graduated.

Online education has become central to nonprofit and for-profit colleges' teaching strategy. The latter currently account for roughly one-third of the enrollment in online courses. The limited evidence to date on the economic effects of online college courses raises concerns that students may learn less from online courses than they do from taking the same courses in person. On the other hand, online courses open educational opportunities for people who otherwise would not pursue education, and they provide effective competition for colleges that offer only in-person courses.

Eric Bettinger and others (2017) studied the performance of students seeking a bachelor's degree at a large for-profit university who took online courses and found that their grades were lower for such courses compared with taking the same courses in person, and that those students were less likely to remain enrolled in the university. In terms of specific grades, students taking the course in person earned a B–, on average, and students taking the course online earned a C, on average. Nonetheless, the authors concluded that online courses may be the only option for some students to access college-level courses because of the distance they live from a college campus.

Joshua Goodman, Julia Melkers, and Amanda Pallais (2017) took a closer look at the effects of online courses on increasing access to education by studying the Georgia Institute of Technology's Online M.S. in Computer Science program, which was developed in partnership with Udacity and AT&T. The online degree costs about $7,000 compared with $45,000 out-of-state students pay for the in-person M.S. degree. The quality of the degrees in terms of coursework, faculty providing instruction, and grading standards are comparable, and comparisons of student achievement across the online and in-person formats suggested that the online students finished their courses with at least as much knowledge as their in-person counterparts. The average in-person degree applicant was a twenty-four-year-old non-American recently out of college, while the average online degree applicant was a thirty-four-year-old mid-career American. The authors found that access to this educational option increased overall enrollment in education, as suggested by the different applicant pools, and that it did not substitute for existing options. By satisfying a large, previously unmet demand for mid-career training, the authors predicted this single program could boost annual production of American computer science master's degrees by about 7 percent. The supply of labor in other fields also might be increased by similar online educational programs.

Finally, for-profit and other colleges that offer online courses represent competitive entry for colleges that offer only in-person courses. David Deming, Michael Lovenheim, and Richard Patterson (2016) found that greater market entry of and enrollment in online institutions reduced enrollment at private nonselective institutions, and increased per-student instructional spending, a broad proxy for quality, at four-year public institutions. The authors concluded that online education could bring competitive pressure to bear that positively affects innovation and productivity in US higher education.

FOR-PROFIT COLLEGES. For-profit institutions, which, as noted, have increased educational options by providing vocational and online programs, also offer traditional college programs leading to associates, bachelors, and master's degrees. Some students who graduate from those programs can increase their annual earnings by a modest amount. But other graduates are not better off over their lifetime, considering the debt as well as the 42 percent of students at two-year for-profit colleges and the 73 percent at four-year for-profit colleges who drop out (Cellini and Turner 2019). Many students have sought to have their student loans cancelled by the government on the grounds that they were deceived about the quality of a for-profit college's program and about the likelihood that it would enhance their future job prospects.[17]

This adverse outcome, however, is attributable to the poor market incentives created by federal student aid programs that provide tens of billions of dollars annually in Pell grants and student loans with very few strings attached (Cooper 2016). For-profit colleges aggressively recruit students to increase revenues (and profits), while the students do not consider their decision to attend those colleges as carefully as they should, because grants and loans are readily available. Indeed, 85 percent of students at for-profit colleges received federal aid compared with 20 percent of community college students. The solution to this inefficiency is for the private sector to play a larger role in education finance because it will have greater incentives than the government to identify students who are prepared and motivated to complete the coursework at a for-profit college to earn their degree, get a job, and repay their loans. The private sector also is more likely than the public sector to determine whether a for-profit college program can help a student get a job and to prevent students from defaulting on their loans.

"CORPORATE" COLLEGES. Private companies eventually may go beyond establishing ties with local high schools and community colleges and expand employee training to the point where they groom their own "college-educated" work force. Corporations have become frustrated with US educational institutions, and some, such as Amazon and Google, may build universities to teach the skills they believe the nation's workforce should acquire (Bruni 2018). Others are working with local colleges to develop programs that better prepare students for work after graduation.[18]

Improving the Quality of Public Schools

Instead of supporting private alternatives to public education, some corporations and foundations have contributed considerable resources to improving public education. Unfortunately, despite good intentions, it is not clear that such efforts have significantly improved student performance.

Two major initiatives are instructive. Facebook founder Mark Zuckerberg donated $100 million to help fix public schools in Newark, New Jersey, to benefit students from varying socioeconomic backgrounds. However, the funding did not produce the hoped-for transformational results in students' performance on state-level math and reading proficiency tests, although it did reveal the difficulty of trying to fundamentally reform traditional public schools (Russakoff 2015). In contrast, charter schools, which received some of the funding but were not encumbered by the bureaucracy and legacy labor costs that adversely affect traditional public schools, were able to devote more of their resources to benefit students, who performed much better than the students attending traditional schools performed on the state-level tests.

The Bill and Melinda Gates Foundation contributed more than $200 million to seven sites in the United States that were attempting to educate a substantial proportion of low-income minority students, to improve teaching effectiveness and student performance outcomes. The RAND Corporation (Stecher and others 2018) conducted an exhaustive assessment of the initiative and concluded that the sites did not hire and retain more effective teachers and that student achievement in math and reading and graduation rates showed negligible improvement. The authors could not explain why measuring teacher effectiveness and using it as the basis for managing and providing incentives for teachers did not appear to lead to gains in student achievement or graduation rates; however, they speculated that a fundamental problem with the initiative—and similar efforts in the future—is that the leaders were better at implementing measures of effectiveness than at using them to improve student outcomes. Large-scale investment initiatives may achieve higher returns in student performance in a competitive private school environment where resources are less likely to be consumed by the types of inefficiencies that exist in public schools and where leaders are more likely to be focused on improving the academic reputation of their schools.

Finally, Dalio Philanthropies have pledged $100 million to strengthen public education and promote greater economic opportunity. Funding will focus on communities where there is both a high poverty rate and a high concentration of youth showing signs of disengagement or disconnection from high school. The results of the Dalio initiative merit a careful assessment.

Reducing Student Costs and Debt

Student debt and growing default rates have become a significant problem in nonprofit as well as for-profit colleges. According to the National Center for Education Statistics, the typical student borrower will average $22,000 in debt by graduation (the average debt for graduate and professional school students is higher), while the default rate on federal student loans has climbed to 16 percent (Miller 2018). Currently, total student debt exceeds $1.3 trillion, with federal loans accounting for more than 90 percent of that amount.

Many expensive private colleges with high graduation rates have reduced the burden of college debt by offering substantial tuition discounts for students from lower-income and even middle-income households. In addition, private firms have taken some responsibility for education finance by paying directly for their employees' or other individuals' college education, helping their employees pay off their college debt, and improving capital markets for student loans. As in the case of wage increases, it is not clear that this assistance represents a long-term commitment or will be provided only in tight labor markets.

DIRECT PAYMENTS FOR EDUCATION. Several large corporations have begun to pay college tuition for their workers. Some prominent recent examples include:

- The Walt Disney Corporation is offering to pay full tuition for up to 80,000 hourly workers who want to earn a college degree, finish a high school diploma, or learn a new skill. The tuition would be paid upfront for employees taking online classes.

- Walmart is offering subsidized college tuition for its 1.4 million employees to take online or on-campus courses to earn degrees in supply chain management or business. Walmart indicated the subsidies would be paid upfront and could be used to take courses at three universities with high graduation rates among part-time students—University of Florida, Bellevue University, and Brandman University.

- Federal Express will offer free tuition to 11,000 employees at its Memphis hub to earn an online degree from the University of Memphis. Employees who do not have a high school diploma would be able to earn a high school-equivalent degree.

- UPS has invested more than $100 million in tuition payments for its employees to attend colleges in Louisville, Kentucky.

- Jeff Bezos, CEO of Amazon, has, along with MacKenzie Bezos, donated $33 million to fund 1,000 college scholarships for Dreamers, undocumented immigrant graduates of US high schools with DACA (Deferred Action for Childhood Arrivals) status.

Starbucks, JetBlue, UPS, Cigna, Fiat-Chrysler, and other large employers also have publicly announced they want to help their employees get a college degree. The employer-sponsored tuition programs have clearly benefited workers, and they have enabled firms to significantly improve their retention rates in a tight labor market and to fill certain positions by promoting their workers internally instead of trying to recruit new workers from outside the firm.

Importantly, the programs also benefit participating educational institutions by strengthening the association between their degree programs and students' employment.

HELPING PAY OFF STUDENT DEBT. Certain firms have benefited their most educated employees by helping them pay off their college and graduate school loans, another perk envisioned as a good recruiting and retention tool.[19] Accounting, financial services, and professional services firms have been among the first to offer this benefit. For example, Fidelity Investments announced it would pay $2,000 a year—up to $10,000 maximum—toward the student loans of anyone employed at the company for more than six months. Fidelity then turned its attention to work with other firms to help them design a way to contribute to their workers' education debt. Similarly, national and regional law firms are helping their new associates pay off law school loans by contributing monthly amounts until the junior lawyers are eligible to receive a bonus from their firm. A handful of companies, including Abbott Laboratories, Travelers, and Raytheon, have either launched or announced plans to prevent workers from falling behind on retirement savings by matching their student-loan repayments with contributions to a 401(k) plan.[20]

IMPROVING THE STUDENT LOAN MARKET. Currently, the US Department of Education has a near monopoly, 91 percent share, on the student loan market, crowding out the private loan market consisting of banks and other private lenders. Emily Top (2018) argues that, in theory, greater competition from the private loan market would reduce the interest rates the government charges students, with individuals who have good credit benefiting more than individuals with poor credit, and would reduce the number of defaults because, in contrast to the government, private lenders would base their loan decisions on an individual's creditworthiness. (Currently, the Department of Education covers defaults by drawing on revenues from taxpayers and by charging interest rates to borrowers who pay off loans that are higher than they otherwise would be absent the defaults.) Finally, the cost of tuition would fall because colleges and universities could no longer count on the government providing unlimited loans to students' parents. Limits on loans especially may reduce demand for the most expensive schools and encourage them to reduce tuition.

Kevin James (2016) considers what an alternative private student loan market for college education would look like without the federal government's loans or guarantees. He argues that private lenders would seek to expand opportunity for education by emphasizing a student's potential rather than the student's economic background. Students would effectively borrow large sums of money against the promise of a future increase in earnings. The challenge is for students to be able to escape an unsecured and possibly growing debt balance if they never experience an earnings bump. High-income students could do so through their families. Lower-income students could obtain loans under an income-share agreement (ISA), where students agree to pay an affordable percentage of their future income over a set time period, subject to an overall cap. The amount students pay, incorporating the interest and the size of the loan, would depend entirely on their income after they graduate. When the college is providing some of the funding for the ISA, its return would be aligned with its students' post-college earnings, giving it economic incentives to make sure its students both graduate and find jobs.

Of course, one could question whether ISAs would be an option for most students who seek a college loan. The answer is that an ISA is very likely to be made available for students' loan requests that align with their past and expected accomplishments, the proposed program of study, the cost of the program, and the availability of more cost-effective options. Undoubtedly, lenders would offer less funding for less lucrative fields, but they also would be able to identify cost-reducing programs, even at the undergraduate level. For example, a lender is likely to balk at loaning MIT tuition to a student who wishes to major in humanities and to encourage the student to attend a strong in-state public university to obtain a humanities degree. The fact that federal loans were available for students who made education investments in programs that did not enable them to increase their earnings represents a cost to the students and taxpayers.

Finally, ISAs represent another example where the government would have to allow a potentially efficient market solution to develop. Policymakers would have to curb the provision of subsidized federal student loans and, as the market develops, they would have to clarify for ISA providers and potential borrowers several legal issues involving taxation, consumer protection, financial regulation, and the like that are likely to arise.

Healthcare

Ironically, market forces that expand output have created additional tasks for markets to safeguard individuals' health because they also may create negative externalities, such as pollution and congestion, which could compromise public health and safety. Technological innovations that could reduce water and air pollution and could benefit lower-income households who live in neighborhoods that have suffered environmental degradation by improving the health of their babies (Currie and others 2013) and by leading to better long-term labor market outcomes (Isen, Rossin-Slater, and Walker 2017) have been discussed. The eventual adoption of electronic autonomous vehicles could reduce the congestion and pollution externalities.

The private sector also has saved billions of lives with innovations in medical technologies and equipment. However, because many workers obtain insurance for medical expenses from their place of work and because ailing workers wish to be treated with the latest innovations, which are more costly than previous technologies, the nation's medical expenditures have increased. Private firms provide insurance for much of the workforce to cover their medical expenses. But they do not provide insurance to all workers and to unemployed individuals; thus, government feels pressured to increase its presence in the health sector to enable all members of society to obtain health insurance.

Market forces improve health without any prodding from the government by generating new medical innovations, providing information that identifies dangerous workplaces and products, and encouraging individuals to take various measures to safeguard their health. Amitabh Chandra and others (2016) argued that the market forces of industry competition and consumer choice have combined to promote health efficiently because: (1) higher-quality hospitals, as indicated by outcome measures such as risk-adjusted survival and patient-reported satisfaction, control greater market share and experience higher growth in market share than do lower-quality hospitals; (2) patients are not simply passive pawns when receiving medical care and will exercise demand-side pressures on healthcare providers; for example, patients who experienced heart attacks were willing to travel 1.8 miles more to receive treatment at a hospital with a risk-adjusted survival rate that was 1 percent higher, and 20 percent of the improvement in heart attack survival for Medicare patients from 1996 to 2008 could be explained by the reallocation of patients to higher-quality hospitals; (3) greater competition among hospitals reduces the distribution of hospital quality because it is easier for patients to switch hospitals; and (4) information about hospital care quality to inform choice is available from many sources, including an individual's social network, family and friends, primary care physician, and even ambulance drivers.[21]

Technological advances in communications and transportation also contribute to improving healthcare. Ride-sharing technologies have provided a lower cost and potentially more reliable option to expensive ambulatory services for patients who need to get to a hospital. Telemedicine has facilitated and expedited patients' interactions with doctors and has led to earlier diagnoses and treatment, especially for patients with poor access to healthcare providers.

Private options appear to reduce the cost of healthcare in certain instances. Healthcare for the US military and veterans has been delivered largely on military bases through public systems run by the Veterans Administration. However, some veterans are able to receive care from private community providers. Michael D. Frakes, Jonathan Gruber, and Timothy Justicz (2020) compare obstetrical care that was provided off-base and find that it is associated with better outcomes—fewer complications and incidences of maternal or neonatal trauma, suggesting efficiency gains from privatization. David Dranove, Christopher Ody, and Amanda Starc (2021) assess the effect of privatizing Medicaid drug benefits, a response by many states to the Patient Protection and Affordable Care Act, on drug prices and utilization by comparing the outcomes with those obtained through public, state-administered programs. Innovation in the private insurance market has increased the use of managed care. The authors find that drug spending would decrease by 21.3 percent if private insurers administered all drug benefits. One-third of the decrease is driven by private insurers' ability to negotiate prices with pharmacies, and the other two-thirds are driven by the greater use of lower-cost drugs, such as generics. Privatization does not reduce prescriptions per enrollee.

Finally, John Goodman (2018) illustrates how a free market in healthcare could work. MediBid, an online platform, operates as a medical tourism market for Americans where a patient seeking a procedure, such as a knee or hip replacement, hernia repair, or colonoscopy, is willing to travel, pay up front, and not involve an insurance company after the fact. Doctors (and, effectively, hospitals) offer competitive bids on the full cost of procedures, and they provide critical information about their qualifications. The patient then chooses among competing bids. MediBid currently has more than 250,000 paid subscribers to their services; comparisons between average MediBid prices and third-party payments indicate large cost savings; at least 30 percent and as much as 50 percent. MediBid has served a useful purpose even if it ceases to exist because it has forced physicians and hospitals to engage more explicitly in price-quality competition.

A PERSONAL ANECDOTE. While I was writing this book, I developed sciatica, and I had to get lumbar surgery to repair my L5 disk. I discussed the matter with a highly recommended neurosurgeon out of my insurance network, and only at the end of the discussion did I ask him how much the surgery would cost. He said his charge would be $7,000. The hospital expenses would be covered by my insurance, with a small deductible, because the hospital participated in my insurance plan. I did not consider whether I could find a lower price for the surgery because I was in considerable pain; I wanted the surgery immediately; I was convinced the neurosurgeon was highly competent; and I could afford the expense. I had surgery three days later, and I did not regret my failure to engage in time-consuming price-quality comparisons.

As a robustness check, I developed painful symptoms of long-standing problems in my cervical disks shortly after recovering from sciatica. The appropriate treatment would require fusion of my spinal disks C3 to T2. The surgeon who originally treated me for sciatica indicated that the sticker price for the surgery was $80,000, so I consulted with five neurosurgeons who participated in my insurance network. In the meantime, my original surgeon offered me a discounted price on the surgery of $20,000, with my insurance covering roughly half the cost. Given that I was confident this surgeon could perform a difficult surgery and that competition had undoubtedly helped reduce the price, I asked him to perform the cervical spinal-disk fusion.

The surgery took roughly eight hours, and two days later, while I was still recovering in the hospital, I developed blood clots in my lungs, which caused me to have a pulmonary embolism. The nurses were slow to react to my condition, so my wife called my primary physician, who immediately got the head nurse on the phone and told her to examine me and administer blood thinners. He then contacted my surgeon, and I was diagnosed further and taken to the ICU. My primary physician is an excellent out-of-network (concierge) doctor, and I was fortunate I was able to have immediate access to him and that he responded so quickly to my wife's insights and concerns about my deteriorating medical condition. If I were unable to obtain such a physician because private insurance was eliminated and because all physicians had to work under a government-run insurance system, where it is likely they would have a greater workload and be less accessible and responsive, it is not clear that I would have received the same quality of timely care.

HEALTH INSURANCE. If I was not aware before my surgeries, I am fully aware now that I am fortunate to have excellent health insurance and to have access to high-quality physicians. I am also more cognizant that the lack of available health insurance for all citizens is a social problem of the highest order and that it is motivating government's intervention in healthcare and frightening the business sector.

The Affordable Care Act (ACA) passed under the Obama administration can be interpreted as applying, to a certain extent, market principles of competition and choice (subject to minimum standards) to provide insurance to individuals instead of requiring a single government insurer. The ACA has increased the number of individuals covered by insurance, but its effects on the cost and quality of healthcare continue to be debated, and the act itself continues to face legal challenges.

As a private-sector alternative, Warren Buffett, the head of Berkshire Hathaway, and the chief executives of Amazon and J.P. Morgan Chase indicated they would form an independent company aimed at lowering the burden that healthcare places on the economy while improving the system for their employees (Gelles 2018). The executives claimed they had a broad vision of the problem and that their approach, which was not explained, would address the complexity and huge costs of the nation's healthcare system and could, potentially, benefit all Americans. Other large companies, such as Comcast and Walmart, are exploring distinctive approaches to lowering healthcare costs without reducing employees' earnings or the quality of coverage and care. Generally, the private sector is frustrated with government policy in this area and is engaged with ameliorating the growing costs of healthcare and with costly social programs, including Medicare,[22] Medicaid, and Social Security.[23]

Of course, a fundamental question is whether the private sector is, in fact, interested in cost-saving measures for particular companies or if it could be incentivized such that market forces contribute to providing social insurance for the population as a whole. That issue is discussed later.

Criminal Activity

The primary mechanism in the United States used to deter crime is the police and the judicial system. Market forces can help the public sector by reducing the benefits and increasing the costs of committing a crime (Becker 1968). New technologies have reduced the probability of getting away with a crime (that is, reduced expected benefits) while improvements in labor markets have increased the relative cost of spending time in illegal activities (that is, increased the cost of crime).

TECHNOLOGY. Facial recognition software, linked surveillance cameras, wireless devices, and drones are the latest technologies developed by the private sector and used by private firms and law enforcement to detect criminal behavior and apprehend criminals.[24] Notwithstanding the absence of hard empirical evidence, police believe enhanced surveillance of locations and individuals has been effective in reducing crime.[25]

Households also are using surveillance technology to help reduce crime. Amazon's Ring and Google's Nest are internet-connected cameras that enable homeowners to use their phone to be a personal security force that guards against porch pirates and suspicious strangers (Harwell 2020). Homeowners can discourage potential criminal activity by posting signs letting visitors know they are under audio and video surveillance by their device, and by using the devices to prosecute crimes involving theft or break-in, should they occur. In fact, some cities offer rebate and voucher programs for the cameras in hope that more surveillance footage will make crimes easier to solve. Police agencies have access to these cameras in nearly all states.[26]

Tesla updated its software to turn its cameras, used for backing up, parking, and cruise control, into a 360-degree video recorder. Geoffrey Fowler (2020) discusses an accident where the cameras captured a swerving city bus that hit his Tesla; the driver failed to stop and report the accident. Tesla refers to the camera function as Sentry Mode. When the vehicle was struck, it sent a message to the owner's cell phone. Other vehicle models, including Cadillacs and Corvettes, have this feature. The video clip in the Tesla case, and in other, similar cases, can be used to make the miscreants pay for vehicle damage and to convict criminals.

Households and businesses have invested hundreds of billions of dollars to deter crime by hiring private security, installing burglar alarms, and the like. More recently, they also have used modern technology, such as smartphone apps and LoJack systems, to help deter crime and apprehend criminals. Lena Edlund and Cecilia Machado (2019) find that the expansion of cellular phone service reduced homicide rates in the 1990s. Their explanation is that cell phones may have reduced the profits of turf-based drug dealers and reduced the propensity of violent street gangs to engage in crime. Google's database, Sensorvault, provides information on communication devices used near crimes and enables investigators to know their location and help make arrests.

Finally, DNA blood typing was introduced in the United States by the private sector and subsequently used by the FBI during the 1980s as a powerful adjunct to forensic science to increase arrests and convictions. DNA databases were subsequently developed in every state to catalogue the genetic fingerprints of criminal offenders to enable law enforcement to quickly and accurately match known offenders with crime scene evidence, thereby deterring those offenders from committing more crimes and incarcerating serial offenders more quickly. Jennifer Doleac (2017) found that by increasing the probability that an individual who is arrested of a crime will be convicted, the development of DNA databases has been an important deterrent and reduced both the violent and property crime rates. The databases also are more cost-effective than the traditional law enforcement tools of hiring more police and setting longer prison sentences because individuals who are deterred from committing a crime in the first place do not have to be identified, captured, prosecuted, sentenced, and incarcerated.

LABOR MARKETS. The opportunity cost of criminal activity is noncriminal activity, so in addition to its other benefits, a higher probability of employment and larger earnings act as deterrents to crime by increasing its opportunity cost. Aaron Chalfin and Justin McCrary (2017) surveyed the evidence and concluded there is an important relationship between unemployment rates and property crime, but little impact of unemployment on violent crime. In contrast, higher average wages reduced both property and violent crime, indicating that market actions that have raised earnings appear to have reduced crime. For example, as discussed previously, improved educational opportunities could increase the potential earnings of children when they become adults and could make a life of crime less attractive to those among them who might have become criminals.

COMMUNITY ORGANIZATIONS. Citizens have banned together to form community organizations to fight crime in their neighborhoods. In addition to citizen watch groups, organizations such as the nonprofit Youth Guidance developed a program called Becoming a Man, which engaged young people with summer jobs programs and other activities. Sara Heller and others (2017) find that the program helped reduce crime arrests and improved school engagement. Patrick Sharkey, Gerard Torrats-Espinosa, and Delaram Takyara (2017) report that the proliferation of nonprofit organizations that focus on reducing violence and building stronger communities can make a city safer. The Cure Violence program, for example, uses professionals to defuse violence by mediating in conflicts and altercations (Butts and others 2015). Sharkey (2020) recommends a demonstration project tailored for a bold mayor and a bold philanthropist that would allow community organizations and leaders to take over primary responsibility for creating a safe community, provided they are given resources equivalent to those given to the police.

Immigration

The US has humanitarian goals for its immigration policy, such as reuniting families and providing political asylum, and economic goals, such as attracting foreign talent that increases the nation's global competitiveness and filling jobs Americans do not want to perform at the wages employers are willing to pay. The government sets the goals, but it has allowed firms to pick foreign workers with the skills and productivity they demand.

Employers determine the level and composition of skilled immigration in accordance with visa guidelines. The H-1B visa allows US employers to employ foreign workers in occupations that require theoretical and practical application of a body of highly specialized knowledge in a field of human endeavor, including but not limited to biotechnology, chemistry, architecture, engineering, mathematics, physical sciences, social sciences, medicine and health, education, law, accounting, business specialties, theology, and the arts, and requiring the attainment of a bachelor's degree or its equivalent as a minimum (with the exception of fashion models, who must be "of distinguished merit and ability"). The L1 visa allows temporary immigration of employees of an international company with offices in both the United States and abroad.

Market forces have worked effectively to induce socially beneficial immigration as US leadership in technology and productivity has attracted skilled foreign workers who have helped the nation maintain that leadership. At the highest levels of achievement, nearly half of the US-based Nobel Prizes in medicine, physics, and chemistry during the past decade were awarded to foreign-born individuals. Immigrant entrepreneurs have played a vital role in starting new technology companies that have expanded output and employment.[27] And in 2014, one-third of US workers with a Ph.D. and a job in a STEM (science, technology, engineering, and mathematics) field were foreign-born (Peri 2016).

However, the US has put annual caps on visas, which may limit market forces and productivity growth by preventing employers from hiring the foreign talent they desire. Sari Pekkala Kerr and others (2016) reported that, in some years, applications for H-1B visas outstripped the available annual quota within a couple of days of the opening of the process. Policymakers can enable market forces to make efficient use of high-skilled foreign workers by curtailing ill-advised limits on the immigration of those workers. In December 2020, a federal judge set aside two Trump administration policies that would have effectively reduced H-1B visas by requiring employers to pay foreign workers on those visas significantly higher wages, instead of paying them lower salaries that foreign workers are willing to accept, and by narrowing eligibility for the program.

Peri also reported that 40 percent of workers without a high school diploma are foreign-born. The tension that the Trump administration created with derogatory references to foreign-born and illegal workers, who also tend not to have a high school diploma, has caused some of the public to overlook the large benefits that even low-skilled immigrants have conferred on the nation. US employers could reduce the ongoing tensions by certifying the legality of all new hires, carefully monitoring their status to ensure they do not violate the terms of their visas and remain in the country illegally, and providing full transparency about the composition of their workforce. As their technology warrants, firms should attempt to increase output by employing seasonal or permanent low-skilled foreign workers if domestic workers are unwilling to take those jobs at the prevailing wage rates. Firms could be their own worst enemies if they do not follow the preceding approach because they could give the government cause to further limit low-skilled immigration.[28]

SUMMARY

Merit goods are very costly for the United States to provide because all citizens lay claim to them and because the government lacks incentives to significantly reduce the growing costs of their programs.

Markets are improving on government provision of merit goods by responding to profit opportunities to cater to consumers' varied preferences for education and homeownership; introducing new technologies to meet the public's demand for higher-quality healthcare and safer communities; and attracting immigrants with different skill sets that can be used efficiently in many sectors of the economy. In keeping with their perceived social responsibility, certain firms are attempting to help less-affluent people gain access to higher-quality merit goods.

Generally, markets have the potential to further reduce the cost and improve the quality of merit goods if government allows them to expand their role.

FOURTEEN

Expanding the Role of Markets to Help Address Social Goals Policies

Part II of this book explains how market forces have made piecemeal attempts to help government accomplish social goals and reduce their cost. Most of this activity has occurred because firms have found it in their financial interest to address those problems. Evidence also exists that a growing number of firms have taken it upon themselves to raise wages and extend paid leave to enable individuals to distance themselves from poverty; apply pressure on policymakers to end policies that discriminate against certain groups of people; encourage their employees to acquire more education by reducing the burden of tuition and student loans; provide low-cost housing for their employees and less-affluent households; and improve healthcare coverage for their employees. Some of this activity may help improve firms' reputations with the public.

Given those constructive steps, it may be socially desirable for market forces, led by private-sector firms, to play an even greater role in addressing social goals, either as part of competing in a market environment or by taking actions to improve their reputation among consumers, which may have a financial payoff. However, is it realistic to expect private-sector firms to deviate from profit maximization as their prime objective in favor of an alternative objective consistent with their perceived social responsibility? Would firms necessarily produce positive social outcomes by pursuing an alternative objective? I do not pretend to know the answers to those questions. But government clearly needs help in accomplishing social goals, and considerable evidence exists that markets have the potential to help government address many social problems.

Klaus Schwab (2019) uses the term "stakeholder capitalism" to characterize a corporation's goals that go beyond profit maximization (that is, shareholder capitalism) to be an active trustee of society by responding to social challenges and seeking ways to link various societal benefits with financial returns. Stakeholder capitalism is consistent with the Business Roundtable's recently revised "Statement on the Purpose of a Corporation" to espouse "a fundamental commitment to all of our stakeholders," which include shareholders and employees, suppliers, customers, and affected communities. Pressure on corporations to behave more virtuously also has come from investors. Larry Fink, chief executive of BlackRock, the world's largest investment fund, has put companies on notice that he expects them to serve a social purpose, not just generate dividends for shareholders (Ewing 2019).

However, such idealized visions are likely to take a long time as firms make the necessary changes in incentive pay structures and corporate cultures, and they are unlikely to evolve into a new model of private-sector behavior unless policymakers take two actions: first, eliminate taxpayer-funded subsidies and other disincentives that limit the private sector's involvement in providing merit goods, and second, craft policy changes that incentivize the private sector to expand its efforts to reduce poverty and provide social insurance.

MARKET FORCES AND MERIT GOODS

Market forces play a role in housing, education, and the use of foreign workers. However, government interventions in those markets have created distortions that should be eliminated and that would enable markets to bear more responsibility for allocating those resources in a way that enhances social welfare.

The housing market would equilibrate more efficiently if the United States no longer relied on the tax system to encourage home ownership. Kamila Sommer and Paul Sullivan (2018) estimate that repealing the $90 billion subsidy to homeowners in the form of mortgage interest deductions would decrease housing consumption by the wealthy, increase aggregate homeownership, improve overall welfare, and lead to a decline in aggregate mortgage debt. Eliminating the subsidy would decrease the price of housing because, all else constant, the after-tax cost of occupying a square foot of housing would increase and the demand for housing would decrease. The minimum down payment required to purchase a house would fall, thereby enabling less-affluent households to become homeowners, and enabling other homeowners to reduce their mortgage debt. Aggregate homeownership would also expand because owning would become relatively cheaper than renting. Finally, over-all welfare would improve because housing consumption would shift from higher-income households (the main beneficiaries of the tax subsidy in its current form) to lower-income households for whom the additional consumption of shelter would be relatively more valuable.

Government subsidies in the form of tax expenditures in education have created two distortions. First, they have shielded inefficient public schools and teachers from the consequences of competition. Market forces could significantly reduce the enormous cost of taxpayer-funded subsidies in education if private schools were able to compete fairly with public schools and if they could expand their presence throughout the country while public schools (and failed private schools) exited as those forces dictated. Leaders of private schools who cater to low-income students may be able to make an effective case to the leading technology entrepreneurs, who have recently dominated philanthropic ventures and would like to improve US education, so that they can achieve higher returns in student performance in a more efficient education environment than the public schools have been able to achieve.

The second distortion is that subsidies have encouraged students at non-profit and for-profit colleges to take on an exorbitant amount of debt. Some students have had difficulty paying back the debt and defaulted because they were unlikely to increase their earnings by investing in education and they never should have been approved for a loan. The government should withdraw its presence in education finance so the private sector could develop an efficient capital market that could provide education opportunities for all students who merit a loan and have the potential to pay it back.

Finally, policymakers should allow market forces to fully determine the number of foreign workers in the United States by eliminating the arbitrary caps on immigration.

MARKET FORCES, POVERTY, AND SOCIAL INSURANCE

Anti-poverty and social insurance programs account for trillions of dollars of government spending and a large share of government inefficiencies. The public sector has proposed reforms to reduce the costs of those programs. However, given that some of the nation's leading executives and investors have expressed an interest in trying to reduce poverty and provide social insurance, it is useful to consider the desirability of expanding the role of the private sector to help solve those problems.

Several civic leaders and progressive advocates have spoken favorably about a "universal basic income" (UBI) program, where the government would distribute cash payments to all citizens, regardless of employment status. Robert Reich contends that a universal program that provides enough cash instead of vouchers for people to live on is inevitable.[1] It also would be inevitable that the program, if implemented, would turn out to be far more costly to society than its proponents contend.[2]

Business leaders have been taking modest—but not necessarily permanent—steps to help reduce poverty. But an effective solution to this seemingly intractable problem requires a more concerted and long-term effort that draws on the creativity, determination, and broad support of the nation's private sector and calls for policymakers to carefully assess whether the nation's poverty goals could be achieved more fully at a much lower cost by placing greater reliance on market incentives.

How might that occur? There is no doubt that firms raised the earnings of and provided bonuses to low-wage workers and extended their paid leave because the macroeconomy was expanding, the labor market was tight, and federal corporate taxes were reduced. Accordingly, firms responded to a very favorable economic climate by exploring ways to increase their output and by taking steps consistent with profit maximization in some respects—for example, providing better pay to attract and retain the best workers in a tight economy—but may have deviated from strict profit maximization in other respects—for example, providing large bonuses following the tax reduction—to engender the good will of their workers, the public, and policymakers.[3]

Assume policymakers could make the macroeconomic environment even more favorable to the private sector by proposing further reductions in household and corporate taxes in return for US industry developing a credible program where they would pay higher wages and provide more training to ensure the lowest-paid workers earn a living wage. That is, the private sector instead of the government would effectively create a UBI program, and the reduction in government expenditures on an expensive set of poverty programs would offset the reduction in tax revenues from firms and households.

Obviously, such a program would require considerable thought and analysis. Specific details would have to be provided and potential problems carefully assessed before it could move forward. However, it is useful to briefly raise the possibility here to suggest how the scope for markets, led by the private sector and their interactions with labor, could be expanded to help government accomplish social goals.

Taxpayers also fund expensive social insurance programs. Medicare is funded by a 1.45 percent tax on workers' earnings that is matched by employers, bringing the total tax to 2.9 percent. Social security also is funded by payroll taxes—the employee pays 6.2 percent of income that is matched by the employer, for a total tax of 12.4 percent. And the Medicaid program is jointly funded by the federal government and states. The federal government pays states for a specified percentage of program expenditures, called the Federal Medical Assistance Percentage (FMAP). Apparently, the current taxes to fund Part A of Medicare, which provides inpatient/hospital coverage, and social security are insufficient because there are growing concerns that each program will not meet its obligations in the coming decades unless either funding is increased or spending is significantly reformed.[4] In addition, payroll taxes are inefficient because they reduce incentives to work.

As described by Martin Feldstein (2005), a more market-oriented alternative to the current social insurance programs would rely on (mandated) individual investment-based accounts for unemployment, retirement, and healthcare, with modest government supplements. Feldstein discusses the evidence that such a system would substantially reduce the harmful economic effects of the current system, which include reducing national saving, inducing early retirement, raising the unemployment rate, pushing up the cost of healthcare, and crowding out private health insurance. Such a system also would be potentially attractive because it would not face insolvency. At the same time, it would require a large one-time transition cost to replace the lost funding for current beneficiaries, who are sixty-two years old or more.

Market-oriented universal basic income and social insurance programs are, at best, in their early development, and they would have to undergo considerable experimentation and refinement before they could be presented as credible policy alternatives. Business leaders could play an important role in crafting and implementing possible experiments. At the same time, such bold changes in policy could occur nationwide only in an environment where policymakers and the public had confidence in the markets' ability to solve social problems the government has not been able to solve, and that the potential benefits were worth the risks.

Part III of this book starts to build that confidence by synthesizing the evidence discussed thus far on government policy inefficiencies and how markets have helped government accomplish economic and social goals. Part III also concludes that: (1) the potential benefits of expanding private-sector involvement and developing market approaches are worth the risks because the existence of poverty alone makes it so much harder for the nation to solve other challenging problems, especially the social goals of educating its citizens, providing them with adequate healthcare, and protecting them against crime; and (2) policymakers and the public should give markets additional opportunities to solve challenging social problems that government policy has failed to solve, after experiments show that they have a good chance of succeeding.

PART III

Synthesizing the Evidence

Policy Inefficiencies and Efforts to Explain Them

FIFTEEN

Government Policy Inefficiencies and Efforts to Explain Them

Because this book is not about what government does well but about how markets help government, some readers still may think government is not getting a fair shake because I have given up too easily by not being more proactive about identifying plausible policy reforms that could reduce policy inefficiencies. However, before policies can be reformed effectively, it is necessary to understand the sources of their inefficiencies.

This chapter provides that understanding by outlining a simple framework based on the demand for and supply of government policy, synthesizing the inefficiencies previously discussed, and then assessing how well the various parts of the framework can explain the policy inefficiencies. I conclude that the explanations, while credible, are at best circumstantial in specific policy contexts, and that the lack of evidence on causality prevents the identification of specific steps policymakers could take to significantly improve microeconomic policy performance.

BRIEF OVERVIEW OF POLICY INEFFICIENCIES

The evidence summarized previously certainly is not exhaustive; however, it is consistent with Peter Schuck's (2014) canvassing of more than 270 assessments of government economic policies by the GAO, the OMB, and several think tanks. The inefficient outcomes of government's economic and social policies can be distilled into three categories.

POLICIES THAT DO LITTLE TO IMPROVE WELFARE. Policies that in most cases do not appear to significantly improve consumer welfare include antitrust enforcement, information and technology policies, and labor market policies (when firms take actions to subvert them). At the same time, there is little evidence of large welfare losses from anticompetitive behavior, imperfect information, the current level of technological innovation, and labor market discrimination, which suggests that market forces have complemented government policy to a notable extent to help address those potential problems.[1]

POLICIES THAT IMPOSE LARGE WELFARE LOSSES. Policies that in most cases have reduced economic welfare without improving equity include price and entry regulations. Generally, eliminating those regulations is likely to result in a welfare gain.

POLICIES THAT GENERATE EXCESSIVE COSTS TO PRODUCE BENEFITS. Policies that in most cases have entailed considerable waste and placed an excessive financial burden on firms and taxpayers include externality policies, public production, anti-poverty policies, and policies to provide merit goods. Although government policy has achieved important objectives by, for example, improving air quality, building the highway system, reducing poverty, and protecting the public against criminals and terrorists, market forces could help government accomplish those and other objectives more fully at lower social cost.

The persistence of inefficient microeconomic policies over a lengthy period motivates a puzzle formalized by Gary Becker (1983): Why can't we allocate resources so that an inefficiency is eliminated and everyone shares in the efficiency improvement, with the gainers compensating the losers if necessary? To solve the puzzle, one must explain government performance. But that has proven to be difficult because possible influences, such as lobbying by special interests, could just as well be the outcomes of government performance (Wolf 1979).

GOVERNMENT WORKERS

In his public debates, Milton Friedman often pointed out that people, not governments, make value judgments, and that people, not government institutions, make policy. It is, therefore, useful to provide an overview of the characteristics of the people who work for the government and of their workplace environment to explore some of the possible explanations for policy inefficiencies.

There are two qualifications to this critical assessment. First, many government workers do perform important services for the public: protecting nuclear sites, enlisting in national defense forces, enforcing criminal justice, and the like. Second, the Trump administration contributed to a poor work environment by neglecting much of the government workforce (Lewis 2018). The Biden administration is likely to improve the work environment for government workers.

Government workers include elected officials and civil servants at the federal, state, and local level. Jennifer Bachner and Benjamin Ginsberg (2016) argue that civil servants exercise real power over how governments operate by writing and enforcing rules and regulations. At the federal level, administrative agencies, authorities, and commissions have proliferated—nearly 500 of them are housed in fifteen executive departments—and they have a great deal of autonomy.

The federal civilian workforce, some 2 million strong, is significantly older, more likely to have served in the military, and much more likely to identify themselves as liberal or moderate than the broader US population (Vinik 2017; Bachner and Ginsberg 2016). Including the state and local government workforce of 18 million workers, some of whom administer federal programs, membership in public-sector unions exceeds that in private-sector unions. And salaries for government jobs generally exceed those of comparable private-sector jobs, except for jobs requiring a graduate degree, such as a lawyer or a doctor (Falk 2012).

Government employees also work in an environment where glowing evaluations are the norm and terminations are rare. The results of recent performance reviews in the federal government were that 99 percent of workers were described as really good at their jobs, and nearly 80 percent of high-level civil servants and 85 percent of senior executives were given scores of outstanding (Rein 2016; GAO 2016). Eric Yoder and Lisa Rein (2017) point out that, if performance issues should arise, it is very difficult to terminate a government worker because various legal and union rights come into play. If government jobs are eliminated, employees in those jobs may be able to displace lower-ranked employees while keeping their higher pay. Given their relatively attractive compensation, government employees tend to stay on the job, and aging bureaucrats are difficult to remove.[2]

Because the government simply is not designed to adjust quickly to changing times and demands and hire a modern and highly productive workforce, policy decisions are affected by employees who, given their characteristics and generational makeup, are greatly distanced from the broader populace. Bachner and Ginsberg (2016) indicate that government bureaucrats welcome this distance because they think the public is ignorant about public policy and they should focus on using their best judgment on policy matters instead of considering public opinion. But such judgment is often driven by ideology, because civil servants tend to self-select into agencies based on their own support for an agency's mission. For example, environmentalists are more likely to work for the Environmental Protection Agency than for the Office of Surface Mining (Bolton, de Figueiredo, and Lewis 2016). Presidential elections may increase departure rates of some career senior employees if their views diverge sharply from those of the new president, but vacancies in high-level positions after elections may induce lower-level executives to stay longer in hopes of advancing.

Elected officials control the dominant instruments of public policy by implementing new laws and reforming old ones. A priori, it is reasonable to posit that microeconomic policy performance is affected by elected officials' interactions with the government workforce to formulate and apply laws and regulations (policy supply), and with private lawyers and other advocates for consumers and firms, who try to influence officials to enact policies favorable to their clients (policy demand).

TOWARD AN ANATOMY OF GOVERNMENT FAILURE

In 1958, Francis M. Bator presented an anatomy of market failure identifying the major causes of market failure that we know today. In the sixty-plus years that followed, I am not aware of a comprehensive treatment of government failure that could be used to explain successfully the dearth of efficient policy changes and the persistence of inefficient policies.[3]

Analyzing the causes of policy inefficiencies is difficult because the political consequences of a public policy, not just its costs and benefits, come into play (Acemoglu and Robinson 2013). Accordingly, political economy models of government stress the importance of organized special interests—that is, those agents who attempt to demand policy or resist policy change through lobbying and campaign contributions because they stand to realize substantial gains or losses. Dani Rodrik (2014), however, questions whether a well-defined mapping from special interests to policy outcomes actually exists, especially because it is not clear why efficient changes in policy would leave elites worse off.[4]

Policymakers—that is, the agents who supply policy—are critical to policy outcomes, and it is, therefore, important to consider the characteristics of government employees, elected officials, and civil servants, and of the workplace environment as possible constraints that an efficient policy must overcome. Rodrik (2014) points to examples abroad, such as dual reform in China and democratization in South Africa, where significant efficiency improvements have occurred without threatening the power of elites and making them worse off. Such major policy improvements, however, have been rare in recent decades in the United States.

Available empirical and anecdotal evidence can be used to explore the explanatory power of an anatomy of government failure based on the demand for and supply of government policy. The demand side is reflected in lobbying and campaign contributions by special interests. The supply side comprises government workers' characteristics, which are crystalized in their self-selection to work in the public sector and preferences and ideology, the government workplace environment, including resource constraints, and the role of law and lawyers in the policy process.

Notwithstanding its policy inefficiencies, the US government is not sufficiently corrupt that systematic evidence supports corruption as a broad explanation for government failure.[5] As noted, I am not aware of evidence that indicates that microeconomic policies tend to be systematically more efficient when a particular administration, and, I would add, political party, is in power. Alan Blinder and Mark Watson (2016) provided evidence that the US economy has performed better when the president of the United States is a Democrat rather than a Republican, and they explained that this edge stems mainly from more benign oil shocks, superior total factor productivity performance, a more favorable international environment, and, perhaps, more optimistic consumer expectations about the near-term future. However, they did not attempt to show that those explanations were caused by more efficient microeconomic policies. Similarly, David Leonhardt (2018) claimed that the Democrats are the party of fiscal responsibility because budget deficits have tended to be lower when they have been in power. But the policy inefficiencies I have documented have persisted for decades, and neither party has done much to correct them by implementing efficient policy reforms. To be sure, there are sharp partisan distinctions between Democrats and Republicans, but the parties have not made policy choices that would support the conclusion that one party has consistently promoted microeconomic efficiency more than the other.

The Demand for Policy: Lobbying

Frank Baumgartner and others (2009) conducted an extensive study of lobbying resources and outlays and concluded that they did not have much effect on policy outcomes. To the extent that lobbying for or against a specific policy helped a special interest, it did so by preventing potential losses and by maintaining the status quo rather than by producing new gains. Studies examining corporate profits have concluded that lobbying has improved performance to some extent, but such studies do not identify the specific government policies affected by lobbying and their effects on economic efficiency (Bessen 2016; Brown and Huang 2017).

Circumstantial evidence suggests that lobbyists may have influenced some laws and regulations: bank lobbyists wrote provisions that allegedly weakened some Dodd-Frank regulations; lobbyists may have influenced legislation by moving in and out of government (the revolving door) to work on matters where they have developed a political connection (Blanes i Vidal, Draca, and Fons-Rosen 2012; Bertrand, Bombardini, and Trebbi 2014). Dhruv Khullar (2017) reported that, in 2016, the healthcare industry, including pharmaceutical companies, hospitals, and health professionals, spent more money than any other US industry on lobbying, roughly $500 million (in comparison, the gun lobby spent $10.5 million). But the benefits that the healthcare industry realized from their lobbying expenditures were not identified.

In general, firms have not improved their financial performance by lobbying. In fact, their performance may have suffered if corporate leaders were using company resources to indulge their own ideological preferences (Cao and others 2018). Most firms do not lobby policymakers even when it may appear to be in their interest to do so (for example, Kerr, Lincoln, and Mishra 2014), and, importantly, most members of Congress do not want to hear from a lobbyist (Lipton 2015). In sum, while lobbying is undoubtedly associated with some changes in public policy, it is difficult to identify the specific policy changes that lobbying has caused, and it is, therefore, difficult to conclude from the available evidence that lobbying accounts for a large share of the US economy's inefficiencies. At the same time, lobbying may be desirable if it helps ward off harmful protectionist actions.

The Economist (2019) argued that, under the Trump administration, lobbying for corporate America became even more difficult because Trump was viewed as an outsider; his administration was inefficient; respectable businesses worried about being sullied by association with Trump's entourage or his views; and power in the administration shifted very quickly. In addition, because Trump retaliated against those who criticized him, it was difficult to distinguish between effective lobbying and when lobbying's goal was consistent with Trump's vendettas.[6] It may be easier for corporations to lobby the Biden administration, but the efforts still may not produce significant policy changes.

The Demand for Policy: Campaign Contributions

Stephen Ansolabehere, John M. de Figueiredo, and James M. Snyder Jr. (2003) conducted an extensive survey of the literature on the effects of campaign contributions on legislation, and they found that, in roughly 75 percent of the studies, campaign contributions had no statistically significant effects on legislators' roll call votes or they had the "wrong" sign—suggesting that more contributions lead to less support. The authors then performed their own study, and they, also, found that campaign contributions had statistically insignificant effects on legislators' behavior. Instead, legislators' votes depended almost entirely on their own beliefs and on the preferences of their constituents and their party.

The authors' main finding has not been affected by the Supreme Court's 2010 decision in *Citizens United v. Federal Election Committee*, which allowed corporations to spend unlimited amounts on elections. Both Binjamin Applebaum (2014) and Lee Drutman (2015) reported that the predicted flood of campaign spending by corporations failed to materialize because corporations were generally satisfied with the status quo and because they tended to get involved in campaigns only to defeat a change in policy that would harm them.[7] Drutman indicated that individuals' spending on and participation in campaigns had increased, but the effect on policy outcomes was unclear.

Anthony Fowler, Haritz Garro, and Jorg L. Spenkuch (2020) assembled data from nearly 19,000 elections and nearly 3,000 firms spanning more than three decades to understand the extent to which campaign contributions systematically benefited firms. They find that, on average, firms do not systematically benefit from having an elected candidate to whom they made a campaign contribution, and they find little evidence that public policy is distorted in favor of firms as a result of corporate campaign contributions. Their response to the question of why firms give so much in campaign contributions if they do not systematically benefit from them is that firms do not contribute much. Many large firms do not even have corporate PACs, and many of those that do make only nominal contributions.

From the perspective of policymakers, Pinelopi Koujianou Goldberg and Giovanni Maggi (1999) estimated that campaign contributions were not highly valued by politicians and that the magnitude of political considerations in government's objective function was small. Adam Bonica and others (2013) argued that campaign finance reform is of little value in attacking corruption because politicians are not corrupted by campaign contributions. Thus, like lobbying, campaign contributions do not appear to have played a major role in explaining policy inefficiencies, especially because little evidence exists that money plays an important role in elections and politics in general (Levitt 1994; Milyo 1998).[8]

A valid reaction to the preceding evidence is to ask why lobbying expenditures have grown even if individual firms' expenditures are not large. William Frenzel, a distinguished member of Congress for twenty years and my long-time next-door neighbor at Brookings, repeatedly explained to me that lobbying was primarily defensive—as various policy proposals continue to surface, firms increasingly spend money to maintain the status quo. Jonathan Rauch (1995) makes a similar point.[9]

The inability of lobbying expenditures and campaign contributions to constitute an important empirically supported explanation of government policy inefficiencies may be surprising to those, including me, who were brought up in graduate school to believe that regulatory inefficiencies were the result of regulators who were captured by the industry or interest group they were supposed to regulate (Stigler 1971). Although that explanation struck many economists as intuitively consistent with the economic effects of regulation, evidence that interest groups, either through lobbying or campaign contributions, caused a regulation to be created or to persist actually was lacking.[10] In addition, assessing capture theory in the wake of economic deregulation only stimulated debate instead of engendering additional support.[11]

Because of a lack of comprehensive data or theory or both, supply-side explanations for policy inefficiencies have been advanced much less often than interest group explanations.[12] The supply-side explanations considered here are, therefore, ad hoc to some extent, but various pieces of institutional and empirical evidence can be drawn on to assess whether policy inefficiencies could be plausibly attributed to policymakers' characteristics and their workplace environment.

The Supply of Policy: Self-Selection to Work in Government

People who self-select to work in government are not a random sample of the US population, based on the difference between their characteristics, age, political ideology, military service, union membership, and those characteristics in the general population. I am not aware of objective evidence on the quality of the government workforce. But some of its notable characteristics may suggest how it could affect government policy and performance. For example, an aging government workforce may not be up to date on the latest information technology to develop evidence to shed light on policy issues. In addition, government workers' cognitive characteristics, such as ability and competence, are likely to affect government performance.

Francesco Decarolis and others (2018) built measures of federal bureaus' and agencies' competence, accounting for skills, incentives, and cooperation among employees, to assess contract execution efficiency. The authors found considerable variability in competence across government organizations and estimated that if all bureaus were able to obtain NASA's (high) level of competence, consistent with private management standards, then delays in contract execution and price renegotiations would decline significantly, with annual cost savings approaching $15 billion.[13] The authors also found that differences in individuals' ability to cooperate with each other were more important than their skills. (The lack of interagency cooperation is a well-known explanation for the US government's failure to prevent the September 11 terrorist attacks.)

Skill deficiencies appear to be important in specific situations. For example, a participant in several industry teams bidding on major FAA programs observed that the FAA's electronic systems engineers were frequently unable to keep up with the levels of technology advancement bidders were offering in their proposals and so took many bidders' claims on faith. The persistent and significant knowledge gap led private industry to identify any promising new people hired by the FAA and lure them away.[14]

Turnover at the FAA left two relatively inexperienced engineers overseeing Boeing's early work on its flawed software known as MCAS. The FAA eventually handed over responsibility for the approval of MCAS to Boeing, which did not have to share details of the system with those engineers. Representative Peter DeFazio, House Transportation chair of a panel investigating the crash of the 737 Max, said that inside the FAA "it has been pretty hard to identify exactly who was in charge of what, and who knew whatever about MCAS and details of the risk analysis."[15]

Similarly, the US patent office does not retain the strongest scientists and engineers to assess patent applications because the pay is not competitive for a strong person in those fields. The most able employees leave the office to work for a law firm or company.

An increasing deficiency of Congress is that congressional staffers with technology expertise do not exist (Moore 2018). Of the 3,500 legislative staff on the Hill, only seven had any formal technical training.[16] The result is that the Senate and House of Representatives are not up to the task of understanding how technology shapes society. During Facebook CEO Mark Zuckerberg's testimony before Congress in April 2018, senior members of Congress did not seem to understand how Facebook made money or how it targeted ads, and some members could not distinguish Facebook from an email platform or an internet service provider. Eric Yoder (2021) discusses a recent report that recommends that the Office of Personnel Management focus on hiring better trained people with the technical skills that government needs.

Clifford Winston, David Burk, and Jia Yan (2021) documented the existence of an intellectual talent gap, based on law school grades and the rankings of degree-granting law schools, between lawyers who worked in the private sector and lawyers who worked in government. Importantly, they found that the government was unable to retain its most intellectually able lawyers. Consistent with that finding, Ed deHaan and others (2015) found in the case of the Securities and Exchange Commission that roughly one-third of their sample of lawyers left to join private law firms and those lawyers were more likely to have graduated from top law schools and to have the best enforcement records at the agency.[17] Finally, Ellen Nakashima and Aaron Gregg (2018) report that the National Security Agency has recently lost its top talent at a historically faster rate as highly skilled personnel have taken higher-paying, more flexible jobs in the private sector.

These fragments of evidence suggest that government policy inefficiencies may be related to the competence of the people who self-select to work and remain employed by the federal government. Policy inefficiencies at lower levels of government may be indirectly affected by the attributes of cities' amenities, because highly-skilled and educated workers are attracted to a city by its amenities (Glaeser, Kolko, and Saiz 2001). Giuseppe Rossitti (2019) applies this idea to study the supply of government officials and finds that, in more remote US state capitals, legislators are, on average, less educated and less experienced. Many legislators do not wish to live in a remote capital city because it is a less attractive city than many alternative cities. At the same time, a remote capital has lower market access and imposes a larger cost of commuting, making a legislative seat less appealing to individuals with a better option. Importantly, Rossitti finds that legislators who attain a lower level of educational attainment are associated with less public good provision and more corruption at the state level.

In the final analysis, government workers, especially at the federal level, who do not depart for the private sector and, instead, remain on their jobs do not live a life of poverty. Accounting for benefits like healthcare and pensions, the average federal worker's compensation is more than 75 percent higher than the average compensation of everyone else.[18] And given that it is very difficult—some would say nearly impossible—to get fired from a government job, the combination of job security and compensation is sufficient to keep many government workers on the job for decades.

At the same time, the subset of government workers who held jobs that required a Ph.D. or a professional degree were paid 18 percent less per hour worked compared with workers in the private sector who had that level of education (Falk 2012), which may help explain why the most intellectually able workers are not attracted to or choose to leave government to work in the private sector. Self-selected (and possibly less-skilled) long-term government employees could hurt policy performance by their tendency to reinforce status quo bias because they do not want to disturb their "sweet gig" by helping advance major policy reforms that might be opposed by the public or by other people in government (Zimmerman 2015).

The Supply of Policy: Preferences

Government policy inefficiencies may arise when government bureaucrats do not rigorously analyze policy alternatives and, instead, follow their own preferences, with their biases and even their religion forming the basis for those preferences. Alexander Hertel-Fernandez, Matto Mildenberger, and Leah Stokes (2018) found that congressional staff fail to correctly estimate constituent preferences, which may explain why Congress appears to be unresponsive to ordinary citizens. Not surprisingly, congressional staff hear from special interests more than they hear from anyone else. The authors point out that congressional staff biases shape their perceptions of constituent preferences, but that those biases tend to be aligned primarily with the input from special interests. Daniel Arnon (2018) explored the effect of senators' religions on their legislative behavior in the Senate, where religion is measured by belonging to a church or synagogue, specific beliefs, and conforming behavior. He found that religious beliefs were a strong predictor of senators' legislative behavior across a wide array of policy areas, controlling for the senators' personal and ideological characteristics and their constituents' political and religious preferences.[19] Religious tradition and behavior were found to be a weak predictor. Finally, Joseph Kalt and Mark Zupan (1990) provide evidence that US senators' ideological preferences help explain certain policy outcomes.

Policymakers who blindly indulge their preferences, however formed, rarely conduct retrospective policy assessments to learn from past mistakes after they have made their decisions. Jonathan Masur and Eric Posner (2016) identified regulatory agencies that have failed to conduct a careful cost-benefit assessment before deciding to implement a regulation or that have issued regulations even when they failed a cost-benefit test—in one case by 1,920 to 1! The agencies proceeded with regulations without conducting cost-benefit tests because, in their judgment, the benefits justified the costs. Richard Epstein (2011) pointed out that the Office of Management and Budget, which is supposed to provide general oversight over regulatory agencies, does not even perform its own cost-benefit analyses of the agencies being reviewed. Instead, it relies on the agencies' own estimates when they are available.

In the language of hypothesis testing, policymakers commit Type I errors by effectively rejecting true null hypotheses that challenge their policies, and they also commit Type II errors by failing to reject false null hypotheses, such as the Federal Drug Administration not approving an effective drug because of excessive concerns about safety. Such behavior is undoubtedly attributable to their policy preferences and to the perceived asymmetries between punishments for unpopular actions and credit for popular ones (Weaver 1986).

During the past decade, Presidents Obama and Trump have used their executive power to finalize hundreds of rules and regulations without evidence that they improve social welfare. Often, one president's actions undoubtedly raised social welfare and the other's actions reduced it, because many of Trump's executive actions primarily sought to undo Obama's executive actions, such as rolling back fuel economy standards. (President Biden is undoing many of Trump's executive actions.) Trump also indulged his own "America First" preferences by initiating harmful protectionist policies, such as invoking tariffs and placing stronger restrictions on legal immigration while failing to initiate a strong effort to repeal the Jones Act, and to spur domestic and international airline competition by granting foreign airlines cabotage rights.

Winston, Burk, and Yan (2021) found evidence of growing ideological polarization for or against business firms among justices on the Supreme Court, which could have adverse consequences for policy. Richard Posner (2008) rationalized such a finding by arguing that when policymakers are not committed to a logical premise for making a decision (for example, by using cost-benefit analysis), those decisions are ideological because they cannot be anything else.

Although policymakers may make judgments with the best of intentions, those judgments still may have unanticipated adverse consequences. For example, the US Department of Transportation thought commercial airline carriers should provide compensation to passengers when they overbooked their flights and had to find volunteers willing to take a later flight. But DOT also decided to put a cap on the maximum compensation an airline could award. This constraint led to the widely publicized incident discussed in the introduction where United Airlines was unable to use a bidding process to determine the minimum compensation passengers would be willing to accept to voluntarily deplane an overbooked flight and wait for the next available flight. Instead, United forcibly removed and injured a passenger who had low boarding priority and had not volunteered to deplane the flight.

The Supply of Policy: Workplace Environment
The government workplace environment may inhibit constructive change and promote waste because of poor morale and resource constraints. Generally, the government's share of total employment has been declining, espe-

cially the federal government's share, and is, according to the Bureau of Labor Statistics, at its lowest point since the 1950s. The decline in employment could affect how the government performs some socially desirable tasks.

Low morale and resource constraints were exacerbated by the Trump administration's efforts to shrink the federal bureaucracy without assessing how policy enforcement may be affected (Rein and Ba Tran 2017). To take some specific examples:

- Trump's political appointees shut down government studies and reduced the influence of government scientists over policy decisions, prompting many to depart (Plumer and Davenport 2019). In the first two years of the Trump administration, more than 1,600 federal scientists left government; at the Environmental Protection Agency, nearly 700 scientists had left, while EPA hired 350 replacements (Gowen and others 2020).

- Mick Mulvaney, the former acting director of the Consumer Financial Protection Bureau, weakened the agency by allowing the staff to shrink and enforcement to dwindle (Confessore 2019).

- The erosion of morale at NASA during the government shutdown and afterward was reflected in workers' sentiments that "We didn't get PhDs just to sit around" (Robertson 2019).

- Researchers at the Department of Agriculture into the economic effects of climate change, trade policy, and food stamps claim that the secretary of the department was pressuring them into leaving the agency by moving them outside of Washington, DC, because their assessments raised questions about Trump's policies. The researchers said that moving them would adversely affect their work because they draw on information from other department divisions, members of Congress, and other stakeholders in Washington (Crampton 2019).

- The administration's plan to relocate more than 20 percent of the Bureau of Land Management's Washington, DC, workforce to west of the Rockies risked resignations and a loss of expertise because the move was too disruptive for many families.

On the other hand, there are cases where there is little doubt that an entire agency or program or subset of employees is contributing very little of social value, but they cannot be eliminated. Examples include:

- The National Technical Information Services (NTIS) agency has more than 75 percent of its documents on the internet and sales of only 8 percent of its documents from 1990 to 2011. Closing the agency would save the government $50 million per year (Ehley 2015).

- Agriculture and airline service subsidy programs are costly but provide few benefits for small farmers and for air travelers to small communities. Both programs' justification is clearly outdated because agricultural subsidies are provided for farmers who earn more than 75 percent of their household income from nonfarm sources, and air service subsidies are provided to airports that are less than 100 miles from a hub airport.

- Some federal employees have been paid not to come to work because they do not have enough work to do, but their positions have not been terminated (Ehley 2014; Rein 2015).

Clearly, one of President Biden's biggest challenges is to revive US agencies and, more generally, institutions after Trump's assault on them. At the same time, Biden should be open-minded that certain inefficiencies may be pared by shrinking the bureaucracy.

Given their environment, it is not surprising that many government workers have low morale even with their relatively high compensation and benefits. Survey research indicates that less than 50 percent of state and local employees are fully engaged in their jobs, which affects productivity and performance.[20] Private-sector employees suffer from similar issues, but they are more likely to quit when they are dissatisfied because they are less likely to enjoy the pension and healthcare benefits most government workers receive. The US Office of Personnel Management's Federal Employee Viewpoint Survey for 2015 indicated that US federal agencies are generally perceived by their own employees as not basing promotions and recognition on merit, not allowing autonomy in the use of individual talent, and not rewarding individuals for innovative approaches and solutions. And in the Office of Personnel Management's 2014 survey, only 38 percent of employees agreed that senior leaders inspired a high level of motivation and commitment to their jobs.

Studies of specific government agencies have pointed to poor management and worker morale as contributing to failure in public sector Arctic expeditions (Karpoff 2001), identifying defects in automobile safety (Ivory 2015), and preventing New Orleans flooding in the aftermath of Hurricane Katrina (Robertson and Schwartz 2015). Lawyers indicated their dissatisfaction with working in the US Department of Justice because they felt President Trump undercut them and eroded the credibility of the department (Barber 2019).

Resource constraints also affect the workplace environment in ways that may contribute to policy inefficiencies. For example, *Government Failure* pointed out that OSHA, the Mine Safety and Health Administration, and the Consumer Product Safety Commission provided weak regulatory enforcement because they did not have enough personnel to carefully inspect the safety of workplaces, mines, and consumer products.

More recent evidence can be provided. With 0.3 staff members for every 100 fatalities in automobile crashes, the National Highway Traffic Safety Administration is not staffed to monitor and regulate complex car software (Gelles, Tabuchi, and Dolan 2015). In comparison, the FAA has over 10,000 staff members for every 100 fatalities on commercial aircraft. Before generic drugs can enter the market to compete with branded drugs and reduce prices, the FDA must approve that generic manufacturers' drugs have the same strength, purity, and stability as the branded drug. However, the FDA's workforce has had a difficult time keeping up with applications, as indicated by the typical lag of four years between the initial application and approval (Ip 2016). Similarly, the US Patent and Trademark Office has been overwhelmed with roughly 650,000 patent applications in recent years, and they do not have enough examiners to spend sufficient time to carefully review the applications, some of which will subsequently be challenged (Nocera 2018). Finally, Winston, Burk, and Yan (2021) find in a study of the US Office of the Solicitor General that the same set of top lawyers performed worse in cases before the Supreme Court when they were working for the Office than when they were working for a private law firm because they were constrained by the available resources to focus on a limited number of the most important government cases.

As discussed previously, the government faces a severe shortage of employees with an appropriate technical background because workers with that background do not tend to self-select to work for the government. This shortage has become a significant resource constraint. Bill Pascrell Jr. (2019), a congressman from New Jersey, argues that there is a lack of resources, capital and staff, and technical assistance from other congressional offices. He adds that people on congressional committees that deal with science and technology issues often do not have a technical background in the subject area. For example, until Eddie Bernice Johnson became chairwoman of the House Committee on Science, Space, and Technology in 2019, that committee had not had a chairperson with a scientific background since the 1990s. The lack of skilled workers, especially in information technology and cybersecurity jobs, can be attributed to poor management and few opportunities for career development (Makridis 2018).

The Supply of Policy: The Role of Law and Lawyers

Law and lawyers are essential for formulating and applying public policy, but both have features that sow the seeds of government policy inefficiencies. The strength of law is that it establishes boundaries—that is, identifies illegal behavior—and governs interactions among and between people and firms. Its weakness is that proposed laws that offer constructive change can be vetoed. For example, the Senate and the House of Representatives are veto players because, without their consent, no bill can become a law. Alfred Stepan and Juan Linz (2011) pointed out that the more veto players in a political system— and the United States has an exceptionally high number of them—the more difficult it is to avoid status quo bias and to adopt socially beneficial policy reforms.

Lawyers understand and respect the policymaking process and account for a large share of policymakers, especially in Congress, where 42 percent of the seats in the House and 59 percent of the seats in the Senate in the 113th Congress were held by lawyers. However, lawyers, like economists, can be slaves to their training and professional culture, which can adversely affect policy. For example, administrative lawyers are comfortable with, and, indeed, may welcome, highly detailed regulations and statutes. The point is illustrated by examples such as the Federal Register approaching 68,000 pages in 2018; the Dodd-Frank Act spawning an additional 14,000 pages on top of its initial 2,300 pages; and the Affordable Care Act amounting to 2,700 pages and 1,327 waivers. Some lawyers can be so preoccupied with administering regulations that they neglect to consider whether the regulations are enhancing or harming social welfare.[21]

Phillip Howard's (2019) critique of the legal profession points out that lawyers share a philosophy of the correctness of the law, such as compliance with a rule, regardless of the law's actual economic and social effects. For more than three years, the Veterans Benefits Administration intentionally stopped redacting names, Social Security numbers, and other personally identifiable information on third-party individuals in claims records provided to veterans. Although people could face substantial harm if their information were misused, the Veterans Affairs' General Counsel's Office said there was legal support for not redacting the data (Corrigan 2019).

Winston, Burk, and Yan (2021) argue that the pervasive role of lawyers in all levels of government has had an adverse effect on the efficacy of public policies in general because lawyers' training and career development have occurred in an environment shaped by regulations that reduce competition and innovation and foster status quo bias. In addition, legal training and practice does not encourage policymakers to acknowledge and correct their policy inefficiencies by subjecting previous decisions to rigorous retrospective cost-benefit analyses.

SYNTHESIS AND CONCLUSIONS BASED ON THE EVIDENCE

The preceding sections of this chapter have outlined possible explanations for policy inefficiencies based on factors underlying the demand for and supply of policy. This section briefly summarizes and integrates the evidence on policy inefficiencies and attempts to explain it. The first column of table 15-1 indicates a specific economic policy to accomplish an economic goal (that is, correct a market failure) or a social goal policy to accomplish a social objective. The second column summarizes the government policy inefficiency, as indicated by the effect of the policy on welfare. And the final column indicates possible explanations for the inefficiency based on the various explanations discussed.

This approach differs from that taken by George Stigler (1981), who claimed that if one cannot explain why some regulations appear and some regulations do not appear, then one does not know what questions to ask about their effects. However, the important economic effects of many microeconomic policies, including regulatory policies, have been measured, and they could shed some light on the influences on policymakers that may have caused them.

Direct Effects of Policy Inefficiencies
The direct effects of policy inefficiencies can generally be characterized as X-inefficiencies (deviations from efficient behavior) caused by policies that require excessive taxpayer spending to cover inflated subsidies; fail to reduce externalities efficiently; and increase costs and prices, possibly by suppressing innovation.

As noted, antitrust, information, R&D and innovation, and labor market policies have produced small welfare improvements, while generating costs, such as court-related costs for firms; higher prices for services subject to occupational licensing; and wasteful taxpayer-funded R&D spending. Regulatory, externality, public production, anti-poverty, and merit goods policies have produced benefits that have generally fallen short of the excessive costs incurred by consumers, firms, and taxpayers in general. Labor market regulations and social goals policies that discourage work have also raised unemployment (Mulligan 2012).

Interactive Effects of Policy Inefficiencies

The cost of policy inefficiencies also has been magnified by creating adverse interactions. The following are examples of policy inefficiencies that have created negative interactions within economic and social goals policies:

- Tariffs restrict the entry of products made by foreign firms, which could limit potential abuses of market power by US firms that raise prices and antitrust concerns.

- By reducing agricultural exports, tariffs that lead to retaliation by countries such as China have hurt the US farm economy, increased bankruptcies, and spurred calls for more subsidies. And by reducing freight flows between the US and foreign countries, tariffs could significantly hurt the financial performance of the deregulated railroad industry and jeopardize its goal to become revenue adequate.

- SEC regulations have heightened firms' regulatory burdens by requiring more compliance employees. Higher costs cause weaker firms to exit and increase industry concentration (Wu 2020).

- Suboptimal highway investments increase road roughness, which reduces fuel economy and increases emissions (Wang and others 2019). Greater road roughness also may reduce highway safety.

- Zoning increases home prices, pushes people further from jobs, and increases traffic congestion. The failure to reduce urban congestion has led to larger vehicle sizes, which reduces highway safety and air quality (Winston and Yan 2021).

- Ineffective anti-poverty policies that fail to enable certain individuals to escape a life of poverty may result in a higher crime rate. Even well-intentioned policies, such as raising the minimum wage, can increase property crime because younger people have fewer employment opportunities and work fewer hours (Fone, Sabia, and Cesur 2019).

Inefficient economic policies also may adversely affect social goals policies and vice versa. Examples of the former include:

- Although I have argued that anticompetitive behavior is limited, the anticompetitive behavior that exists in product and labor markets and is unaddressed by policy raises prices and reduces wages, which places additional burdens on anti-poverty policies, such as food stamps, and makes it harder to combat poverty through employment if a job pays low wages.

TABLE 15-1. Policy Inefficiencies and Potential Explanations

Economic or Social Goals Policy	Government Policy Inefficiency	Potential Explanation For Policy Inefficiency
Goal: Correct Market Failure		
Antitrust enforcement to promote competition	There is little evidence of consumer welfare gains from antitrust enforcement.	Preferences/ideology for lax or stronger enforcement could lead to inefficient policy. Resource constraints limit enforcement activity.
Regulation to prevent destructive competition or monopoly pricing	Price regulations have created deadweight losses and transferred resources from consumers to producers.	Inefficient programs cannot be eliminated or substantially reformed. Preferences/ideology lead to inefficient regulations (for example, President Trump setting new tariffs, pulling out of the TPP, and seeking to replace NAFTA).
Information policies to enable consumers and workers make more-informed decisions about products and workplaces	There is little evidence that government actions have improved consumers' and workers' welfare. In addition, policies such as occupational licensing have raised consumer prices.	Resource constraints limit inspections of products and workplaces. Legal process contributes to complexity and cost of financial regulations.
Reduce negative externalities efficiently	Externalities are addressed at excessive cost or unaddressed.	Preferences/ideology favor quantity-based regulations instead of efficient pricing.

Objective		
Increase positive externalities from R&D and innovation efficiently	There is little evidence that government subsidies have spurred R&D and innovation that would not have been undertaken anyway. The welfare effects of the patent system are not clear. Academic research is, in all likelihood, underfunded.	Preferences/ideology affect who gets government funding.
Provide socially desirable services that would not be provided by the private sector	Management of public infrastructure and services has been extremely inefficient and strained the budgets of all levels of government.	Preferences/ideology for increasing public expenditures instead of adopting efficient policy reforms
Goal: Accomplish Social Objective		
Reduce poverty at the least cost to society	The cost of antipoverty programs has been inflated by waste and fraud.	Preferences/ideology oppose reform Resource constraints limit efficacy
Promote fairness in labor markets	Firms have adjusted their behavior to subvert government policies.	Preferences/ideology oppose reform
Provide merit goods efficiently	Merit goods have been provided at excessive costs.	Preferences/ideology oppose reform

- Regulations that lead to increases in commodity prices and increase the price and reduce the availability of housing place additional burdens on anti-poverty policies. Specifically, they place a greater burden on in-kind benefits that subsidize food and housing, and they weaken efforts to encourage homeownership, a merit good.

- Individuals seeking employment in a profession that requires occupational licensing could be harmed by restrictions on the interstate movement of workers, which is one way workers could reduce the shock of job loss caused by a recession, and by laws preventing ex-offenders from working in a profession that requires a license (Kleiner and Vorotnikov 2018; Johnson and Kleiner 2020). Any increase in unemployment among such workers adds to the burden of social insurance. And by raising prices and limiting service, occupational licensing also makes it more difficult for vulnerable people to get valuable legal and medical assistance and advice, which in the long run could increase the cost of various social programs.

- Land use controls increase housing prices and prevent less-affluent Americans from moving to the most productive labor markets in the country, improving their job matching, and possibly reducing the costs that anti-poverty programs incur.

- Excessive excise taxes on cigarettes force lower-income individuals to spend more of their income on cigarettes and less on food and preventive healthcare. Of course, people should be encouraged to stop smoking, but if elevated cigarette taxes are primarily shifting expenditures shares toward less healthy consumption, then they will increase the cost of healthcare provided by Medicaid and Medicare unless the elevated taxes lead to a reduction in smoking that reduces the cost of treating lung cancer.

Similarly, inefficient economic policies that are justified to allegedly help accomplish a social goal would be unnecessary if social goals policies were more effective. For example:

- Large subsidies for public transit, with fares well below costs, are justified as benefiting low-income travelers—that is, urban transportation is treated as another in-kind benefit when, in fact, transit subsidies largely benefit travelers who have above-average incomes.

- Congestion pricing is opposed because of its adverse effect on the poor, when it could benefit the poor by improving job-matching and highway safety.

▪ Amtrak has received over $200 billion in federal subsidies since 1970, but it offers discounts to veterans, presumably because of their service to the country. Amtrak hopes to end this in-kind benefit to improve its fiscal situation, but it is receiving harsh criticism from various members of Congress. Such criticism could be deflected if an adequate veterans program were part of the nation's enormous military spending.

The prevalence of adverse interactions between inefficient economic and social goals policies indicates that efficient policies would not necessarily have to reduce equality. In contrast to Arthur Okun (1975), efficient policies could help the United States accomplish both goals simultaneously.

Possible Explanations for Policy Inefficiencies

Policy inefficiencies tend to generate large welfare costs throughout the economy, both directly and by exacerbating other inefficiencies. Consistent with the discussion of the evidence on demand-side explanations, it is difficult to claim that lobbying and campaign contributions constitute a potent explanation for any of the effects of the specific policy inefficiencies discussed.

Even when studies conclude that policymakers were captured by a particular interest group, it is possible to offer a plausible explanation of the subsequent policy inefficiency based on supply-side explanations. For example, Haris Tabakovic and Thomas Wollmann (2018) argued that revolving door patent examiners at the United States Patent and Trademark Office awarded more patents to firms that subsequently hired them. They also argued that those patents were of lower quality based on subsequent citations, and concluded that the government inefficiency to award such low-quality patents was consistent with regulatory capture.

However, it also is plausible that the government inefficiency could be attributed to the personnel, supervision, and resource constraints in the patent office because, as noted, the office does not attract and retain the strongest scientists and engineers to examine patents; the patent examiners are overwhelmed with applications and under pressure to move through the applications quickly without spending much time on any one application; and the patent examiners have supervisors who, apparently, are unable to spend much time checking for possible errors by the examiners. The authors focused on firm outcomes when it was certainly possible that the examiners who remained in the patent office also approved lower-quality patents to firms that hired their colleagues.

Similarly, in the wake of two crashes by the Boeing 737 Max, critics claimed the FAA was captured by Boeing because it was too slow to ground the plane and because the original certification process to approve the aircraft was flawed.[22] However, instead of being captured, I noted that the FAA suffered from resource constraints because it did not have the personnel to evaluate the safety of the 737 Max. Boeing took responsibility for assessing the safety of its aircraft, and it is suffering the financial consequences of the design flaws.

Given the evidence, the welfare costs from government policy inefficiencies appear to be primarily X-inefficiencies and inconsistent with the frequent claim that inefficiencies are primarily the result of redistribution that benefits interest groups. Indeed, deregulation of US industries revealed that the major inefficiencies of price and entry regulation were not the result of resources being distributed from consumers to firms and labor in the protected industry, but they were the result of inflated costs and prices because efficient operations and technological advance were constrained and not incentivized (Winston 1998, 2010).

Most government policy inefficiencies appear to reflect status quo bias caused by some combination of policymakers' preferences/ideology and resource constraints. Status quo bias inhibits policymakers from learning about the effects of their policies and how they could be improved, and enables X-inefficiencies in one area to persist and interact with inefficiencies in other areas. The self-selection of people who choose to work in government and the legal process undoubtedly strengthen status quo bias and make it less likely that government will reform inefficient policies and implement efficient ones.

Status quo bias may be an unsatisfying explanation for government policy inefficiencies because it encompasses so many factors. Nonetheless, it plausibly reflects the difficulty of providing a more accurate and defensible explanation of most government policy inefficiencies and captures policymakers' inertia and lack of vision about the potential for policy inefficiencies to be compounded. Peter Schuck's 2014 study of why government fails concluded that, "the political process is so complex and opaque, and the role of ideological zeitgeist is so pervasive, that it is usually impossible—even after the fact—to know for sure how weighty each of the many politically relevant factors might have been in determining the policy outcome."

Consider the challenging and frustrating effort in the United States to adopt a comprehensive highway congestion pricing policy in major metropolitan areas. After decades of resistance, road pricing gained popularity in New York City among some politicians and the public because it could reduce congestion and delays and raise revenues to help fund badly needed improvements in bus and rail transit. Historically, politicians have expressed their opposition to congestion pricing on the grounds that it would place an undue burden on a large share of their constituents, who commute by auto and do not have the option to use other modes to avoid a high peak-hour toll. But as pointed out in an editorial in the *New York Daily News*, Assemblyman David Weprin was the most vocal opponent of the New York City tolling plan sponsored by Robert Rodriquez of East Harlem even though only 4.2 percent of Weprin's constituents, the same share of Rodriquez's constituents, would have to pay the new toll.[23] One can only speculate why the two assemblymen took such polar positions on this issue. In any case, Weprin's opposition prevailed, as congestion pricing was rejected in 2018 by New York state lawmakers.

Yet, one year later, a shock appears to have overcome the perplexing political opposition to congestion pricing—namely, the increasingly desperate financial situation of New York City's transit system. It now appears more likely that some form of congestion pricing eventually will be implemented in Manhattan, with much of the toll revenue used to finance transit operations and improvements. However, as noted earlier, city officials have yet to satisfy federal information requirements, and the Trump administration delayed the city's congestion pricing plan by more than a year. City officials hope that the Biden administration will expedite adoption of the policy.

As another example, consider the multiyear effort by former Congressman Bill Shuster to spin off air traffic control from the FAA and run it as a private nonprofit corporation to improve its efficiency and spur technological advance. Surprisingly, Shuster pulled the plug on his bill to corporatize ATC before it was voted on by the House of Representatives. As reported by Robert Poole (2018), President Trump had made strong statements about the failure of FAA to modernize the ATC system and said that ATC reform would be part of his administration's infrastructure bill. However, air traffic control was absent when the administration's infrastructure plan was released, and the White House informed Shuster that the president would not make any efforts to enable the FAA authorization bill, which included ATC corporatization, to pass. So, Shuster pulled the ATC section from the bill. Again, one can only speculate why President Trump would suddenly not act on an opportunity to reform air traffic control and why Congressman Shuster did not persist in trying to persuade Congress to pass his bill.[24]

Still another example is that President Trump was going to significantly ease the Jones Act regulations of ocean shipping, but he decided to leave the law intact. One could speculate about several possible influences on Trump's decision, including congressional Republicans aligned with the shipbuilding industry who supported protection; former administration officials Peter Navarro, the president's trade adviser, and Elaine Chao, the US Secretary of Transportation, who supported protection of US industries; national security hawks who wanted to keep foreign vessels from US shores; and even Mark Buzby, the Maritime Administrator. In the final analysis, Trump did not even hint at an alternative explanation to status quo bias as to why he decided not to reform an act he had allegedly long opposed.

SUMMARY

Government policy inefficiencies have been widespread, costly, and persistent. But the evidence available to explain them does not indicate that we have a confident understanding of why the inefficiencies have occurred so policy-makers could be given sound guidance on how to reform and increase the social benefits of government interventions. If making government interventions more efficient were a viable option, the case I have made for expanding market approaches to help government would not be so important.

Nonetheless, some analysts may believe they understand the cause of a particular policy's inefficiency, and may propose efficient policy reforms along with strategies to overcome opposition to them. Others, including myself, believe it is reasonable to speculate about the causes of government policy inefficiencies but misguided to think one has "the" causal explanation that can guide a policy reform that is actually implemented. I believe more constructive progress can be made toward accomplishing economic and social goals by providing what is, in fact, a progress report—not a final report—on how markets have used the tool kit of competition, incentives for efficiency, and innovations and technological advance to help government in many different areas, and how they could provide additional help to stimulate thinking about future possibilities.

SIXTEEN

Markets Helping Government

This chapter synthesizes and summarizes the evidence that shows how markets have helped government accomplish economic and social goals. Because both types of policy goals are included in the analysis, I show that the actual and potential effects of market forces often have important spillovers that positively affect both goals. The chapter concludes by providing a long-run perspective of markets helping government.

SYNTHESIZING AND SUMMARIZING THE EVIDENCE

The evidence is distilled in four tables: the actual direct and spillover benefits of markets helping government accomplish economic goals (table 16-1) and social goals (table 16-2), and the potential direct and spillover benefits of markets helping government accomplish economic goals (table 16-3) and social goals (table 16-4). Tables 16-3 and 16-4 identify the government and, where appropriate, the market constraint that currently prevents market forces from converting potential benefits into actual benefits.

Table 16-1 shows that the competition and technical advance unleashed by market forces have helped improve on government economic policies, generating trillions of dollars of direct and spillover benefits in lower costs and prices, higher-quality products, and new products and services. The cu-

TABLE 16-1. Market Forces Helping Government to Accomplish Economic Goals

Government Policy	Market Forces	Direct Benefits	Spillover Benefits
Price and entry regulations of the communications industry	Competition among firms in a deregulated environment	Lower telecommunications prices New services, including voice mail, cellular, the internet, and services available online and through mobile apps	Lower prices and greater variety from online competition
Price, entry, and exit regulations of the transportation industry	Competition among firms in a deregulated environment*	Lower transport prices Improved service quality	Lower trade costs Lower inventory costs Productive collaborations Improved logistics and distribution
Price and entry regulation of the energy industry	Competition among firms in a deregulated environment	Lower energy prices	Higher wages and employment
Service and entry regulation of the financial industry	Competition among firms in a deregulated environment	Greater loan availability Improved banking services	Increase mortgage access among lower- and middle-income Black households
Price and entry regulation of taxis in most metropolitan urban areas	Competition from digital ride-sharing platforms, such as Uber and Lyft*	Lower fares Greater availability and reliability of services	Lower-cost reliable alternative to ambulance service Alternative to driving under the influence

Antitrust policies to protect competition	Market forces to increase competition, including reducing entry barriers, foreign competitors, challenging industry leaders, and consumers gaining competitive advantages*	Lower prices Greater product variety Better product and service quality	Stronger economic growth
Information policies	Revolution in information technology that has significantly reduced the cost of searching, collecting, and distributing information about products, services, and workplaces	Lower prices Better product and service quality	Improve provision of merit goods
Externality policies	Households' residential sorting such that those who experience the highest costs from the externality are the least exposed to it	Reduce social cost of the externalities	…
Technology policies	Private-sector investments in research and development; ability to attract and manage superior human capital	Lower prices Better product and service quality More product variety	Reduce cost of government policy inefficiencies Spur economic growth

*Indicates that governments have instituted policies that have limited the effectiveness of market forces.

mulative benefits, based on the empirical studies in the preceding chapters, have increased the US annual growth rate by at least one percentage point, if not more.[1] Table 16-2 shows that firms' incentives in a market environment to pursue business opportunities and improve their brands also have helped government social goals policies reduce poverty and labor market discrimination, and provide merit goods, which have helped improve the quality of life for the most vulnerable members of American society.

Market forces are powerful because they can address simultaneous government policy inefficiencies. The revolution in information technology has led to a major improvement over ineffective information policies and has helped expose discrimination and improve healthcare. Intrastate branch bank deregulation from the late 1970s to the early 1990s improved banking services and increased mortgage access for lower-middle-income groups, and young and Black households. The initiation of private van services and ride-sharing has enhanced the quality of urban transportation in general and has, specifically, enabled carless households to have better access to jobs. A limited instance of decontrol of rents in Cambridge, Massachusetts (not shown in a table) caused an overall decrease in crime of approximately 16 percent (Autor, Palmer, and Pathak 2019). And the overall improvement in economic growth attributable to market forces helps people escape poverty by creating additional jobs. Generally, the huge benefits generated by market forces have been widely shared by the public.

Table 16-3 shows that market forces have the potential to benefit consumers by lowering costs and prices and improving service quality in many markets that are subject to partial government regulation, including airlines, ocean shipping, agriculture, international trade, professional services, and ride-sharing. Some of the largest benefits may arise through subtle channels. For example, eliminating tariffs that increase the price of certain inputs could enable firms to increase expenditures on R&D and produce valuable innovations.[2]

Market forces also could produce technological advances that reduce environmental externalities and could develop private markets that replace inefficient public production of various services.

Currently, markets have technological limitations that prevent them from significantly helping to reduce policy inefficiencies that affect electricity markets and the widespread use of alternative sources of energy. A technological breakthrough, such as the development of cell phones that generated new competition in local and long-distance telecommunications, is needed

TABLE 16-2. Market Forces Helping Government Accomplish Social Goals

Government Policy	Market Forces	Direct Benefits	Spillover Benefits
Policies to reduce poverty	Help poor children get a better start in life. Improve poor adults' job prospects. Raise earnings for low-income workers with targeted programs and benefits.	Help reduce poverty and the intergenerational transmission of poverty.	Reduce the cost to taxpayers of related goals, such as reducing crime.
Antidiscrimination laws	Raise the cost to employers who discriminate. Use information technology and social media to counteract discrimination. Pressure states to fight against hate groups who support discrimination.	Provide equal opportunity for all people to achieve their personal goals.	Make the best use of the nation's human resources.
Merit goods	Firms offer affordable housing.	Increase homeownership.	Spur economic growth.
	Several private entities have contributed to reducing students' costs and expanding education alternatives.	Increase the skills and education of the nation's citizenry.	
	Information technology, consumer choice, and competition have combined to improve health by generating medical innovations, encouraging safe workplaces and products, encouraging individuals to safeguard their health, and incentivizing hospitals to provide high-quality and efficient care.	Improve the health of the nation's citizenry.	
	New technologies developed by the private sector have reduced the expected benefits of getting away with a crime and improvements in labor markets have increased the relative cost of spending time in illegal activities.	Improve the safety of the nation's citizenry.	
Immigration	Companies and universities attract skilled foreign workers, some of whom start their own companies.*	Increase productivity, output, and employment.	…

*Indicates that governments have instituted policies that have limited the effectiveness of market forces.

TABLE 16-3. Market Forces Can Potentially Help Government Accomplish Economic Goals

Government Policy	Market Forces	Direct Benefits	Spillover Benefits	Government Constraints	Market Constraints
Continued regulation of international airline markets	Competition among deregulated airlines in international markets	Lower fares Greater flight frequency	Productive collaborations	Continued regulation	…
Prohibiting foreign airlines from serving US domestic routes	Competition among US and foreign airlines in a deregulated environment	Lower fares Seamless international travel	Productive collaborations	Continued regulation	…
Jones Act, which prohibits foreign built ships from calling on two consecutive US ports	Competition among US and foreign ocean shipping companies in a deregulated environment	Lower costs Lower rates	Reduction in freight shipped by truck that damages road pavement	Jones Act not repealed	…
Regulation of parts of the electricity industry	Competition among electric utilities in a deregulated environment	Lower costs of production More innovation Real-time cost-based pricing	…	…	Technical breakthrough to reduce the cost of storing electricity
Agricultural subsidies	Subject farmers to market competition without subsidies	Reduce costs to taxpayers Incentivize farmers to be more productive	…	Agricultural subsidies not eliminated	…
Tariffs and quotas	Free trade	Lower prices More variety of products	Effects on wages and employment are disputed	Tariffs and quotas remain on some products	…

Information policies, such as occupational licensing	Revolution in information technology that has significantly lowered the cost of searching, collecting, and distributing information about products, services, and workplaces*	Lower prices Increase employment	Increase the availability of important services, especially for low-income people	Occupational licensing exists for many services	…
Externality policies	Technological innovations, self-interested actions by firms and consumers, and incentive-based market designs that reduce the cost of externalities	Less oil consumption Less pollution	Less adverse climate change	Excessive solar and wind regulations, insufficient plug-in stations, failure to implement more cap-and-trade policies	Technological breakthroughs in solar panels, power grids, low-cost batteries with more storage
Public production	Provision by private companies in a competitive environment; new providers facilitated by technical advance, such as ride-sharing companies, AVs, and drones*	Eliminate taxpayer-funded subsidies Improve services and safety More advanced technology Greater returns on public lands and structures	Improve job access for low-income workers and spur economic growth	Failure to design and implement privatization experiments; regulatory delays and operating inefficiencies for new technologies	…

*Indicates that governments have instituted policies that have limited the effectiveness of market forces.

to create workable competition in those industries. Regulatory constraints may last until markets innovate and show they can improve on government intervention.

Market forces also could produce spillover benefits, such as improvements in information technology that justify eliminating occupational licensing and increase employment and the availability of valuable services for low-income households. Technological advances that reduce externalities benefit low-income households, which are less able to avoid the externalities by moving to a different neighborhood.

Table 16-4 shows that market forces could help accomplish social goals by introducing autonomous vehicles that improve job access for low-income households and by creating private markets that increase homeownership, improving the educational system so it is less costly and more responsive to consumer preferences, and reducing medical costs and crime. Unfortunately, government constraints pose significant obstacles for markets in most of those areas.

Finally, James Heckman and Gonzalo Schwartz (2018) point out still another way market forces could help produce favorable social outcomes but are constrained by government actions. The authors argue that the family is the most important producer of skills, through effective parenting, which helps develop children's cognitive and noncognitive abilities. Government policies that discourage family formation and effective parenting, such as the marriage penalty, disincentives created by welfare programs, and excessive incarceration, are significant obstacles that market solutions must overcome.

MARKETS HELPING GOVERNMENT: A LONG-RUN PERSPECTIVE

The preceding evidence is a progress report, because changes in consumer preferences, new sources of competition, and technological advances enable markets to continue to help government as they evolve over time. Thus, it is essential to take a long-run perspective of markets helping government.

The ongoing evolution of the US transportation system is useful for illustrating how markets have gradually reduced the cost and improved the quality of transportation as modes have been given greater freedom to compete, had greater incentives and opportunities to become more efficient and to innovate, and developed new ways to engage with and respond to the preferences of heterogeneous travelers and shippers.

TABLE 16-4. Market Forces Potentially Helping Government Accomplish Social Goals

Social Goals Policy	Market Forces' Potential Help	Direct Benefits	Spillover Benefits	Government Constraints
Policies to reduce poverty	Private development of AVs	Improve job access and increase earnings for low-income workers.	Spur economic growth.	Regulatory delays and operating inefficiencies for AVs
	Offer shared equity.*	Increase homeownership and diversify risk.		Dominance of Fannie Mae and Freddie Mac limits competition in the mortgage market.
	Expand private school provision of secondary education.*	Create an education system that is responsive to competitive forces to increase quality and to reduce cost.		The consequences of poor performance by public schools have not been allowed to materialize.
Merit goods	Expand the private market for student loans.*	Reduce student loan defaults, interest rates on loans, and college tuition.	Spur economic growth.	Education Department has a near monopoly on and crowds out the private student loan market by providing federally subsidized loans.
	Competitive bidding for medical procedures.*	Reduce medical costs.		Government-supported social medical programs discourage consumer interest in competitive bidding.
	Legalize and create a private market for drugs.	Reduce crime.		Federal policy and most states have not decriminalized marijuana and other drugs sold by drug dealers.

*Indicates that governments have instituted policies that have limited the effectiveness of market forces.

Economic regulation of the major intercity modes (air, rail, and truck) created significant pricing and service inefficiencies and stymied innovations. The justification for heavy-handed regulation had clearly been eliminated by the 1950s, given that trucking competed with railroads for most commodities, and all the modes could potentially exhaust scale economies at plausible levels of output and operate close to constant returns to scale. Estimates of scale economies reported by researchers generally reflected excess capacity that was caused by government regulations, which prevented carriers from exiting unprofitable markets and reducing fares to attract additional traffic.

Economic deregulation of the major intercity modes began in the mid-1970s, when policymakers were convinced, in large part by experiments in unregulated intrastate airline markets and in unregulated surface freight commodity markets, that competition was feasible.[3] Market forces helped government by replacing economic regulations. The large benefits to consumers were mainly attributable to intense competition and technological change that had been suppressed by regulation. Less-affluent households were better able to afford air travel and to benefit from lower surface freight transport costs that reduced consumer commodity prices. Spillover benefits stimulated growth by reducing inventory and logistics costs and by facilitating greater collaboration among researchers that helped generate new ideas. Further deregulation could enable market forces to further improve airline and ocean freight transportation in international markets and in US domestic airline markets.

Market forces introduced ride-sharing in only the last decade, but it has become a new urban transportation service that is helping government by providing value to affluent and lower-income households. By developing and spurring widespread adoption of autonomous vehicles, market forces could help government address the seemingly intractable problems of highway congestion and safety, and further improve urban and intercity highway passenger and freight transportation. Finally, given that the private sector is currently experimenting with drones and flying cars, market forces have the potential to help government improve transportation for the foreseeable future.

SEVENTEEN

Some Broader Implications of Markets Helping Government

The benefits in specific areas where markets have helped government represent important sources of economic growth and quality of life improvements for the American people. The efficiency gains have simultaneously spurred economic growth and benefited lower-income households during a period when annual growth has slowed since 2000 from 3.5 percent to a "new normal" of closer to 2 percent, and when growing inequality since the 1970s has resulted in a decline in the national income share of the poorest half of the US population, while the share of the top 1 percent has significantly increased.

INCREASING GROWTH

Future innovations, if implemented successfully, have the potential to spur growth and help government solve social problems. Transportation service would be revolutionized by electric vehicles; autonomous vehicles on city streets and interstate highways and, eventually, in the air; and satellite-based air navigation. Logistics and distribution would be transformed by the use of robotics in warehouses and by autonomous trucks, and robots and drones for local deliveries. New, more widely available non-carbon-based energy sources, such as wind and solar, would produce energy cost savings, improve the environment, and facilitate a competitive and more efficient and innovative electricity industry. Individuals would use information technology to enhance their skills through more extensive and more effective online learning courses. And the widespread adoption of artificial intelligence being spurred by global competitive forces would produce large efficiency gains in healthcare, financial services, manufacturing, and retail.[1]

The doubts that Robert Gordon (2016) has expressed about the ability of the United States to produce significant innovations that increase economic growth are overstated, because market forces still have a capacity for creative destruction (Greenspan and Wooldridge 2018), and because those forces have made the United States a place where talented people with ideas and ambition want to live and work. The relevant constraints on growth, which are too often overlooked, have been government regulatory policies that have slowed innovation[2] and discouraged talented and ambitious people from working in the United States.

In the interest of promoting innovation, there may be a number of antitrust actions directed against the leading technology firms, known as Big Tech. Daron Acemoglu (2020) argues that breaking up Facebook, Google, Microsoft, and Amazon will not lead to the diversity and multiple objectives in technologies necessary for broad-based innovation, and he asserts that government needs to reclaim the leadership role it once had in shaping technological change. However, it is not clear where the new innovative firms will come from absent Big Tech. As stressed in various parts of this book, leading firms—even technology firms—must constantly be on guard for new sources of competition, which often come from firms that provide complementary products and services and are led by people whose human capital partly developed at or was influenced by the leading firms.

HELPING THE LEAST AFFLUENT

Market forces will continue to help the poorest individuals in the United States raise their material quality of life by enriching education and training that increases skills, employability, and earnings and by enhancing noncognitive skills that can lead to better life choices. Greater economic growth expands employment opportunities, and more efficient transportation increases access to those opportunities. Instead of increasing the burden on taxpayers, policymakers should rely more on market forces to coordinate the self-interest of entrepreneurs to train and make effective use of the most disadvantaged members of society and the self-interest of those members to seek out programs and firms that could help them improve their lives. In contrast to Zachary Liscow (2018), efficient market forces generally do not redistribute resources to the rich at the expense of the poor.

Emmanuel Saez and Gabriel Zucman (2019) argue "that there are many policies—from the enforcement of antitrust laws to a broader access to education; from the regulation of intellectual property to better corporate governance—that can contribute to curbing inequality in the years to come." But there is little evidence that those policies have had or could have those effects. In fact, government interventions often have created economic rents and made inequality worse. Market forces that increase economic growth improve the quality of life for all, and may even benefit poor people more than others.[3] Saez and Zucman assert that government transfers—whether in the form of income support for families or public health insurance—have a critical role to play. But they ignore the myriad social goals policies already that have been attempted to provide those transfers but, instead, generated considerable waste and produced disappointing outcomes.

Institutions are studied to provide a fundamental explanation for economic growth and inequality and to understand the direction of economic change (North 1991; Acemoglu, Johnson, and Robinson 2005). When institutions are included to help explain the varied economic performance of countries both over time and in the current world, US institutions are perceived relatively favorably. However, those same institutions generally have persisted in maintaining counterproductive policies that contribute to inequality and that adversely affect the sources of growth—technology, innovation, and competition—in the United States.

The public had been steadily losing confidence in government institutions before the Trump administration—in fact, some believe that trend contributed to Trump's election. Daron Acemoglu (2021) points out that institutions should clearly be reformed after Trump to prevent, for example, public officials from firing inspectors general for doing their jobs and presidents from gaining customers for their private businesses. The relevant issue here is whether institutional reform will result in constructive government policy reforms. To be sure, the public is probably even less confident in capitalism and markets than in institutions to solve the critical issues of growth and inequality. However, this attitude is misguided and must change because the evidence indicates that markets, not government interventions, are a more promising source of faster growth and lower inequality.

PART IV

Markets Helping Government

A Robustness Test and Proactive Perspective

EIGHTEEN

Market and Government Responses to COVID-19: A Robustness Test

The novel coronavirus (COVID-19) is thought to have originated in China in late 2019 and then spread throughout the United States at the beginning of 2020. Although COVID-19 is an extraordinary event that is outside of our living experience and its effects and the world's responses continue to evolve, it can serve as a preliminary robustness test of the book's main themes of significant government inefficiencies and markets helping or potentially helping address those inefficiencies. The virus has led to government and market responses that bear directly on those themes.

As of this writing in early spring of 2021, COVID-19 is still rampant and infecting and killing large numbers of people in the United States and throughout the world, vaccines have been developed to protect the public from the virus, and people are slowly being vaccinated. But scholars have yet to provide a comprehensive empirically-based assessment of the full effects of government and market responses. Thus, I provide descriptive evidence indicating that, to date, both the limitations of government responses and the help provided by market responses to the coronavirus in several of the policy areas discussed are consistent with the book's conclusions.

AN OVERVIEW

By eventually encouraging social distancing and instituting quarantine and stay-at-home orders to reduce the spread of COVID-19 infections, government has saved many lives and limited the extent of debilitating long-term illnesses (Ip 2020). Solomon Hsiang and others (2020) acknowledge that anti-contagion policies, such as closing schools and restricting populations to their homes, have imposed costs, but the authors also provide evidence that the policies have substantially slowed the growth rate of infections and generated substantial health benefits. Government also has lessened the economic hardships caused by the virus by providing social insurance in the form of: (1) trillions of dollars of payments to households in accordance with their taxable income, (2) expanded unemployment insurance for furloughed workers, (3) loans to small businesses, and (4) direct aid to certain industries.

Future research will debate the merits of the US government's actions and whether it could have saved a comparable (or larger) number of lives, limited debilitating illnesses, and reduced economic hardships at lower cost by adopting more socially desirable policies. For example, Sweden stood in contrast with the strict stay-at-home policies of other countries, including the United States, by taking a light-touch approach that allowed many educational, economic, and social activities to continue. However, Sweden's chief epidemiologist acknowledged that Sweden should have done more to curb the spread of the virus, which would have reduced its death rate per capita (Henley 2020).

In any event, although Anne Case and Angus Deaton (2020) argue that government shutdowns did not result in a spike in "deaths of despair" associated with a significant recession, US government delays in responding appropriately to the crisis did cause needless deaths. The coronavirus spread unchecked for three weeks in February 2020 while problems plagued the test designed to detect whether Americans were infected. Testing was prevented that might have limited the spread by alerting cities like New York and Seattle to shut down sooner.

Sen Pei, Sasikiran Kandula, and Jeffrey Shaman (2020) estimate that some 36,000 fatalities could have been prevented if the federal government had warned people to socially distance by avoiding large gatherings, and if governors and mayors had declared states of emergency a week earlier. In addition, government's failure to mount an earlier response then required more stringent distancing measures, with their attendant costs, because of the exponential nature of the virus, whereby each infected person passed the disease on to two or three others. This phenomenon caused containment measures to take longer to be implemented, a steeper spike in the numbers of infections and deaths, and greater fear among consumers and workers to engage in economic activities. As the pandemic worsened, the Trump White House declined to purse a national strategy, so governors faced off against lobbyists, health experts, and a misinformed public, adding to the toll of the virus.

Acts of commission or omission that led to a delayed and constructive response, especially by the Trump administration, include the following:

- Although President Trump implemented a travel ban from China in late January 2020, some 40,000 people entered the US from China (under rules that exempted citizens and others) after the travel ban was imposed, but those people were not tested or effectively quarantined and there was no effective tracking and tracing of contacts (Zimmer 2020). The inability of the Centers for Disease Control and Prevention's (CDC) outdated notification system to deliver accurate passenger data to local authorities responsible for tracking potential COVID-19 carriers from China was a harbinger of the CDC's substantial difficulties and limitations in combating the virus in the US, let alone serving as a leader in the global battle against the pandemic (Lipton and others 2020).

- Although top infectious disease specialists inside and outside the administration had warned of the seriousness of the disease, President Trump continued to downplay and even mock its seriousness until March 16, when he finally asked Americans to practice social distancing. By then, however, he had failed by example to encourage voluntary social distancing measures that could have stemmed the spread before states and localities ordered stringent lockdowns. With respect to authoritative recommendations on mask-wearing to limit spread of COVID-19, despite scientific evidence of masks' effectiveness in other countries, the CDC gave contradictory advice, hesitated, and ultimately reversed its position on mask-wearing by the general public. It was not until early April 2020 that the CDC recommended the use of cloth masks by asymptomatic people. The waffling and delay are attributed in part to concerns about the public hoarding the N95 masks needed for healthcare workers (Pike 2020).

- The US Food and Drug Administration and the CDC were inadequately prepared for COVID-19, despite weeks of advance notice from China. CDC's flaws in leadership, guidance, and execution undermined the country's response to the virus (Lipton and others 2020). In particular, the CDC's initial test for the disease failed to work correctly. Moreover, neither it nor the Food and Drug Administration had plans for quickly certifying and allowing the production of tests by others outside the CDC, such as university hospitals and state and private-sector testing labs, which would have enabled much more rapid production and distribution of tests. In contrast, authorities in South Korea engaged with the private sector in advance of this pandemic and were far more successful in tamping down the spread of the infection in its early stages.

- The CDC had been marginalized by policy, as hospital data on coronavirus patients was rerouted to the Trump administration instead of first being sent to the CDC. Importantly, the change made the data less transparent to the public, researchers, and health officials who rely on CDC data.

- Congress and the Fed were quick to provide some relief to the massive numbers of workers laid off or furloughed due to the lockdowns that proved necessary precisely because of the government's late medical responses. However, the aid and loans were disseminated through distribution systems, such as the Small Business Administration and state unemployment insurance programs, that were neither designed nor well equipped to deal with the massive numbers of applications that flooded in after the programs were authorized.

- The federal government gave no assistance to the states to set up contact tracing programs to identify and isolate persons who were infected by others. The important leadership roles taken on by a number of state and local officials left to fend for themselves should not be discounted.

- Many states reopened high-risk venues and businesses too soon and saw a spike in infections and deaths. For example, daily new case incidences were much lower in northeastern states, which were initially hit hard by the virus and were careful not to open early, than the rest of the US during the end of July. A new surge of COVID-19 cases spiked in the fall of 2020, producing the highest number of new daily infections since the pandemic began.

Losing precious time before the pandemic really took hold turned out to have disastrous effects. An exasperated William Burns, a former US diplomat, summed up government's performance in an article by Edward Luce (2020) as causing America to be "first in the world in deaths, first in the world in infections, and standing out as an emblem of global incompetence." America is currently not first in the world in deaths and infections per capita, but that fact does not change the conclusion that government performed poorly.

GOVERNMENT MICROECONOMIC POLICY INEFFICIENCIES

The US government is responsible for using its vast powers and resources to reduce the social costs of a global pandemic by safeguarding public health and providing social insurance to mitigate economic losses. Private entities can provide assistance in different ways, but market forces are too decentralized and isolated to respond fully to such an enormous shock to society and the economy. Policymakers lacked an overarching systematic strategy to combat the virus effectively and in a timely fashion and to distribute doses of the vaccines as they became available. Furthermore, inefficiencies that have persisted in several specific microeconomic policies, including international trade, agency regulations, occupational licensing, externalities, technology policies, public production, and the provision of merit goods, undermined government actions in response to COVID-19.

International Trade
The Trump administration maintained its hostility to free trade that could enrich the global effort to fight the coronavirus by initiating US production of certain goods that could be quickly imported, and by imposing import and export bans. The administration signed a $354 million four-year contract with Phlow Corporation to manufacture generic medicines and pharmaceutical ingredients needed to treat COVID-19, even though these are widely produced overseas, mostly in India and China (Stolberg and Thomas 2020).

N95 masks are critical for first responders who treat infected patients, and the masks can help infected patients reduce the spread of the virus. However, the US has experienced a shortage of N95 masks because it has mismanaged domestic production and eschewed foreign supply. Panthera Worldwide, a small US company that had no prior experience producing N95 masks, was given a $55 million contract to deliver 10 million masks, which it failed to do, causing its contract to be cancelled in May 2020. Four months earlier, the government passed up an opportunity to contract with a domestic N95 manufacturer, Prestige Ameritech, to ramp up production to make an additional 1.7 million N95 masks per week at a much lower price per mask than Panthera's price. China's version of the N95 mask is the KN95 mask; according to 3M, the largest US producer of N95 masks, the two masks are equivalent in their effectiveness. Nonetheless, the FDA delayed allowing KN95s into the country and then later authorized some of them for emergency use only.

Trump used the Defense Production Act (DPA) to ban 3M from exporting N95 masks to Canada. Alexander Tabarrok (2020) points out that Canada could retaliate by not selling the US the paper pulp used in the manufacture of surgical masks and gowns. Given increasingly tighter supply chains, it has not been in the US interest to alienate its trading partners. At the same time, Trump failed to use the DPA early on to ensure the availability of a wide range of medical supplies or their inputs, including ventilators, personal protection equipment for front-line healthcare and other workers, and test kits.

Federal Economic Regulation

Federal agencies enforce regulations to improve information about risks to safety and consumer welfare that may be caused by imperfect information about goods, suppliers, and workplaces. However, many agencies have been unable to shed their rulebooks to think "outside the box" and take prompt and constructive action to mitigate growing threats to public health from the coronavirus. The FDA is responsible for approving accurate tests for COVID-19, but it approved a flawed test, stymied an effective test by requiring the developer to submit his request both electronically and by mail, and delayed another potentially effective COVID-19 test by demanding that its developer see if its test worked against other coronaviruses. In addition, the FDA shut down a testing regime developed by the Seattle Flu Study because it lacked correct licensing requirements, and halted work on the COVID-19 testing program supported by Bill Gates (Baker 2020). In the latter, researchers and public health authorities had tested thousands of samples and found dozens of previously undetected cases.

The FDA also had failed to adjust its regulations to expedite care. It took roughly two months to lift a key regulatory hurdle and let private lab companies and hospitals more easily test patients for the virus. Its regulations on the use of ethanol had limited the amount of hand sanitizer available to the public. Congress had to overturn FDA regulations to permit hospitals to purchase N95 masks previously approved only for industrial use. And the FDA failed to immediately denounce Trump's claims that hydroxychloroquine and chloroquine were effective treatments (or, as Trump reportedly using them, prophylactics) for COVID-19, even though there was insufficient evidence for such a claim and credible evidence that those drugs had potentially harmful side effects. The increased demand for those drugs caused shortages for patients who had long used them to treat chronic autoimmune diseases. The FDA then had to allow overseas manufacturing facilities that were previously sanctioned for quality violations to begin producing those drugs for US patients.

The United States Department of Agriculture (USDA) is responsible for responding to school closures caused by COVID-19 by switching to summer feeding programs and waiving regulatory requirements. But USDA waivers included other onerous conditions. For example, Oregon was allowed a waiver with the requirement that each school district work with a state agency to target the most-needy students. But school districts have been impeded by USDA's bureaucratic approach because the target of "most-needy" has steadily moved as the economy has collapsed (Stephens 2020).

Hal Scott (2020) argues that the Dodd-Frank Act has constrained financial responses by limiting the Federal Reserve's lender of last resort powers for nonbanks; preventing the FDIC from expanding guarantees to bank depositors without congressional approval; prohibiting the Treasury from guaranteeing money market funds; and making it harder for financial firms to lend to each other. Congress should remove those constraints by restoring all the powers it took away from the Fed, FDIC, and Treasury during the 2008 financial crisis.

The Occupational Safety and Health Administration has not significantly influenced employers to improve the safety of their workplaces. OSHA has been criticized during the pandemic for being invisible and failing to fully use the tools it has to protect the workforce (Telford 2020). Instead, OSHA has issued only voluntary guidance on coronavirus mitigation and resisted calls to mandate social distancing. And it has yet to issue a single pandemic citation under its general duty clause that requires employers to provide a workplace "free of recognized hazards." Beginning with Virginia, states have proposed their own set of coronavirus-era safety rules that companies must implement to protect workers from infection, in large part because of a lack of guidance and enforcement from OSHA to uphold workplace safety.

Government agencies even have taken steps that have jeopardized their own workers' safety. For example, the Transportation Security Administration withheld N95 masks from staff and exhibited "gross mismanagement" by leaving airport security workers and travelers vulnerable to infection (Mak 2020). By delaying a decision on whether airports can use some of their funds to screen passengers for the coronavirus, the FAA had increased the risks to health for both workers and travelers.

Ironically, some regulations that were relaxed raise questions as to whether they should ever be restored. For example, HIPAA regulations were relaxed to allow doctors to use personal phones for telemedicine. The USDA and the FDA deregulated labeling and packaging for sixty days to allow food to be redistributed, resulting in fewer USDA food recalls than normal. Other regulations also are unlikely to cause harm if they were relaxed, such as Jones Act restrictions to help lower freight costs and open up more distribution channels for consumer and producer goods, and FAA restrictions on the use of drones for home delivery, especially given the dramatic reduction in air traffic.

Occupational Licensing

Occupational licensing is alleged to protect the public from unqualified service providers, but the evidence indicates its main effect is to limit the supply of valuable services and raise their cost. Healthcare workers are invaluable during the pandemic, yet their supply is constrained because occupational licensing is ubiquitous in healthcare—nearly 44 percent of workers are licensed (Timmons, Bayne, and Norris 2020). Many healthcare professionals, such as physician assistants (PA) and nurse practitioners (NP), are not allowed to practice their full skill sets and apply their full training because of scope-of-practice laws. In many states, PAs and NPs are not allowed to practice without a supervising physician. If a physician becomes sick with COVID-19, that physician's PA or NP will be able to do little in those states. Although a handful of states waived licensure requirements in the case of unmet need arising from COVID-19, America's current regulatory policies do not allow the supply of healthcare workers to respond to sudden, sharp changes in demand. Along the same lines, several states have relaxed their Certificate of Need (CON) requirements for medical facilities. CON requirements are another example of regulations that limit supply and raise costs while producing questionable benefits.

Externalities

The federal government neglected an opportunity to significantly reduce the externality that arises when a contagious individual infects other people with the virus. The government's mixed messaging confused instead of informed people about the benefits of wearing masks for themselves and others. And, instead of taking a systematic approach to ensure that enough N95 masks were initially available to first responders and then the general public, the Trump administration created a chaotic environment characterized by "Try Getting it Yourselves" (Bender and Ballhaus 2020). Finally, the federal government eschewed a mandatory mask requirement, although many states and counties have issued such requirements.[1]

Technology Policy

The federal government's most important action to help the US and global economies is to encourage and facilitate an effective treatment for the novel coronavirus and, more importantly, an effective vaccine to be distributed worldwide as soon as possible. As noted, the share of R&D in the federal budget has declined significantly over time, and government policy has recently done little to spur innovation. Economists generally agree that policymakers must reverse course and allocate resources to increase health investments in testing; equipment to treat infected patients; medicines that will mitigate illness or eliminate the virus; and vaccines to prevent infection.

Lawrence Summers (2020) urges the federal government to take the proactive steps of identifying the most promising vaccines and producing them at scale. Thoughtful yet enormous expenditures are not out of bounds. At the same time, policymakers should eliminate obstacles to innovation created by patents and regulatory licensing.

Public Production and Distribution

Operation Warp Speed was the Trump administration's initiative to speed the development of vaccines and therapeutics. In December 2020, the United States began to vaccinate people with the Pfizer-BioNTech and Moderna vaccines. (Arguably, the Trump administration deserves credit regarding the public-private partnership with Moderna, which received two grants through Operation Warp Speed.) However, production of the vaccines has far outpaced vaccinating people. Health officials had hoped that additional vaccines would be released from reserves that had been stockpiled, but they were disappointed when Health and Human Services Secretary Alex Azar announced that no stockpile actually existed and that the available supply from the manufacturing lines had been immediately released.

The vaccine rollout caused considerable confusion and frustration among the public in securing appointments and matching supply with demand. Barrett and Greene (2021) point out that poor intergovernmental relations caused much of the problem as the federal government left it to state leaders to make decisions about how to involve lower levels of government, particularly counties, to distribute and administer the vaccine. However, many counties were given inadequate information on what they were expected to do and guidance on how to do it. In addition, the CDC's website, called VAMS (Vaccine Administration Management System), was plagued by problems and abandoned by most states.

The US Postal Service inefficiencies were discussed earlier in this book. A new postmaster general, Louis DeJoy, was appointed on June 15, 2020, to improve the efficiency of postal operations. However, DeJoy's strategy was to push mail trucks to keep close to their schedules, an action that conflicted with the increased parcel volumes and labor shortages due to the pandemic. Although trucks left on time, processing plants experienced backlogs and mail deliveries were delayed because extra delivery trips were not allowed.

Social Goals Policies

The public has turned to government for help as a provider of social insurance to reduce the economic hardships caused by the unanticipated global pandemic, and policymakers have responded with trillions of dollars of aid. However, the enormous expenditures have not been guided by a coherent effort to minimize their cost and maximize their benefits. Future research will undoubtedly quantify considerable waste, but such waste is already evident as, for example, roughly half of all unemployed US workers have stood to earn more in augmented unemployment benefits than they did at their jobs before the coronavirus shut down swaths of the US economy, complicating efforts of employers to reopen businesses (Morath 2020).[2] In addition, as a condition for aid, airlines have been incentivized to fly, even with extremely low load-factors on many routes.

Governments also have managed to thwart the provision of merit goods, such as education. For example, online schools are the definition of social distancing. Yet, the Oregon Department of Education restricted accepting additional students to the state's online public charter schools under the governor's order to close public schools. Inadequate health insurance has further strained the healthcare system by discouraging people from immediately seeking testing and treatment, likely increasing the number of patients who require hospitalization, and possibly increasing the spread of the virus.

Finally, government reimbursement policies have provided distorted incentives for nursing homes. Federal support, through Medicare and Medicaid, has long influenced the services that nursing homes provide to generate revenues. However, adopting stringent infection control and hiring more registered nurses, which are critical to fighting the pandemic, have not been high priorities because they are low-revenue services.

EXPLAINING GOVERNMENT INEFFICIENCIES

I have argued that status quo bias is the best explanation for government's inadequate policy performance. Given the government's lack of retained learning from experience with previous viruses and its lack of preparation for new ones, status quo bias is relevant for understanding government's poor response to COVID-19. SARS, H1N1, and the Ebola viruses suggested it was always a matter of when—not if—a global pandemic would make it to America. The core purpose of the CDC is to control and prevent the spread of infectious diseases. But, in recent years, it has strayed from that mission, focusing more on influencing people's lifestyle choices, such as sounding the alarm about youth vaping, than on pandemic preparedness. The CDC's actions during COVID-19 have not assured the public that the nation will be any better prepared for the next pandemic.

The H1N1 influenza pandemic of 2009 triggered the largest deployment in US history of the Strategic National Stockpile, the federal government's last-resort cache of drugs and medical supplies. The stockpile distributed 85 million N95 respirators along with millions of other masks, gowns, and gloves (Reinhard and Brown 2020). The International Safety Equipment Association warned there would be significant shortages of N95 masks if another pandemic caused demand for masks to surge. But the stockpile's reserves were not significantly restored after the 2009 pandemic.

President Trump compounded all of those problems by dismantling, in 2018, a National Security Council directorate at the White House charged with preparing the nation for a pandemic, and by failing to take advantage of and act expeditiously on the advice of the leading infectious disease specialists within various agencies of the federal government. It also has been claimed that presidential advisor Jared Kushner was working with a team to launch a large-scale national plan to bring the pandemic under control; however, he concluded, for unspecified but allegedly political reasons, that a national plan was unnecessary and focused on reopening the country as soon as possible.

Resource constraints in both capital and labor have added to government inefficiencies. Testing was slowed by equipment shortages; tracking was limited by aging IT and computer systems and the inadequate use of cell phone data; and the talent pool to execute the delivery of assistance has shrunk to the point where much of the work is done by nongovernmental employees who are not well supervised.

Political forces also may have exacerbated inefficiencies. For example, places that did not have stay-at-home orders tended to receive a disproportionate share of federal bailout money for small business compared with places that did have stay-at-home orders. Aaron Glantz (2020) reports the percent of a state's small businesses that got a share of the $350 billion in Paycheck Protection Program loans was: 58 percent in North Dakota, 56 percent in Nebraska, 53 percent in South Dakota, 48 percent in Iowa, and 44 percent in Arkansas, compared with 15 percent in California, 18 percent in New Jersey and New York each, 20 percent in Oregon and Washington each, 27 percent in Connecticut, 28 percent in Illinois, 33 percent in Ohio, and 34 percent in Louisiana. On a per worker basis, North Dakota got $8,000, while California and New York got roughly $5,000 despite their higher cost of living.

The political forces that have caused inefficient allocation of public funds in transportation infrastructure reappeared in the $10 billion in funding set aside for airports as part of the Coronavirus Aid, Relief, and Economic Security Act. Cape Cod, Massachusetts, and nearby island airports, which have little air travel, received $26 million in funding, while both Providence, Rhode Island, and Manchester, New Hampshire, airports, which in a normal year have far more enplanements than the small Massachusetts airports combined, received less money.

MARKETS HELPING GOVERNMENT REDUCE THE SOCIAL COSTS OF COVID-19

Markets have responded in several ways to the challenge of simultaneously reducing the public's exposure to the virus and facilitating as much economic and leisure activity as possible. The latter is critical because extreme social distancing creates risks to health by reducing earnings and damaging physical and mental well-being.

First, mobility data networks based on GPS data from cell phones indicate that consumers and households have curtailed certain activities in advance of announced shutdowns, and they have been cautious about resuming activities when shutdowns have been lifted. Firms have responded to this behavior when making their adjustments, and generally have not tried to exploit opportunities to raise prices. High prices are generally a useful market signal that new suppliers should enter the market instead of a reflection of price gouging. Efforts to prevent markets from working by alleging price gouging has led, for example, to vast supplies of masks being purchased by foreign buyers who were willing to pay the higher market prices.

Second, by allowing employees to work remotely, firms have enabled their employees to be productive and continue to earn a living while maintaining social distancing. Facebook plans to let some current employees work from home permanently. Other companies, such as Twitter, have announced a similar policy for their employees. Even the nation's freight railroads provided a safe environment for employees by allowing many to telework. In addition, most employers have helped their employees by not forcing them to bear the burden of rising healthcare costs by increasing co-payments and raising deductibles (Carns 2020).

Third, markets also have protected the public by enabling supply chains to function more normally. The surface freight transportation network of truck and rail continued delivery of e-commerce and store goods and essential industrial inputs and critical products, including disinfectants, chemicals for medicines, and toilet paper. To be sure, there are still consumer shortages of certain items, such as disinfectant wipes and N95 masks, due to production limitations and reserving those for healthcare and other frontline industries. Home delivery services for food and healthcare items have been significantly expanded, although this has been criticized as putting warehouse and delivery service workers at higher risk. Finally, transportation companies have supported first responders by discounting their travel and shipping expenses.

Fourth, many firms across the country have redeployed thousands of workers into new jobs in one of the fastest labor shifts in postwar history (Weber 2020). For example, CVS Health partnered with firms such as Gap, Hilton Hotels, and Delta Airlines to employ their laid-off workers to meet the surge in demand for healthcare products and services by stocking warehouses and stores, staffing phones at call centers, and stepping in for CVS staff who were sick or quarantined. Gap encouraged its furloughed workers to take temporary jobs at CVS and other companies. Similar collaborations are occurring to enable firms in urgent need of workers to tap laid-off and furloughed workers to reduce unemployment.

Fifth, some firms have completely changed their product lines and services to continue to operate. For example, Balsam Hill, a company that sells artificial Christmas trees, seasonal wreaths, and flower arrangements, has used its e-commerce infrastructure to sell bulk food to consumers from distributors who normally serve restaurants (Castaneda 2020).

Sixth, households are exploring alternative leisure activities and home repairs to reduce the stress during the pandemic, and suppliers are responding. Dance studios are holding online classes, bars are selling cocktails to go, maintenance companies are offering over-the-phone, do-it-yourself guided repairs, online meeting services have burgeoned as a form of socially distant socialization, and the like.

Finally, consistent with the central thesis of this book, market forces have assisted government to improve market efficiency by enabling consumers to make more-informed choices, reducing externality costs from transmission of the virus, and increasing innovative activity. Markets also have helped government accomplish social goals by improving the provision of education and healthcare in the challenging environment of a global pandemic.

Providing Information to Make More-Informed Decisions

During the pandemic, the internet has been an invaluable source of direct information and personal advice by facilitating virtual meetings with healthcare providers, business associates, and other professionals. Cloud services' flexibility and extra capacity has handled the 25 percent increase in internet traffic since the pandemic began (Fishman 2020), and have enabled valuable conference and meeting services such as Zoom. As vaccines have become available, the private sector has improved vaccine websites that had not provided clear guidance for registering and receiving a vaccine in an orderly fashion. For example, Salesforce and Skedulo have developed the technology for a website in California that enables residents to learn when they are eligible to be vaccinated and find a place to make an appointment. Similarly, in response to failed city and state vaccine websites, people in New York with technology skills built their own vaccine websites (Otterman 2021).

Reducing Externality Costs

Dozens of major retailers and chains across the country, including but not limited to Walmart and McDonalds, have reduced the externality of people infecting others by requiring customers to wear face coverings, even in places where the local government does not require it.

Market forces also are sorting mask- and non-mask-wearers to some extent to help reduce the total externality costs of the virus. People who choose not to wear masks expose both themselves and others who do not wear masks and do not socially distance, to the virus. However, their costs from catching the virus are partially offset by the benefits revealed by their preferences not to wear a mask. Mask-wearers attach a much higher cost to catching and spreading the virus, and a lower cost to wearing a mask, as revealed by their preferences to wear a mask. Mask-wearers are probably inclined to distance themselves from non-mask-wearers at both indoor and outdoor events, while non-mask-wearers are more inclined to associate with other non-mask-wearers at those events. Thus, the people who attach a lower net cost to catching and spreading the virus are more likely to become infected, and the people who attach a higher net cost to catching and spreading the virus are less likely to become infected and to infect their associates.

Private companies, including but not limited to Dollar General, Instacart, and Trader Joe's, are also reducing the virus from spreading by paying workers as an incentive to get a COVID-19 vaccine.

Logistics Innovations by Firms and Third Parties

Firms have developed new ways to keep selling and delivering their products. For example, confronted with the sudden closures of its primary distribution channel to restaurants and institutions, Sysco, a big food-distribution firm, built an entirely new supply chain and billing system to serve grocery stores (*The Economist* 2020). Nike made a digital pivot to increase its internet sales of sporting goods, and HP accelerated the roll out of "3D as a Service." The increased use of drones (discussed below) also can enable firms to deliver more of their products in a timely manner.

Sydney Page (2020) describes the efforts of FarmLink, a third-party logistics project started by college students, to reduce food waste and improve efficient allocation of the nation's food by connecting farms that experience a surplus due to reduced commercial orders with food banks that face excess demand and shortages of donated food. FarmLink has delivered millions of meals in dozens of states. Government agricultural programs generally do not interact with the food banks experiencing the greatest shortages; thus, USDA distributors are reaching out to FarmLink for assistance with identifying those food banks.

Education

The technology sector has played a vital role in enabling the public to continue its formal education during the pandemic, by facilitating online instruction at all grade levels through internet-based courses and/or collaboration tools like

Zoom. In some cases, distance learning at lower grade levels has improved in-class learning by providing a less disrupted environment, and it may continue to be used after the pandemic. The technology sector's presence in higher education is likely to grow as it forges partnerships with certain universities to help them increase their student body by offering both in-class and online degrees.

Interest in for-profit online colleges also has increased during the pandemic. Those schools potentially can fill an important gap by helping educate low-income, nontraditional college students. As a qualification, those students tend to have lower completion rates and larger unpaid debts than students who attend college full time do.

Healthcare

Markets' most important response to the virus's threat to human health has been to conceive and bring to market in less than a year two new mRNA COVID-19 vaccines, which instruct cells to make the coronavirus spike protein that the immune system learns to attack. Additional vaccines also are being developed and gaining adoption throughout the world. Bill Gates, among others, has played an important role in expediting vaccine development and production by picking the top seven vaccine candidates and, rather than waiting for the "winners," building manufacturing capacity for all the candidates.

Markets also have improved healthcare by (1) distributing protective equipment for first responders and the public, (2) implementing testing and contact tracing for individuals who potentially were infected with the virus, and (3) producing ventilators and therapies for seriously ill patients.

3M planned ahead for surge capacity and, as noted, is the largest US producer of N95 masks. In addition, Honeywell and Stratasys, among other companies, have produced N95 masks and face shields, and Ford and HP Inc. have converted production operations to increase the supply of masks and shields. The New England Patriots even contributed to the effort when the team plane delivered 1.2 million N95 masks from China to Boston.

Other entities have developed new ways to increase the availability of protective equipment. Budmen Industries, which makes 3D printers for architects and artists, designed a face shield; Eclipse International, a New Jersey bedding maker, and Aunt Flow, an Ohio-based tampon producer, made face masks using materials for mattresses or maxi pads; the Professional Association of Diving Instructors (PADI) partnered with Rash'R to turn plastic water bottles that pollute oceans into protective face masks; and sewing hobbyists networked online to coordinate do-it-yourself mask-making.

Bizagi, a business process management and automation platform, launched CoronaPass, a digital solution to offer healthcare organizations and workplaces a way for people to demonstrate immunity to COVID-19 based on antibody testing.[3] Private labs, such as LifeHope Labs, are helping with COVID-19 testing by selling at-home kits and processing the tests, and Thermo Fisher Scientific has shipped millions of tests to customers. Finally, Apple and Google are partnering on COVID-19 contact tracing technology using a Bluetooth-based platform.[4]

The United States was clearly caught off guard about the lethality of COVID-19, and the nation's hospitals did not have an adequate supply of ventilators for patients whose infection caused their lungs to fail. Firms including Ford and General Motors shifted their production activities to make additional ventilators for hospitals, and Dyson designed the CoVent ventilator quickly and proceeded to make thousands of them.

Potential Benefits from Markets

The innovations in transportation, drones and autonomous vehicles, have the potential to facilitate both social distancing and economic activity in the current and future pandemics, but policymakers must take prompt actions to expedite the adoption of those modes of transportation.[5]

Drone companies can move medical supplies quickly and reduce human contact. However, the FAA requires drones to be certified as a Part 135 air carrier, a process that can take months or years to achieve. Zipline, a medical drone delivery business, has been active in Africa for years. It has been getting calls for help in the United States, but is not certified by the FAA to make deliveries. Finally, at the end of May, Zipline's partner, the hospital system Novant Health in North Carolina, received an FAA waiver to enable Zipline to make its first US delivery of medical supplies from a field in Kannapolis, North Carolina, to a designated spot fifteen miles away, near Novant Health's Huntersville Medical Center. The FAA should allow all drone companies to expand their operations in a prompt and orderly fashion.[6]

Autonomous cars and trucks also can help with social distancing while reducing the disruption to economic and other activities because they enable people to get to work in a solo-occupied vehicle rather than one shared with a driver, and enable freight to be delivered without exposing a driver. Small, autonomous vans have been used in China to deliver medical equipment to first responders. Nuro is the first autonomous vehicle operator in the United States that has been approved to mass-produce its delivery robots without traditional controls like steering wheels, and it also has been approved to transport pharmaceuticals to CVS customers in Houston, Texas. Policymakers should expedite the expanded use of autonomous vehicles and trucks for several reasons, already noted; an additional reason is that they can help reduce the social costs of a pandemic.

SUMMARY

The novel coronavirus (COVID-19) has provided an unanticipated and extremely unfortunate opportunity for me to conduct an informal robustness test that generally confirms the central conclusions of the book. The federal government bears prime responsibility for policies to reduce the social costs of the virus and, while it has taken some helpful actions, such as initially encouraging stay-at-home policies and providing social insurance, it has maintained status quo bias by failing to learn from past outbreaks of new viruses and respond quickly before the pandemic took hold. As a result, the pandemic unnecessarily cost additional lives and generated greater social costs. In addition, the federal government failed to develop a coordinated plan to distribute vaccines that have been approved by the FDA.

Market forces have responded constructively, where possible, to reduce the social costs of the virus and, with the adoption of drones and autonomous vehicles, could be more helpful in future pandemics. Markets and nongovernmental actions are mitigating some of the current burdens on the public and, through the development of new treatments and vaccines, they are providing hope that we will soon return to life as we once knew it.

In the meantime, it is useful to gain perspective about the progress attributable to market forces by considering if the pandemic had occurred only twenty years ago. Economic activity would have declined much more than it has because we had not developed or adopted the innovations that facilitated remote work and that created an efficient supply chain and distribution system for home e-commerce and industrial deliveries. In addition, social isolation would have been much less tolerable for many people without the innovations in communications, social media, and entertainment.

NINETEEN

Conclusion: Advancing the Perspective of Markets Helping Government

The US will need resilient and creative market forces to provide greater assistance to government as it enters the post-coronavirus environment. Unfortunately, neither the public nor the policymakers are likely to have changed their negative views about capitalism any time soon, and they are likely to have little interest in promising market approaches to address economic and social problems.

Resistance to market approaches—or at least a lack of enthusiastic support—also comes from academics in different ways.[1] For example, consider the 2018 economics Nobel Prize committee report explaining that Paul Romer's and William Nordhaus's "findings put the spotlight on a specific market failure. Both laureates thus point to fundamental externalities that—absent well-designed government intervention—will lead to sub-optimal outcomes."[2] I certainly agree that underfunding R&D to produce innovations and knowledge spillovers and creating environmental externalities are market failures. But this book has provided considerable evidence that markets have become sufficiently robust to reduce the cost of those failures better than have policymakers who are mired in the status quo. Surely market forces are doing more than government officials to generate important innovations to spur economic growth, and they are making significant efforts to develop technological advances that could significantly reduce pollution and slow climate change.

Naomi Oreskes and Eric Conway (2018), two scholars in the history of science at Harvard and Caltech, respectively, assert that the private sector is not capable of addressing climate change without a substantial government role. They support their view by claiming that "major technological transformations of the nineteenth and twentieth centuries involved significant interventions by the visible hand of the government, and that none were delivered by the "invisible hand" of the marketplace." I agree that government financial support may have helped the development of those advances. However, consider the extent that deregulation exposed how government economic regulations came to adversely affect the efficiency of railroads and telecommunications and that, someday, deregulation will expose similar inefficiencies in electricity.

Government deserves credit where it has provided financial support for a socially valuable innovation and where its taxpayer-funded support did not crowd out support the innovation would have received from the private sector. But those who believe government should be given a substantial role to address climate change without the valuable help of markets are ignoring what history has taught us about the long-run effects of regulatory interventions. To paraphrase George R. R. Martin, if you think new government regulations are going to have a happy ending, you haven't been paying attention.

Similarly, I could be rightfully accused of not paying attention if I thought policymakers would immediately heed my recommendation to give greater consideration to market forces to help solve economic and social problems. Indeed, Robert Samuelson (2019) asserts that the hoped-for gains from policy entrepreneurs, including scholars, have been conspicuous by their absence. But Samuelson does not distinguish between: (a) policies that reform or expand government interventions, and (b) socially beneficial policies and private actions that reduce the alleged justification for those interventions in favor of more help from markets. It is important for the policy community to recognize and appreciate the difference.

To this end, it would be useful to have a large commission composed of a group of authors who would write detailed and granular proposals in several areas where markets potentially could help government and present those proposals for a debate among academics, policymakers, and the business community. The commission would recommend a set of policy experiments that would explore how markets could help government, which could be assessed, say, five years later by another commission. Such an effort hopefully would spur a fundamental change in the mindset of the policy community to regularly consider how markets could contribute to accomplishing economic and social goals by providing incentives for efficiency, various sources of competition, and innovations that lead to technological advance. To channel Albert Einstein, markets should be given a greater opportunity to solve problems using forces that are different from the forces that created them.

NOTES

Chapter 1

1. Binyamin Appelbaum (2019), a business journalist, criticizes the influence of economists, especially Chicago economists, for advancing policies during the 1960s and 1970s that placed greater reliance on the market than on the government to solve social problems. Appelbaum claims the "economists' hour" ended in 2008 when the Great Recession took hold.

2. Tankersley and Hirsh, who also are journalists, argued that the American public lost faith in the economics profession for failing to predict how asset bubbles and a wave of complex new financial products could bring the world economy to its knees. Jim Tankersley and Michael Hirsh, "Neo-Voodoo Economics," *National Journal*, May 20, 2011.

3. Citizens also have goals, such as freedom of speech, freedom of worship, and the like, that are more closely related to political rather than economic problems. But the way in which society awards such rights may be heavily influenced by the costs and benefits of rival systems of organization. For example, the US Constitution's guarantee that "Congress shall make no law abridging freedom of speech . . . or of the press" embodies a judgment that decentralized choices about various forms of expression are a better way to protect rights than would be the establishment of, say, a Free Speech Commission.

4. William Baumol and William Bowen used the term "merit good" in the case of opera as a designation for the value judgment that the arts are good for society and, therefore, deserve financial support. However, they indicated that the merit

good approach indicates a desire to provide support rather than a justification for support. Musgrave's approach to merit goods suggests a justification for support. William J. Baumol and William G. Bowen, *Performing Arts: The Economic Dilemma* (New York: The Twentieth Century Fund, 1966).

5. A potential Pareto improvement indicates that someone cannot be made better off without making someone else worse off.

6. Clint Rainey, "Stranded Amtrak Passengers Waited So Long, They Ordered Pizza," Grubstreet, www.grubstreet.com/2017/05/stranded-amtrak-passengers-ordered-pizza.html. Domino's also has attracted attention for helping government with its "Paving for Pizza" initiative: Domino's pays for nominated towns' pothole repairs, to prevent a pothole from ruining a pizza en route to a consumer. In return, Domino's receives publicity for the work.

7. This did not turn out to be an idle promise. Bureau of Transportation statistics indicated that carriers responded quickly by posting a bumping rate of 0.34 per 10,000 passengers in 2017, which was the lowest in decades and a significant decline from the bumping rate of 0.62 per 10,000 passengers in 2016. See Bureau of Transportation Statistics, "2017 Airline Bumping Rate Lowest in Decades," BTS (n. d.), www.bts.dot.gov/bts/bts/newsroom/2017-airline-bumping-rate-lowest-decades. During 2018, the US Department of Transportation reported that United Airlines involuntarily bumped only thirteen passengers per 1 million boarded. See Prachi Bhardwaj, "Airlines are Guilty of Bumping the Most Passengers," *Money*, March 31, 2019, http://money.com/money/5639829/sorry-but-you-cant-board-this-flight-these-airlines-are-guilty-of-bumping-the-most-passengers/.

Chapter 2

1. Recent work in behavioral economics has identified potential welfare gains from nudges made by the government. Hunt Allcott and Judd Kessler (2019) provide evidence that it is important for assessments of nudges to identify their full costs to consumers, which can substantially affect a welfare assessment.

2. The Biden administration took office after this book was completed.

3. The National Bureau of Economic Research is a nonpartisan, nonprofit organization that encourages and disseminates economic research but does not take policy positions. However, many of its publications have policy implications.

Chapter 4

1. Jose Azar, Ioania Marinescu, and Marshall Steinbaum (2017) claimed that antitrust enforcement has paid little attention to whether anticompetitive behavior has adversely affected labor markets by reducing wages. But the authors overlook the role of market forces by not explaining why skilled workers would accept reduced wages when they could explore higher-paying jobs in other cities and why less-skilled workers, who are not tied to a particular occupation, could not consider many potential employers.

2. The government's argument was that the merged AT&T–Time Warner entity would withhold Time Warner-owned networks, such as HBO, TNT, and CNN, from rivals and would raise the price consumers would have to pay for them. The defense's argument was that AT&T–Time Warner would have no incentive to

withhold networks because they would lose significant licensing and advertising revenue. In addition, the defense claimed they would have a legally binding commitment to continue to license those networks after the merger for seven years without any drops in service, and to resolve any disputes about licensing terms through arbitration.

3. This section draws on material in Winston (2021 forthcoming).

4. Patent attorneys have developed sophisticated practices that specialize in successful design-around patent strategies for competitors. A specific example of case law where a successful design-around occurred is contained in Shyla Shirodkar (2004). Naturally, patent attorneys have also developed strategies to counter a potential design-around.

5. Laura Depta, "Latin American Countries Producing the Most MLB Players," Bleacher Report, Alone Together, May 1, 2015, http://bleacherreport.com/articles/2450131-latin-american-countries-producing-the-most-mlb-players.

Chapter 5

1. Under Ramsey pricing, the percentage markup of prices above marginal costs is inversely related to consumers' demand elasticity to minimize the welfare loss from inefficient substitution.

2. Congressional Budget Office, June 2017 Baseline for Farms Program, CBO, June 2017, www.cbo.gov/sites/default/files/recurringdata/51317-2017-06-usda.pdf #page=9.

3. The costs of tariffs may be understated because they do not account for the disruption associated with destroying global value chains. This is especially true because much of trade today is in intermediate goods.

4. A waiver to the Jones Act enables foreign built or rebuilt small passenger vessels that are authorized to carry no more than twelve passengers to operate in US waters and docking facilities. The Secretary of Transportation must determine that employment of the vessel in coastline trade will not adversely affect US vessel builders or the coastwise trade business of any person who employs vessels built in the United States. I have not identified any foreign built or rebuilt vessels that are operating under the small vessel waiver program.

5. At the local level, an important regulation is that some governments control the price of selected rental housing. Evidence of the inefficiencies caused by rent control in New York City and San Francisco can be found in Edward Glaeser and Erzo Luttmer (2003) and Rebecca Diamond, Timothy McQuade, and Franklin Qian (2018), respectively. New York City has recently announced that it will permanently stabilize rents for nearly 1 million apartments housing 2.4 million tenants.

6. By workably competitive, I mean that enough competition exists to protect consumers from monopoly abuses and to generate higher welfare than would imperfect regulation. The economic explanation for regulation, above, abstracts from other considerations that may have played a role. In any case, it is fair to say that federal regulatory authorities were dubious for many decades that workable competition was possible in the industries they regulated.

7. This chapter draws on and extends material discussed in Litan (2014). Litan used that material to make a strong case that economists' ideas, which arguably

influenced policymakers to pursue regulatory reform, have greatly contributed to the nation's welfare.

8. Government has been criticized for relying on antitrust policy to initiate deregulation when the Federal Communications Commission could have implemented regulatory reform earlier to spur competition in long-distance telecommunications.

9. Diana Carew and others (2018) estimate that allocation of the unlicensed spectrum in the 5.9 GHz frequency band could generate additional welfare gains from WiFi communications.

10. The Telecommunications Act of 1996 also deregulated the television broadcast industry. Jessica Stahl (2016) found that industry consolidation followed deregulation, which improved profitability, and that consolidation and deregulation appear to have boosted viewership.

11. Allcott and others (2020) point out that Facebook, while providing large benefits to users, has downsides that include addictive online activity, depression, and political polarization. The costs have not been quantified, but they suggest caution that Facebook's benefits not be overstated.

12. Amtrak and commuter rail passenger services were not deregulated because they are in the public sector and would first have to be privatized. Private passenger rail service does not appear to be profitable in the United States because of its high costs and competition from cars and planes.

13. Oracle, Amazon, and Uber have opened digital freight-brokerage departments to lessen the need for a middleman when companies try to move their goods.

14. According to Rakuten Intelligence, from 2017 to 2019, the time from purchase to delivery has, on average, declined from 5.2 days to 4.3 days, with Amazon at 3.2 days.

15. As an early example, Erik Brynjolfsson, Y. Hu, and Michael Smith (2003) pointed out that the number of book titles available at Amazon.com was more than twenty-three times larger than the number of books on the shelves of a typical Barnes and Noble superstore, and fifty-seven times greater than the number of books stocked in a typical large independent bookstore. The authors estimated that the increased product variety of online bookstores enhanced consumer welfare by as much as $1 billion in the year 2000.

16. The accuracy of the prediction turned out to be distorted by the global pandemic, which drove the United States into a recession.

17. The US energy sector is already filling some of the gaps in OPEC's production. During 2017–2018, OPEC tried to curb crude oil output at some 33 million barrels a day, but US companies pumped more crude and were on track to produce a daily record of 10 million barrels.

18. Fracking also has been criticized for having adverse environmental impacts because it generates considerable wastewater. However, the industry has tried to address the problem by recycling wastewater from fracking jobs in larger amounts to reduce the burden for further wastewater treatment and disposal.

19. Interstate banking that has led to national bank consolidation has aggravated the "too big to fail" problem, which the Dodd-Frank legislation has attempted to address by making it much more difficult for government to bail out creditors of

large banks. We will not know whether that policy will be effective until we assess its effects during the economic crisis caused by COVID-19.

20. For example, advances in information technology could transform ocean shipping. CargoMetrics is using Amazon's high-performance computing network to consolidate and organize all available shipping data—GPS, cargo manifests, and satellite tracking—to gain a global understanding of the movement of raw and finished goods in real time. The tools offer potential improvements to shippers, including pricing transparency, assistance in finding more fuel-efficient routes, identification of lost ships and cargo, and the like.

21. Nicholas Buchholz (2018) points out that some 45,000 customers in New York City fail to find cabs during the weekday due to search frictions exacerbated by regulated fare structures.

22. Uber's effect on congestion is controversial because, on one hand, it reduces congestion caused by taxis that cruise for passengers in dense urban areas, but it could also cause congestion if it generated more trips during peak travel periods. In any case, the efficient policy is not to limit Uber operations but for policymakers to set an efficient congestion toll for all motor vehicles. Similarly, Benjamin Leard and Jianwei Xing (2020) conclude that the availability of ride-sharing has led to modest increases in total vehicle-miles traveled and greenhouse gas emissions; but efficiency calls for setting emission charges on all motor vehicles to reduce the social costs of pollution.

23. Mears Transportation, a Florida taxi company, has announced plans to create an app to compete vigorously with ride-sharing companies in the largest metropolitan markets across the country.

24. Utility commissions can add to the challenge by forcing utilities to buy back higher-cost electricity generated by residential solar projects.

25. In the wake of the severe arctic cold front in February 2021 that caused many Texas households to lose their power for several days, some have blamed the problem on electricity deregulation and claimed that it has raised, not lowered, electricity prices. However, I am not aware of a counterfactual study that has performed a clean analysis of this issue by controlling for differences in the costs of supplying different customers and differences in wholesale markets. MacKay and Mercadal (2021) stress the importance of market design in creating a deregulated electricity sector and point out that poor design can increase electricity prices even if deregulation reduces costs to utilities.

26. Blockchain technology could facilitate peer-to-peer energy trading, which would enable customers to switch power suppliers more quickly, but it is unclear how soon that technology could be scalable (Basden and Cottrell 2017).

27. Autor and others (2020) have raised another concern with rising imports from China by finding that the imports caused a decline in innovation, measured by US firms' patents, with the largest effects among less profitable and less capital-intensive firms. Their finding contrasts with the effect of imports on innovation in other parts of the world, so it is likely that, similar to the effect of Chinese imports on employment, alternative findings will emerge and additional research will be necessary to resolve the debate.

28. TAA provides workers who have lost their jobs as a result of increased

imports with job training, relocation allowances, and income maintenance while they attempt to shift into new occupations. However, assessments of TAA have found that this assistance and training to acquire new job skills has not improved earnings. Sarah Dolfin and Peter Schochet (2012) built on previous assessments of TAA and found that, compared with a statistically matched group of workers in the manufacturing sector who were from the same local areas, TAA participants received more unemployment insurance benefits, were more likely to exhaust their unemployment insurance benefits, and had lower annual earnings when they returned to work. Overall, the authors' cost-benefit analysis found that the net loss to society of TAA was roughly $50,000 per participant.

Chapter 6

1. Ginger Jin and Phillip Leslie (2003) found that the enactment of restaurant hygiene grades in Los Angeles county restaurants in 1998 caused a 20 percent decrease in hospitalizations in Los Angeles compared with the rest of California. Daniel Ho, Zoe Ashwood, and Cassandra Handan-Nader (2019) collected a new expanded data set and found that Jin and Leslie's positive finding failed to hold. Jin and Leslie's (2019) reply acknowledges that foodborne hospitalizations did not decline in Los Angeles relative to other southern California counties after LA adopted restaurant hygiene grade cards in 1998, but that foodborne hospitalization did decline relative to central and northern California. Jin and Leslie speculate that spillover effects could account for the difference. But another explanation, in Winston (2008), is that Jin and Leslie did not control for other important changes in food safety in southern California during that period.

2. But Marshall Lux and Robert Greene (2016) claim that Dodd-Frank credit card regulations reduced lower-income Americans' access to credit cards.

3. Matthew Johnson (2020) explores whether OSHA could be more effective in improving workplace safety and reducing accidents if it issued press releases about facilities that violated safety and health regulations. Johnson finds that OSHA's issuing of such a press release about the most egregious violators had a much greater effect on employers' compliance with safety regulations than additional inspections did. However, he did not find that press releases led to a reduction in injuries and illnesses that was statistically significant at conventional levels.

4. See Red's Best, Fishermen First, www.redsbest.com/redsbest/.

5. For example, restaurants inspected in San Francisco by the Department of Public Health receive a hygiene score. However, instead of forcing the restaurant to post the score, the department shares the information with Yelp, who posts it. Weijia Dai and Michael Luca (2020) find that Yelp's posting of low hygiene scores and a "hygiene alert" that indicates high-risk hygiene violations decreases the probability that restaurants will receive low hygiene scores again after the alert, possibly because those restaurants tend to exit at a faster rate than other restaurants exit.

6. States' "lemon laws" give consumers who have purchased a hopelessly defective vehicle an opportunity, typically for one year, to request either a full refund or a replacement vehicle from the manufacturer. The evidence that indicates those laws have been ineffective is summarized in *Government Failure*, pp. 40–41.

7. As with any rating system, fraudulent positive and negative reviews do

appear. Most consumers develop their own strategy to evaluate reviews and filter biased information. For example, I look at the lowest ratings and assess whether the criticisms are plausible, and I also consider the other reviews that critical individuals have made.

8. During the pandemic, people have relied on food delivery apps to order from companies like DoorDash, Grubhub, and Uber Eats, which are not required by the FDA to display calorie and nutrition information in their online menus because of a legal loophole for foods from chain restaurants.

9. FDA, "Examples of Software Functions for Which the FDA Will Exercise Enforcement Discretion," US Food and Drug Administration, September 26, 2019, www.fda.gov/medicaldevices/digitalhealth/mobilemedicalapplications/ucm368744.htm.

10. Nick Sibilla, "Florida House Passes Bill to Slash Licensing Red Tape," Institute for Justice, January 15, 2018, http://ij.org/press-release/florida-house-passes-bill-reform-repeal-dozen-job-licenses-2/.

11. Recent theoretical work is raising concerns about government efforts to address information problems. For example, Berk and van Binsbergen (2021) develop a theoretical model in which government attempts to use regulation to reduce the number of professionals who do not deliver the service that they sell (charlatans). The authors find that the regulation does not help consumers because the cost of reduced competition outweighs any improvement in service providers.

Chapter 7

1. The full $7,500 federal tax credit for electric vehicles was phased out for General Motors and Tesla vehicles, and was eliminated as of April 2020. Subsidies for other EV models depend on their battery capacity and the manufacturers' vehicle limit.

2. The US Department of Transportation made a significant attempt in the early 1970s to encourage automakers to conserve energy by imposing Corporate Average Fuel Economy (CAFE) standards. CAFE's economic effects continue to be controversial in large part because analysts disagree on whether consumers undervalue fuel economy; but there is no controversy that increasing gasoline taxes would be a more efficient policy to reduce energy consumption than imposing CAFE because by improving fuel economy, CAFE encourages people to drive more, not less. The magnitude of the so-called rebound effect also has not been resolved. The methodological challenge is to estimate a model of vehicle choice and vehicle-miles-traveled (VMT) that allows consumers to change their vehicles in response to CAFE standards and adjust their VMT to their new vehicle. Ashley Langer, Vikram Maheshri, and Clifford Winston (2017) compare the efficiency and distributional effects of a VMT tax, which accounts for vehicle congestion and environmental and safety externalities, with increasing the federal gasoline tax. Several states are currently conducting VMT tax experiments, including Oregon, Washington, Utah, Wyoming, and the seventeen states and Washington, DC, that comprise the I-95 Eastern Transportation Coalition.

3. States also have enacted residential building energy codes to reduce the use of electricity and natural gas. Arik Levinson (2016) calculated the energy savings from

energy codes in California by estimating how much energy would have been used in the absence of the codes. He then compared his findings to the projected savings in electricity and natural gas when the regulations were enacted and found that the estimated savings fell far short of the projected savings. He could not explain, however, why the gap occurred.

4. Clifford Winston and Jia Yan (2021) report evidence that congestion pricing could address complementary externalities—congestion and the fuel consumption and safety externalities associated with larger vehicle sizes—by inducing motorists to drive smaller cars, thereby improving safety by reducing the vehicle fatality rate and reducing fuel consumption by improving vehicle fleet fuel efficiency.

5. Policymakers have begun to show some interest in more efficient road pricing by instituting high-occupancy-toll (HOT) lanes in several metropolitan areas, where solo commuters can pay an electronic toll that varies with traffic volume to use high-occupancy-vehicle (HOV) lanes. Recently, New York City announced its intention to implement congestion pricing of vehicles traveling below 60th Street. However, city officials have yet to indicate to the federal government, which funds much of the roadways, the toll levels they will set or provide estimates of the toll's effects on congestion. As a result, the Trump administration delayed the New York City congestion pricing plan by at least a year. The Metropolitan Transportation Authority has expressed hope that the Biden administration will quickly approve the congestion pricing plan.

6. Government policy also has attempted to reduce the externalities associated with smoking and drug use, which include higher healthcare costs, life insurance premiums, and crime; however, it is not clear what policies could work in practice. Some people call for raising cigarette taxes, but Benjamin Hansen, Joseph Sabia, and Daniel Rees (2015) found little evidence of a negative relationship between cigarette taxes and youth smoking; thus, increasing excise taxes just forces lower-income individuals to spend more of their income on cigarettes, and less on food and preventive healthcare. The United States has fought a long, unsuccessful war against the illegal use of drugs. Indeed, some states have decided that conditional surrender is a better course of action by taking steps to legalize recreational and medical marijuana use. Recently, the US has experienced an epidemic of opioid abuse that has elevated annual fatalities from opioid overdoses to roughly the same level as annual automobile fatalities. States have attempted to reduce the lethal effects of opioids by passing laws that enable opioid users to have access to Naloxone, which is a drug that can reverse an opioid overdose if administered quickly. However, Jennifer Doleac and Anita Mukherjee (2018) found that broadening Naloxone access has led to more opioid-related crime and emergency room visits and to no reduction in opioid fatalities.

7. Kirk Maltais (2019) reports farmers have begun to use solar panels to generate revenue and to diversify their production. Solar panels are being installed across the Farm Belt for personal and external use on land where farmers are struggling. Local utilities pay the farmers for operating the solar panels on their land, and farmers can use the solar panels to reduce their energy bills.

8. Google Maps can show electric vehicle drivers real-time availability of charging stations.

9. Stephen Holland and others (2020) find that significant declines in the air pollution from electricity generation indicate that electric vehicles are now cleaner on average than gasoline vehicles.

10. Loren McDonald, "US Electric Car Range Will Average 275 Miles by 2022, 400 Miles by 2028—New Research (Part 1)," CleanTechnica, October 27, 2018, https://cleantechnica.com/2018/10/27/us-electric-car-range-will-average-275-miles-by-2022-400-miles-by-2028-new-research-part-1/.

11. Figures on the number of public electric vehicle charging stations can be found at www.statista.com/statistics/416750/number-of-electric-vehicle-charging-stations-outlets-united-states.

12. William Yeatman, "Obama's Electric Car Money Grab," *Wall Street Journal*, November 1, 2016, characterized the settlement as a coercive overreach by President Obama to substitute his agenda to promote electric vehicles with government subsidies, which Congress rejected. The settlement, however, may have a constructive outcome if the private sector efficiently develops the electric vehicle infrastructure. The number of fast chargers installed by Electricity America is reported at https://media.electrifyamerica.com/en-us/releases/120#:~:text=Electrify%20America%20plans%20to%20continue,By%20the%20end%20of%202021.

13. As an example of the latter, California regulators recently have approved new rules that all vans and trucks must be electric by 2024. However, a shortage of charging stations, for example, could upset EV van and truck users and cause an uproar that, as in the case of solar, sets back the adoption of EVs in California.

14. The Long Island projects will be built by a division of Equinor, the Norwegian oil and gas company, and a joint venture between Orsted, a Danish company, and Eversource Energy, an American firm.

15. NET companies include Global Thermostat, Carbon Engineering, Climeworks, and Indigo AG. Climeworks, a Swiss start-up, has built several air capture plants in Europe and has had more than fifty corporate clients pay the company to capture and store carbon dioxide. Because agriculture is a major source of greenhouse gas emissions, Indigo AG seeks to remove carbon dioxide by transforming farming practices. BioCellection and Opus 12 are companies attempting to recycle pollutants into beneficial uses.

16. Cap-and-trade programs and command and control regulations also affect labor markets by reducing employment in the industries that are subject to the environmental policies. However, Mark Curtis (2018) found that the nitrogen oxide emissions trading program reduced employment by a smaller amount than did the command and control regulations used in the past.

17. Sam Ori (2017) points out that a market-based trading mechanism also can allocate scarce water resources more efficiently among farmers in a climate-stressed future. Oliver Browne (2017) found that the increase in water rights trading in Idaho moved water to relatively more productive uses and increased total crop acreage.

18. The Council of Economic Advisers (CEA) (2019) reports that deregulatory efforts by the Trump administration during its first two years in office will have raised real annual incomes of US households by $3,100 per year by as early as 2022, or more than $400 billion per year in total. Such a gain would amount to a

2 percent increase in GDP growth, or account for virtually all economic growth in the pre-pandemic economy, which is implausible. Cary Coglianese, Natasha Sarin, and Stuart Shapiro (2020) have critiqued that report and concluded that the CEA's claims are overstated. It also is important to understand that the deregulatory efforts in the report are not economic deregulation in the traditional sense of withdrawing price, entry, and exit regulations in specific industries. As pointed out in chapter 5, the federal government has yet to pursue remaining opportunities for economic deregulation. One regulatory area the report identifies as having potentially large costs relates to emission and fuel economy standards for automobiles; but to be conservative, cost savings from deregulatory actions in this area were not included. However, regulatory reform but not complete deregulation is appropriate for addressing the externalities caused by automobile emissions and fuel consumption. At the same time, there are serious methodological challenges in determining optimal regulatory reform. Alternatively, I argue, it would be more efficient for the government to set a VMT tax that accounted for all the relevant automobile externalities instead of using a command and control regulation.

19. Editorial, "Can You Guess These Three Surprising Energy Trends?" *New York Times*, July 14, 2018, www.nytimes.com/interactive/2018/07/14/opinion/edi torials/Can-You-Guess-These-Three-Surprising-Energy-Trends.html?action=click &pgtype=Homepage&clickSource=story-heading&module=opinion-c-col-left -region&region=opinion-c-col-left-region&WT.nav=opinion-c-col-left-region.

20. Larry Ellison, who owns 98 percent of the Hawaiian island Lanai, may provide a test case of transitioning from oil-based to solar and wind energy (Markind 2020).

Chapter 8

1. The federal government's management of other public services also is marked by inefficiencies. For example, Thomas Hazlett (2008) argued that the Federal Communication Commission has mismanaged the allocation of the electromagnetic spectrum by wasting space and delaying licensing, which thwarts competition.

2. Gary Libecap (2018) discusses the historic reasons the federal government became such a large landowner, and he points out that no strong supportive evidence of market failures existed that justified government ownership.

3. Private-sector firms have helped fund highway investments that have the potential to benefit them. For example, Google and Facebook helped finance $500 million express lanes between San Francisco and the Peninsula. Truck-only lanes, which would be owned and managed by trucking companies, are also a possibility.

4. Rules about radio spectrum access for vehicle telematics and communications protocols also will have to be established.

5. Private investors recently provided funding to help Paine Field in Washington State offer air service to the public.

6. Many cities throughout the world also have privatized their ports, and some evidence exists that this action has led to efficiency gains (Tongzon and Heng 2005). US policymakers should consider conducting privatization experiments for ports in selected coastal regions of the country. Apparently, private-sector users of ocean transportation are willing to make investments to improve US ports. For example, a trio of American energy logistics firms wishing to increase their oil exports is

preparing to build a terminal at the Port of Corpus Christi in Texas that is capable of handling very large crude carriers (Paris 2018).

7. Siyabulela Fobosi (2020) discusses the importance of South Africa's deregulated minibus taxi industry. The industry accounts for 75 percent of all daily transport, and the minibuses are used by the majority of commuters even though they are more expensive than buses and trains, because they provide an efficient service, especially over shorter routes. They also are more widely available, reaching places buses and trains do not.

8. France is home to the first federal postal service to deploy drones for deliveries on regular routes. See April Glaser, "France is Going to Let Drones Start Delivering the Mail," Vox, December 19, 2016, www.recode.net/2016/12/19/14009398/france-mail-drones-delivery-dpdgroup-postal-service.

9. Hannah Downey and Holly Fretwell (2017) describe alternative approaches, including charters, outsourcing, and franchises, for enabling the private sector to help manage public lands more efficiently.

10. It is possible that current government policies toward public lands and structures are motivated by a public goal besides economic efficiency. But I do not know what that goal may be or its justification.

Chapter 9

1. Poor quality patents create a hostile climate for innovation because they are more likely to be challenged in court and because high levels of litigation depress venture capital investment (Tucker 2014).

2. Consider stock price movements: a pharmaceutical company announces positive trial results and its stock price pops up, say, 9 percent, an amount in the billions of dollars, while the entire S&P 500 pops up, say, 4 percent, an amount close to a trillion dollars.

3. For discussions of how another first-rate private university in the United States could substantially increase innovation and improve social welfare, see Brian D. Wright and others, "Technology Transfer, Industry-Funded Academic Inventions Boost Innovation," *Nature*, March 19, 2014, www.nature.com/news/technology-transfer-industry-funded-academic-inventions-boost-innovation-1.14874; and Justine Pope, "Could a Private University Have Made a Difference in Detroit?" *The Atlantic*, July 27, 2013, www.theatlantic.com/national/archive/2013/07/could-a-private-university-have-made-a-difference-in-detroit/278148/.

4. See the Pioneer company website, https://pioneer.app/.

5. See the Mercatus website, www.mercatus.org/emergentventures.

Chapter 10

1. In contrast to the Friedman doctrine about business, Andrew Sorkin (2020) notes that the Business Roundtable, an industry group that includes the leaders of roughly 200 of the nation's leading companies, such as Apple, Amazon, and Walmart, recently changed its "Statement on the Purpose of a Corporation" to espouse "a fundamental commitment to all of our stakeholders." Stakeholders include not just shareholders but also employees, suppliers, customers, and affected communities. Oliver Hart (2020) argues that shareholders may be interested in

more than the bottom line, and he cites climate change as an example where the majority of shareholders may want a company to sacrifice some profit to reduce its carbon footprint. Binyamin Appelbaum (2020) dismisses the Business Roundtable's revised statement and reverts to government solutions to create stronger incentives for "good" behavior, such as increasing the federal minimum wage instead of pleading with McDonald's to raise wages. However, Appelbaum ignores the evidence on the efficacy of the actions government has taken, discussed in this book.

Chapter 11

1. The Census Bureau uses a set of money income thresholds that vary by family size and composition to determine who is in poverty. If a family's total income is less than the family's threshold, then that family and every individual in it is considered in poverty. The official poverty thresholds do not vary geographically, but they are updated for inflation using the Consumer Price Index (CPI-U). The official poverty definition uses money income before taxes and does not include capital gains or noncash benefits (such as public housing, Medicaid, and food stamps).

2. The OECD's measure of the poverty rate is the ratio of the number of people (in a given age group) whose income falls below the poverty line; taken as half the median household income of the total population.

3. Angus Deaton (2018) reported World Bank data that among the world's poorest people who lived on less than $1.90 a day in 2013, 3.2 million of them lived in the United States. When the data are adjusted to reflect needs-based absolute poverty—it is easier to get by with little clothing and transportation in an Indian village than it is in a metropolitan area in America's northeast—the figure rises to 5.3 million. Ryan Briggs (2018) claimed those figures are off by an order of magnitude because poor people in the United States receive noncash benefits, such as food from the Supplemental Nutrition Assistance Program, which boost consumption without boosting income. However, poor people may not receive those benefits because, as noted in other contexts later, they are discouraged from applying for them. Bruce Meyer and others (2019) also challenge the extent of extreme poverty in the US. Of the non-homeless households with cash income below $2/person/day, they find that more than 90 percent are not in extreme poverty once they include in-kind transfers, use administrative records instead of survey reports, and account for the ownership of substantial assets. Of the households remaining in extreme poverty, 90 percent consist of a single individual.

4. The Congressional Budget Office (2018) reported that in 2014, the poorest 20 percent of households received, on average, $12,000 in government transfers, and the richest 20 percent of households paid, on average, $75,000 in federal taxes.

5. The disincentive effects of poverty programs on employment are not homogeneous across different parts of the population. Manasi Deshpande (2016) found that most youth who were removed from the Supplemental Security Income program had a small earnings response and experienced minimal earnings growth over time. In contrast, single mothers who were removed from welfare after the 1996 welfare reform law had higher employment and income after removal (Blank 2002).

6. See Greg Mankiw, "An Effective Marginal Tax Rate," Greg Mankiw's blog,

June 25, 2018, http://gregmankiw.blogspot.com/2018/06/an-effective-marginal-tax
-rate.html.

7. Given that annual transfers constitute 84 percent of the disposable income of
the poorest quintile of American households and 58 percent of the lower-middle-
income households (Gramm and Early 2018), the nation's redistribution programs
have failed to make poor households more self-sufficient.

8. Eric Morath, "The Federal Minimum Wage Doesn't Really Matter Anymore,"
Wall Street Journal, August 11, 2019, www.wsj.com/articles/the-federal-minimum
-wage-doesnt-really-matter-anymore-11565515801.

9. Several states recently have raised their minimum wage to $15 per hour. It
will be useful to determine whether that increase has done more good than harm
for low-wage workers.

10. Jorge Garcia and others (2020) question the methodology in Patrick Klein
and Christopher Walters (2016) and argue its approximations of benefit/cost ratios
have questionable validity.

11. Dale Farran and Mark Lipsey's (2017) assessment of the evidence casts a critical light on some pre-kindergarten programs. The authors argue that only two rigorous studies of pre-K participation have followed children into third grade: the Head
Start Impact study (Michael Puma and others, OPRE Report 2012-45, October 2012,
www.acf.hhs.gov/sites/default/files/opre/head_start_report.pdf) and the Tennessee
Voluntary Pre-K study (Mark Lipsey and others, "Evaluating the Effectiveness of
Tennessee's Voluntary Pre-K Program," Vanderbilt University, https://my.vanderbilt
.edu/tnprekevaluation/#_ftn1). Each of those studies found that the early gains at the
end of pre-K were not sustained even as long as to the end of kindergarten. Children
to whom the pre-K participants were compared caught up quickly.

12. There is some debate on whether the average return on investment in poverty programs is greatest for the youngest recipients. David Rea and Tony Burton
(2019) question whether this is always the case by using data based on the Washington State Institute for Public Policy and finding that programs targeted early in
individuals' lives do not have high returns. The so-called Heckman curve allegedly
indicates that the highest social returns from poverty programs are obtained for the
youngest recipients, but Heckman disagrees with that characterization. See James
Heckman, "Heckman Curve Update Update," StatModeling, comments section,
August 12, 2020, https://statmodeling.stat.columbia.edu/2020/08/12/heckman
-curve-update-update/.

13. David Jaeger, Theodore Joyce, and Robert Kaestner (2020) criticized Melissa
Kearney and Phillip Levine (2015), and Kearney and Levine (2016, 2018) responded
to those criticisms.

14. Brian D. Ray, "Research Facts on Homeschooling," National Home Education Research Institute, March 23, 2020, www.nheri.org/research-facts-on-home
schooling/.

15. *Sesame Street* is a nonprofit that receives funding from corporate grants and
royalties and licensing deals. The US government contributes very little funding.

16. See Honest Jobs website, https://honestjobs.co/.

17. Some parents also leave the workforce because they spend a sizable fraction

of their household income on child care (Levitz 2018). To address this problem and retain employees, Lee Container, for example, purchased a former school building in Iowa and partnered with a day care provider to open a child care center.

18. Other nonprofit private training companies include Year Up and Skillful.

19. Canice Prendergast (2017) describes a market mechanism based on auctions that Feeding America uses to allocate 300 million pounds of food each year.

20. A large government contractor, Conduent, which runs the food stamp network in twenty-five states, has taken actions to block the public's access to Propel's app (Lohr 2018).

Chapter 12

1. One might advocate a non-gender-neutral tenure policy to benefit women, but that is likely to prompt strong legal challenges.

2. Businesses have also expressed their opposition to voting laws that effectively discriminate against Blacks and other minority groups by making it more difficult for them to vote. Major League Baseball moved the 2021 all-star game from Atlanta to protest Georgia's new voting law and American Airlines and Dell Technologies announced their opposition to a possible new voting law in Texas.

Chapter 13

1. Paid leave provided by firms is not a means-tested program, but it could help reduce poverty, so I include that topic with other anti-poverty actions.

2. I include immigration in the discussion of merit goods as part of crime prevention because the Trump administration attempted to significantly curtail immigration, partly on the belief that it would provide protection against violent criminals and terrorists.

3. The government may have gone too far in trying to cut back the costs of student loan debt by appearing to renege on the Public Service Loan Forgiveness program, enacted by Congress in 2007, which encouraged people to pursue low-paying government and public service jobs by allowing them to discharge the remainder of their federal student debt after ten years. According to the US Department of Education, of the 28,000 borrowers who applied to have their loans forgiven in 2018, only 1 percent, a mere 289, were approved. Apparently, students have found the requirements of the program to be convoluted and confusing. For example, although borrowers must make ten years of on-time payments while working at qualified public service employers, the Department of Education had no process for tracking qualified employment for the first five years of the program (Sloan 2018).

4. Notwithstanding the help provided by the program, it is clearly not efficient for a crime prevention program to originate in the military and to transfer surplus equipment to police agencies.

5. The Supreme Court has allowed the Trump administration to enforce its "public charge" immigration restriction, which restricts immigrants entering the United States if the government believes they will rely on public assistance, such as housing or healthcare benefits. The Biden administration is likely to reconsider this restriction and take a less hostile approach to immigrants.

6. Crime and terrorism committed by immigrants is an inflammatory issue because people use different benchmarks—the absolute level of crime and acts of terrorism committed by immigrants or the relative level of crime and acts of terrorism committed by immigrants compared with native born Americans.

7. Recall that I pointed out in chapter 5 that financial deregulation also can create risks that investors fail to fully understand.

8. Capenet, "Facts and Studies, Private School Facts," Capenet (n. d.), www .capenet.org/facts.html.

9. Lam Thuy Vo, "How Much Money Does the Government Spend to Send a Kid to School?" NPR, June 21, 2012, www.npr.org/sections/money/2012/06/21/ 155515613/how-much-does-the-government-spend-to-send-a-kid-to-school.

10. This estimate would be less if vouchers allowed parents to transfer public moneys to private schools. However, most private school students do not use vouchers.

11. Jennifer Fisher, "How Much Money Each State Saves Thanks to Home-schooling," *The Libertarian Republic*, July 22, 2017, https://thelibertarianrepublic .com/much-money-state-saves-thanks-homeschooling/.

12. Dennis Epple, Richard Romano, and Miguel Urquiola (2017) do not include charter schools in their review of the evidence because of state requirements classifying charter schools as public schools, whereas all the voucher programs they review permit the use of vouchers in private schools.

13. Atila Abdulkadiroglu, Nikhil Agarwal, and Parag Pathak (2017a) show that improvements in the matching algorithm for school choice could help improve student welfare.

14. Abdulkadiroglu, Pathak, and Christopher Walters (2018) find that participation in the Louisiana Scholarship Program, a voucher plan that provides public funds for disadvantaged students to attend private schools, lowered math scores and reduced achievement in reading, science, and social studies, possibly because of the selection of low-quality private schools into the program.

15. See the Lambda School, https://lambdaschool.com/.

16. Tyler Cowen, "Conversations with Tyler – Larry Summers," Medium.com, Mercatus Center, September 20, 2017, https://medium.com/conversations-with -tyler/tyler-cowen-larry-summers-blog-secular-stagnation-twitter-421a69ed84c8.

17. For-profit colleges also can fail, like any business. Recently, Education Corporation of America shut down its chain of schools, leaving almost 20,000 students with partially completed degrees, and credits that many other schools will not accept.

18. For example, major businesses in the Washington, DC, region are working with universities in the area, such as George Mason and Virginia Commonwealth, to design a digital tech credential that certifies that graduates have knowledge and skills in such fields as statistics, data visualization, and cybersecurity. Students, therefore, take a sequence of courses that cover knowledge and skills that businesses are demanding.

19. Those perks could be partially offset by lower wages.

20. Robert Smith, founder of Vista Equity Partners, committed to paying off the

student debt for the entire 2019 graduating class at Morehouse College, which was estimated to amount to $40 million.

21. Annetta Zhou Ruohua and others (2017) found that, given their constraints, uninsured individuals consume healthcare in a rational way and do not "overuse" the emergency department.

22. Vilsa Curto and others (2019) compare public and private Medicare spending using available claims from Medicare Advantage, which enrolls the over-65 Medicare population in private insurance plans. Almost a third of Medicare beneficiaries are enrolled in Medicare Advantage. The authors find that healthcare spending per enrollee is 9 to 30 percent lower than in traditional Medicare controlling for "comparable enrollees." Medical Advantage encourages substitution to less expensive care. That is, lower health spending reflects lower utilization of services, not lower payment for the same services—for example, more outpatient and less in-patient surgery. Based on revealed preference, health outcomes also should be better for people who choose Medicare Advantage over traditional Medicare.

23. Anne Tergesen (2019) reports that a growing number of employers are helping workers build their savings accounts to supplement any payments they may receive from Social Security and to enhance their ability to retire. In particular, the goal of the companies is to encourage people to save for retirement by saving for emergencies and by paying down debt. By reducing their workers' financial stress, companies hope to improve labor productivity.

24. BNSF Railroad has used drones to identify trespassers on its facilities and to notify the police.

25. Similar to labor-intensive approaches to reducing crime (that is, the police), new technologies can raise concerns about racial bias, and they also can raise concerns about privacy.

26. Again, this can raise concerns about privacy.

27. Dane Stangler and Jason Wiens, "The Economic Case for Welcoming Immigrant Entrepreneurs," Ewing Marion Kauffman Foundation, March 26, 2014, www.kauffman.org/what-we-do/resources/entrepreneurship-policy-digest/the-eco nomic-case-for-welcoming-immigrant-entrepreneurs.

28. The Trump administration periodically announced that they would increase the number of visas for high-skilled foreign workers and H-2B visas for guest workers. However, market forces instead of the preferences of government officials would be a more efficient way to determine the annual number of visas that are granted.

Chapter 14

1. Catherine Clifford, "Ex-Labor Secretary: Some kind of cash handout 'seems inevitable'," CNBC, Make It, Life with A. I., July 13, 2018, www.cnbc.com/2018/07/12/robert-reich-us-will-need-some-kind-of-universal-basic-income.html.

2. Milton Friedman's (1962) proposal of a negative income tax has the same goal as a UBI program.

3. COVID-19 ended the macroeconomic expansion and led to a recession. But the economy is slowly recovering, and it will resume expanding. In the meantime, there are fewer examples of firms providing generous bonuses.

4. Medicaid and the rest of Medicare do not have trust funds and are not at risk of running out of money.

Chapter 15

1. To be clear, when I say there is little evidence of large welfare losses, I mean I cannot point to studies that find large welfare losses or, for example, in the case of antitrust, I can point to Robert Crandall and Clifford Winston (2003) and Clifford Winston (2021) that surveyed the evidence and found no large welfare losses from anticompetitive behavior or large welfare gains to consumers from antitrust policy. I did point out that labor market discrimination still exists, but could not find estimates of large welfare losses that have been generated by it. Of course, there are large welfare gains from greater technological advances, but I argued previously that the private sector is developing and has the potential to continue to develop significant innovations.

2. President Trump issued executive orders in May 2018 that would have made it easier to fire federal employees, but a federal district judge in Washington, DC, struck down its key provisions.

3. Charles Wolf Jr. (1979) develops a theory that offers explanations for government (nonmarket) failure that parallel those given for market failure. However, he does not subject those explanations to empirical evidence on inefficient policies. Public choice theory attempts to explain government failure in terms of self-interested elected and unelected government officials and their interactions with the public. However, that line of research has not produced a comprehensive anatomy of government failure, which is well-supported by causal empirical evidence.

4. Allan Drazen and Nuno Limao (2008) develop a bargaining model between the government and special interest groups where restrictions on the use of efficient and inefficient policies reduce the surplus over which the government and special interests can bargain but improve the government's bargaining position.

5. The Transparency International Corruption Index, which ranks 180 countries and territories by their perceived levels of public-sector corruption, ranked the United States the 16th least corrupt country in 2017 and among the top twenty least corrupt countries since it started its index in 1995. See www.transparency.org/research/cpi/overview.

6. For example, the $10 billion Pentagon cloud computing contract known as Joint Enterprise Defense Infrastructure, or JEDI, has been the subject of competition involving Amazon, Microsoft, Oracle, and IBM. Amazon has been the target of a national lobbying campaign by Free and Fair Markets, which is funded in part by Amazon's competitors, Oracle and Walmart. President Trump indicated he would intervene in awarding the JEDI contract in response to complaints about Amazon. However, Trump's interest in the matter was personal because it was well-known that he had feuded with Amazon's founder, Jeff Bezos, because Bezos owns the *Washington Post*, which was highly critical of Trump. Thus, it is difficult to conclude that lobbying played much of a role when Microsoft instead of Amazon was awarded the JEDI contract in October 2019. In fact, Amazon filed a lawsuit to challenge the Pentagon's decision to award the JEDI contract to Microsoft, citing

"unmistakable bias" because the Pentagon was improperly influenced by Trump (Greene and Gregg 2019).

7. This explanation was provided by political scientist Michael Munger in Applebaum's article.

8. This is not to say politicians are not rewarded with greater campaign contributions for taking certain actions. For example, Zack Cooper and others (2019) found that members of Congress representing districts where hospitals were awarded an increase in Medicare payments through waivers subsequently received more campaign contributions from the healthcare industry. Similarly, politicians gain support when they spend public funds on roads, subways, and the like.

9. Alma Cohen and others (2019) provide evidence that business leaders have marked political preferences. Based on a sample of political contributions made by 3,500 individuals who served as CEOs of S&P 1500 companies during 2000–2017, the authors found that those political contributions display substantial partisan preferences in support of Republican candidates. The authors claim that CEOs are important players in the policy process because they take a public role on policy issues, act as informal and formal advisors to policymakers, and advocate views as part of the Business Roundtable. However, CEOs' political contributions could be aligned with their desire to maintain the status quo. Indeed, the authors do not provide any evidence that the CEOs' contributions had even a partial effect on specific policy changes.

10. For example, George Stigler (1971) offered a circumstantial interest group explanation for how states set weight limits for trucks by estimating a regression where measures of weight limits for different sizes of trucks were a function of trucks' use in farming, the quality of the road system, and the average length of haul of railroad traffic. Stigler interpreted the positive coefficient for rail's average length of haul as evidence that regulations on truck weight were less onerous the less competitive (that is, the longer the rail hauls) the trucks were to railroads. Clearly, by today's standards of identification, all of the explanatory variables are endogenous; in particular, the structure of rail's network was influenced by growing competition from trucks that was eroding its market share.

11. Sam Peltzman (1989) offered a case for capture theory explaining economic deregulation, and Michael Levine (1989) and Roger Noll (1989) made trenchant criticisms of that case.

12. Capture theory has indicated that interest groups have conferred benefits on the suppliers of regulation, and the public choice literature has stressed the self-interested behavior of government officials. Noll (1989) critiqued the public choice explanation for regulatory policy.

13. NASA's reputation as a high standard of comparison has recently suffered given that SpaceX and other private satellite firms are out-competing it.

14. Robert Poole, Air Traffic Control Newsletter #151, Reason Foundation, February 22, 2018, https://reason.org/atcreform/air-traffic-control-newsletter-151/#g.

15. Andy Pasztor and Andrew Tangel, "Internal FAA Review Saw High Risk of 737 MAX Crashes," *Wall Street Journal*, December 11, 2019, www.wsj.com/articles/internal-faa-review-saw-high-risk-of-737-max-crashes-11576069202.

16. The number of legislative staff with technical training was considerably higher before Congress defunded the Office of Technology Assessment in 1995.

17. The SEC's competence was severely criticized because its lawyers were unable to digest a dossier compiled by Harry Markopolos, which exposed Bernard Madoff's extensive fraud. Andrew Clark, "The Man Who Blew the Whistle on Bernard Madoff," *Guardian*, March 24, 2010, www.theguardian.com/business/2010/mar/24/bernard-madoff-whistleblower-harry-markopolos.

18. Chris Edwards, "Reforming Federal Worker Pay and Benefits," Downsizing the Federal Government.org, August 2, 2019, downsizinggovernment.org/federal-worker-pay.

19. At the same time, the authors did not provide evidence of specific inefficient policies that were influenced by specific special interests.

20. Katherine Barrett and Richard Greene, "How Government Workers Differ from Private-Sector Counterparts," *Government Technology*," June 9, 2016, www.govtech.com/opinion/How-Government-Workers-Differ-from-Private-Sector-Counterparts.html.

21. The Civil Aeronautics Board is a classic example, making World Airways wait for six years when it applied during the regulatory era to provide a low fare on the New York-Los Angeles route only to reject it (Button 2015).

22. Theo Leggett, "What Went Wrong Inside Boeing's Cockpit?" BBC News, May 17, 2019, www.bbc.co.uk/news/resources/idt-sh/boeing_two_deadly_crashes.

23. Editorial, "Stand Up for the 96% and Support Congestion Pricing," *New York Daily News*, January 30, 2018, www.nydailynews.com/opinion/stand-96-support-congestion-pricing-article-1.3786696.

24. A rumor that has gained currency among my air transportation research colleagues is that Trump was convinced by his (private) jet pilot that the change in ATC governance was a bad deal.

Chapter 16

1. Litan (2014) titles his book *Trillion Dollar Economists* because of economists' influential contributions that led to economic deregulation, which generated trillions of dollars in social benefits.

2. For example, automobile companies have argued that the tariffs imposed by the Trump administration are harming their progress to develop autonomous vehicles by raising the cost of inputs, such as steel, and forcing them to reduce their expenditures on R&D.

3. Other factors, such as the high inflation rate during the 1970s, also played a role in garnering policymakers' support for deregulation.

Chapter 17

1. A summary of the potential economic value of artificial intelligence worldwide is contained in Irving Wladawsky-Berger, "The Economic Value of Artificial Intelligence," *Wall Street Journal*, October 26, 2018, https://blogs.wsj.com/cio/2018/10/26/the-economic-value-of-artificial-intelligence/.

2. Eli Dourado (2019) points out that highly regulated sectors tend to discourage investments by venture capitalists.

3. Russ Roberts (2018) points out that it is critical to measure the incomes of the same people over time to see if they share in the gains from economic growth,

instead of taking snapshots at different points in time and comparing different people in different parts of the income distribution. Roberts summarizes evidence indicating that, when one follows the same people over time, the largest gains from economic growth go to the poorest workers; the richest workers make relatively less progress.

Chapter 18

1. As with any externality policy, mask requirements have costs and benefits. People who do not want to wear a mask, for any number of reasons, including discomfort, facial dermatitis, desire to make a political statement, and so on, incur costs from a mask requirement. But they also impose costs on other people if they infect them, and a mask requirement would provide benefits by eliminating that externality. People who wear a mask reduce the probability of getting infected and of infecting others. Timothy Taylor (2020) outlines the scientific evidence on the costs and benefits of wearing a mask, but he is cautious about drawing a strong policy recommendation based on the evidence.

2. It could be argued that there are benefits from policies that encourage people to stay home to limit transmission of the virus, to take care of children when schools were closed, and so on. However, those benefits could be achieved at lower cost by not paying unemployed people more money than they earned while they were working.

3. The CDC has urged caution about the accuracy of antibody tests for COVID-19.

4. These are works in progress in terms of efficacy and adoption.

5. Policymakers also have been slow to take straightforward actions that could benefit the traveling public during the pandemic. For example, American Airlines wanted to give out hand sanitizer to its passengers, but it had to have two separate meetings with FAA inspectors before they could even write a letter asking permission that explicitly satisfied the Code of Federal Regulations. Only after completing that process could American distribute hand sanitizer.

6. Drones with thermal sensors also could help identify sick people walking around in public places, enforce social distancing by identifying miscreants, and even walk a dog.

Chapter 19

1. Raul Magni-Berton and Diego Rios (2019) argue that academics tend to oppose the market because they are among the best students of their cohort, but markets are only contingently sensitive to school achievement.

2. "Economic Growth, Technological Change, and Climate Change," The Royal Swedish Academy of Sciences, October 8, 2018, p. 2, www.nobelprize.org/uploads/2018/10/advanced-economicsciencesprize2018.pdf.

REFERENCES

Aaronson, Daniel, Eric French, Isaac Sorkin, and Ted To. 2018. "Industry Dynamics and the Minimum Wage: A Putty-Clay Approach." *International Economic Review* 59 (February), pp. 51–84.

Aaronson, Stephanie R., Mary C. Daly, William L. Wascher, and David W. Wilcox. 2019. "Okun Revisited: Who Benefits Most from a Strong Economy?" *Brookings Papers on Economic Activity* (Spring), pp. 333–404.

Abdulkadiroglu, Atila, Nikhil Agarwal, and Parag A. Pathak. 2017a. "The Welfare Effects of Coordinated Assignment: Evidence from the New York City High School Match." *American Economic Review* 107 (December), pp. 3635–89.

Abdulkadiroglu, Atila, Parag A. Pathak, Jonathan Schellenberg, and Christopher R. Walters. 2017a. "Do Parents Value School Effectiveness?" NBER Working Paper 23912 (October).

———. 2017b. "Do Parents Value School Effectiveness?" NBER Working Paper 23912 (October).

Abdulkadiroglu, Atila, Parag A. Pathak, and Christopher R. Walters. 2018. "Free to Choose: Can School Choice Reduce Student Achievement?" *American Economic Journal: Applied Economics* 10 (January), pp. 175–206.

Acemoglu, Daron. 2020. "Antitrust Alone Won't Fix the Innovation Problem." *Project Syndicate* (October 30).

Acemoglu, Daron. 2021. "US Institutions After Trump," *Project Syndicate* (January 20), www.project-syndicate.org/commentary/repairing-us-institutions-after-trump-by-daron-acemoglu-2021-01?barrier=accesspaylog.

Acemoglu, Daron, and James A. Robinson. 2013. "Economics versus Politics: Pitfalls of Policy Advice." *Journal of Economic Perspectives* 27 (Spring), pp. 173–92.

Acemoglu, Daron, Simon Johnson, and James A. Robinson. 2005. "Institutions as a Fundamental Cause of Long-Run Growth." In *Handbook of Economic Growth, Volume 1A*, edited by Philippe Aghion and Steven N. Durlauf, pp. 385–472, Elsevier, North-Holland.

Agan, Amanda Y., and Michael D. Makowsk. 2018. "The Minimum Wage, EITC, and Criminal Recidivism." SSRN. https://ssrn.com/abstract=3097203.

Agan, Amanda Y., and Sonja Starr. 2018. "Ban the Box: Criminal Records and Racial Discrimination: A Field Experiment," *Quarterly Journal of Economics* 133 (February), pp. 191–235.

Agarwal, Sumit, Souphala Chomsisengphet, Neale Mahoney, and Johannes Stroebel. 2015. "Regulating Consumer Financial Products: Evidence from Credit Cards." *Quarterly Journal of Economics* 130 (February), pp. 111–64.

Aikins, Matthieu. 2016. "The Bidding War," *New Yorker*, March 7.

Ailworth, Erin. 2017. "Fracking 2.0: Shale Drillers Pioneer New Ways to Profit in Era of Cheap Oil," *Wall Street Journal*, March 30.

Akerlof, George A. 1970. "The Market for 'Lemons': Quality Uncertainty and the Market Mechanism." *Quarterly Journal of Economics* 84 (August), pp. 488–500.

Akerlof, George A., and Robert J. Shiller. 2015. *Phishing for Phools: The Economics of Manipulation and Deception.* Princeton University Press.

Alden, Edward, and Robert E. Litan. 2017. "A New Deal for the Twenty-First Century." Council on Foreign Relations Discussion Paper (May).

Allaire, Maura, Haowei Wu, and Upmanu Lall. (2018). "National Trends in Drinking Water Quality Violations." *Proceedings of the National Academy of Sciences* (February 27). www.pnas.org/content/early/2018/02/06/1719805115.

Allcott, Hunt, Luca Braghieri, Sarah Eichmeyer, and Matthew Gentzkow. 2019. "The Welfare Effects of Social Media." NBER Working Paper 25514 (March).

———. 2020. "The Welfare Effects of Social Media." *American Economic Review* 110 (March), pp. 629–76.

Allcott, Hunt, and Judd B. Kessler. 2019. "The Welfare Effects of Nudges: A Case Study of Energy Use Social Comparisons." *American Economic Journal: Applied Economics* 11 (January), pp. 236–76.

Almond, Douglas, Janet Currie, and Valentina Duque. 2018. "Childhood Circumstances and Adult Outcomes: Act II." *Journal of Economic Literature* 56 (December), pp. 1360–446.

Amiti, Mary, Mi Dai, Robert C. Feenstra, and John Romalis. 2017. "How Did China's WTO Entry Benefit U.S. Consumers?" NBER Working Paper 23487 (June).

Amiti, Mary, Stephen J. Redding, and David E. Weinstein. 2019. "The Impact of the 2018 Tariffs on Prices and Welfare." *Journal of Economic Perspectives* 33 (Fall), pp. 187–210.

Anenberg, Elliot, and Edward Kung. 2015. "Information Technology and Product Variety in the City: The Case of Food Trucks." *Journal of Urban Economics* 90 (January), pp. 60–78.

Ansolabehere, Stephen, John M. de Figueiredo, and James M. Snyder Jr. 2003. "Why Is There so Little Money in U.S. Politics?" *Journal of Economic Perspectives* 17 (Winter), pp. 105–30.

Antecol, Heather, Kelly Bedard, and Jenna Stearns. 2018. "Equal but Inequitable: Who Benefits from Gender-Neutral Tenure Clock Stopping Policies?" *American Economic Review* 108 (September), pp. 2420–41.

Applebaum, Binyamin. 2014. "Who Wants to Buy a Politician?" *New York Times* (December 9).

———. 2019. *The Economists' Hour: False Prophets, Free Markets, and the Fracture of Society*. New York: Little Brown and Company.

———. 2020. "Blaming Milton Friedman." *New York Times* (September 19).

Arnon, Daniel. 2018. "The Enduring Influence of Religion on Senators' Legislative Behavior." *Journal for the Scientific Study of Religion* 57 (3), pp. 1–18.

Auerbach, Alan J., and Laurence J. Kotlikoff. 1987. *Dynamic Fiscal Policy*. Cambridge University Press.

Autor, David H., David Dorn, and Gordon H. Hanson. 2016. "The China Shock: Learning from Labor Market Adjustment to Large Changes in Trade." NBER Working Paper 21906 (January).

Autor, David, David Dorn, Gordon H. Hanson, Gary Pisano, and Pian Shu. 2020. "Foreign Competition and Domestic Innovation: Evidence from U.S. Patents." *AER: Insights* 2 (September), pp. 357–74.

Autor, David H., and Mark G. Duggan. 2003. "The Rise in the Disability Rolls and the Decline in Unemployment." *Quarterly Journal of Economics* 118 (February), pp. 157–201.

Autor, David H., Christopher J. Palmer, and Parag A. Pathak. 2019. "Ending Rent Control Reduced Crime in Cambridge." *AEA Papers and Proceedings* 109 (May), pp. 381–84.

Azar, Jose, Emiliano Huet-Vaughn, Ioana Marinescu, Bledi Taska, and Till von Wachter. 2019. "Minimum Wage Employment Effects and Labor Market Concentration." NBER Working Paper 26101 (July).

Azar, Jose, Ioana Marinescu, and Marshall I. Steinbaum. 2017. "Labor Market Concentration." NBER Working Paper 24147.

Babcock, Pamela. 2019. "Tech Start-Ups Look to Disrupt the Affordable Housing Industry." *Washington Post* (July 11).

Bachner, Jennifer, and Benjamin Ginsberg. 2016. *What Washington Gets Wrong*. New York: Prometheus Books.

Bai, Liang, and Sebastian Stumpner. 2019. "Estimating U.S. Consumer Gains from Chinese Imports." *AER: Insights* 1 (September), pp. 209–24.

Baily, Martin Neil, Aaron Klein, and Justin Schardin. 2017. "The Impact of the Dodd-Frank Act on Financial Stability and Economic Growth." *Russell Sage Foundation Journal of the Social Sciences* 3 (January), pp. 20–47.

Bailey, Martha J., Tanya S. Byker, Elena Patel, and Shanthi Ramnath. 2019. "The Long-Term Effects of California's 2004 Paid Family Leave Act on Women's Careers: Evidence from U.S. Tax Data." NBER Working Paper 26416 (October).

Baker, Jonathan. 2019. *The Antitrust Paradigm: Restoring a Competitive Equilibrium*. Harvard University Press.

Baker, Mike. 2020. "F.D.A. Halts Coronavirus Testing Program Backed by Bill Gates." *New York Times* (May 15).

Barber, C. Ryan. 2019. "A Very Difficult Time: Challenges for Career Lawyers at Trump's DOJ." *Wall Street Journal* (July 15).

Barrett, Katherine, and Richard Greene. 2021. "If Your State Is Struggling with the Vaccine Rollout, This Is Probably Why." Route Fifty (March 9), www.route-fifty.com/health-human-services/2021/03/if-your-state-struggling-vaccine-rollout-probably-why/172567.

Barrios, John M. 2018. "Occupational Licensing and Accountant Quality: Evidence from the 150-Hour Rule." Becker Friedman Institute, University of Chicago Working Paper 2018-32.

Bartik, Alexander W., Janet Currie, Michael Greenstone, and Christopher R. Knittel. 2019. "The Local Economic and Welfare Consequences of Hydraulic Fracturing." *American Economic Journal: Applied Economics* 11 (October), pp. 105–55.

Basden, James, and Michael Cottrell. 2017. "How Utilities Are Using Blockchain to Modernize the Grid." *Harvard Business Review* (March 23).

Bator, Francis M. 1958. "The Anatomy of Market Failure." *Quarterly Journal of Economics* 72 (August), pp. 351–79.

Baumgartner, Frank R., Jeffrey M. Berry, Marie Hojnacki, David C. Kimball, and Beth L. Leech. 2009. *Lobbying and Policy Change: Who Wins, Who Loses, and Why.* University of Chicago Press.

Baumol, William J., and William G. Bowen. 1966. *Performing Arts: The Economic Dilemma.* New York: The Twentieth Century Fund.

Baumol, William J., and Robert D. Willig. 1986. "Contestability: Developments since the Book." *Oxford Economic Papers* 38 (November), pp. 9–36.

Becker, Gary S. 1957. *The Economics of Discrimination.* University of Chicago Press.

———. 1968. "Crime and Punishment: An Economic Approach." *Journal of Political Economy* 76 (April), pp. 169–217.

———. 1983. "A Theory of Competition among Pressure Groups for Political Influence." *Quarterly Journal of Economics* 98 (August), pp. 371–400.

Bell, Alexander M., Raj Chetty, Xavier Jaravel, Neviana Petkova, and John Van Reenen. 2017. "Who Becomes an Inventor in America? The Importance of Exposure to Innovation." NBER Working Paper 24062.

Ben-Shahar, Omri. 2016. "The Surprising Failure of Food Labeling." *Forbes* (April 18).

Ben-Shahar, Omri, and Carl E. Schneider. 2014. *More Than You Wanted To Know: The Failure Of Mandated Disclosure.* Princeton University Press.

Bender, Michael C., and Rebecca Ballhaus. 2020. "How Trump Sowed Covid Supply Chaos. 'Try Getting It Yourselves.'" *Wall Street Journal* (August 31).

Berk, Jonathan B., and Jules van Binsbergen. 2021. "Regulation of Charlatans in High-Skill Professions." Stanford University Graduate School of Business working paper (February).

Bernard, Tara Siegel. 2018. "Getting Down Payment Help Now. Sharing Home's Gain (or Loss) Later." *New York Times* (June 1).

Bertrand, Marianne, Matilde Bombardini, and Francesco Trebbi. 2014. "Is It Whom You Know Or What You Know? An Empirical Assessment of the Lobbying Process." *American Economic Review* 104 (December), pp. 3885–920.

Bessen, James. 2016. "Accounting for Rising Corporate Profits: Intangibles or Regulatory Rents?" Boston University School of Law, Law and Economics Research Paper 16-18. SSRN. https://ssrn.com/abstract=2778641.

Bessen, James, and Michael J. Meurer. 2008. *Patent Failure: How Judges, Lawyers, and Bureaucrats Put Innovators at Risk.* Princeton University Press.

Bettinger, Eric P., Lindsay Fox, Susanna Loeb, and Eric S. Taylor. 2017. "Virtual Classrooms: How Online College Courses Affect Student Success." *American Economic Review* 107 (September), pp. 2855–75.

Bilton, Nick. 2014. "Tinder, the Fast-Growing Dating App, Taps an Age-Old Truth." *New York Times* (October 29).

Birch, Andrew. 2018. "How to Halve the Cost of Residential Solar in the United States." Gtm. www.greentechmedia.com/articles/read/how-to-halve-the-cost -of-residential-solar-in-the-us#gs.lWHm85s.

Bitler, Marianne, and Hilary Hoynes. 2016. "The More Things Change, the More They Stay the Same? The Safety Net and Poverty in the Great Recession." *Journal of Labor Economics* 34 (January), pp. S403–S444.

Blanes i Vidal, Jordi, Mirko Draca, and Christian Fons-Rosen. 2012. "Revolving Door Lobbyists." *American Economic Review* 102 (December), pp. 3731–48.

Blank, Rebecca. 2002. "Evaluating Welfare Reform in the United States." *Journal of Economic Literature* 40 (December), pp. 1105–66.

Blinder, Alan S. 2018. *Advice and Dissent: Why America Suffers When Economics and Politics Collide.* New York: Basic Books.

Blinder, Alan S., and Mark W. Watson. 2016. "Presidents and the US Economy: An Econometric Exploration." *American Economic Review* 106 (April), pp. 1015–45.

Bloom, Nicholas, Kyle Handley, Andre Kurmann, and Philip Luck. 2019. "The Impact of Chinese Trade on U.S. Employment: The Good, The Bad, and The Apocryphal." Stanford University Working Paper (July).

Bloom, Nicholas, Charles I. Jones, John Van Reenen, and Michael Webb. 2018. "Are Ideas Getting Harder to Find?" Stanford University Working Paper, March.

Boadway, Ira. 2020. "Batteries for Electric Cars Speed Toward a Tipping Point," *Bloomberg*, December 16, www.bloomberg.com/news/articles/2020-12-16/ electric-cars-are-about-to-be-as-cheap-as-gas-powered-models.

Boldrin, Michele, Juan Correa Allamand, David K. Levine, and Carmine Ornaghi. 2011. "Competition and Innovation." CATO Papers on Public Policy 1, pp. 109–71.

Boldrin, Michele, and David K. Levine. 2008. *Against Intellectual Monopoly.* Cambridge University Press.

Bolton, Alexander, John M. de Figueiredo, and David E. Lewis. 2016. "Elections, Ideology, and Turnover in the U.S. Federal Government," NBER Working Paper 22932 (December).

Bonica, Adam, Nolan McCarty, Keith T. Poole, and Howard Rosenthal. 2013. "Why Hasn't Democracy Slowed Rising Inequality?" *Journal of Economic Perspectives* 27 (Summer), pp. 103–24.

Bordo, Michael D., and John V. Duca. 2018. "The Impact of the Dodd-Frank Act on Small Business." NBER Working Paper 24501 (April).

Bove, Vincenzo, and Evelina Gavrilova. 2017. "Police Officer on the Frontline or a Soldier? The Effect of Police Militarization on Crime." *American Economic Journal: Economic Policy* 9 (August), pp. 1–18.

Bowles, Nellie. 2019. "An Online Preschool Closes a Gap but Exposes Another." *New York Times* (July 7).

Bradley, Sebastien, and Naomi E. Feldman. 2020. "Hidden Baggage: Behavioral Responses to Changes in Airline Ticket Tax Disclosure." *American Economic Journal: Economic Policy* 12 (November), pp. 58–87.

Brady, David, Ryan M. Finnigan, and Sabine Hubgen. 2017. "Rethinking the Risks of Poverty: A Framework for Analyzing Prevalences and Penalties." *American Journal of Sociology* 123 (November), pp. 740–86.

Braun, R. Anton, Karen Kopecky, and Tatyana Koreshkova. 2017. "Old, Sick, Alone, and Poor: A Welfare Analysis of Old-Age Social Insurance Programmes." *Review of Economic Studies* 84 (April), pp. 580–612.

Briggs, Ryan. 2018. "Millions of Americans as Destitute as the World's Poorest? Don't Believe It." *Vox* (February 4).

Brown, David W., Amanda E. Kowalski, and Ithai Z. Lurie. 2020. "Medicaid as an Investment in Children: What Is the Long-Term Impact on Tax Receipts?" *Review of Economic Studies* 87, no. (March), pp. 792–821.

Brown, Jeffrey R., and Jiekun Huang. 2017. "All the President's Friends: Political Access and Firm Value." NBER Working Paper 23356 (April).

Browne, Oliver. 2017. "The Economic Value of Clarifying Property Rights: Evidence from Water in Idaho's Snake River Basin." University of Chicago Working Paper.

Bruni, Frank. 2018. "Corporations Will Inherit the Earth." *New York Times* (February 10).

Brynjolfsson, Erik, Y. Hu, and Michael Smith. 2003. "Consumer Surplus in the Digital Economy: Estimating the Value of Increased Product Variety at Online Booksellers." *Management Science* 49 (November), pp. 1580–96.

Brynjolfsson, Erik, and JooHee Oh. 2012. "The Attention Economy: Measuring the Value of Free Digital Services on the Internet." Presented at the 33rd International Conference on Information Systems. Orlando, Florida.

Buchholz, Nicholas. 2018. "Spatial Equilibrium, Search Frictions, and Dynamic Efficiency in the Taxi Industry." Working Paper. Department of Economics, Princeton University (July).

Burkhauser, Richard V., Kevin Corinth, James Elwell, and Jeff Larrimore. 2020. "Evaluating the Success of President Johnson's War on Poverty: Revisiting the Historical Record Using a Full-Income Poverty Measure" (April).

Butcher, Kristin F., and Anne Morrison Piehl. 2007. "Why Are Immigrants' Incarceration Rates So Low? Evidence on Selective Immigration, Deterrence, and Deportation." NBER Working Paper 13229 (July).

Button, Kenneth. 2015. "A Book, the Application, and the Outcomes: How Right Was Alfred Kahn in the Economics of Regulation about the Effects of Deregulation of the U.S. Domestic Airline Market?" *History of Political Economy* 47, pp. 1–39.

Butts, Jeffrey A., Caterina Gouvis Roman, Lindsay Bostwick, and Jeremy R. Porter. 2015. "Cure Violence: A Public Health Model to Reduce Gun Violence." *Annual Review of Public Health* 36, pp. 39–53.

Byrne, Elizabeth. 2019. "Safety at Risk: Future of Texas Plumbers' Licensing and Regulation Uncertain After Legislative Impasse." *Texas Tribune* (May 28).

Byrne, David, and Carol Corrado. 2019. "Accounting for Innovation in Consumer Digital Services: IT Still Matters." NBER Working Paper 26010 (July).

Caliendo, Lorenzo, and Fernando Parro. 2015. "Estimates of the Trade and Welfare Effects of NAFTA." *Review of Economic Studies* 82 (January), pp. 1–44.

Calomiris, Charles W. 2000. *US Bank Deregulation in Historical Perspective*. Cambridge University Press.

Cao, Zhiyan, Guy D. Fernando, Arindam Tripathy, and Arun Upadhyay. 2018. "The Economics of Corporate Lobbying." *Journal of Corporate Finance* 49 (April), pp. 54–80.

Caplin, Andrew, James H. Carr, Frederick Pollock, Zhong Yi Tong, Kheng Mei Tan, and Trivikraman Thampy. 2007. "Shared-Equity Mortgages, Housing Affordability, and Homeownership." *Housing Policy Debate* 18, issue 1, pp. 209–42.

Caplin, Andrew, Noel B. Cunningham, and Mitchell Engler. 2009. "Rectifying the Tax Treatment of Shared Appreciation Mortgages." *Tax Law Review* 62, pp. 505–38.

Caplan, Bryan. 2019. "Big Business: Recasting the Anti-Hero." The Library of Economics and Liberty (April 29). www.econlib.org/big-business-recasting-the -anti-hero/.

Carew, Diana, Nicholas Martin, Marjory S. Blumenthal, Philip Armour, and Jesse Lastunen. 2018. *The Potential Economic Value of Unlicensed Spectrum in the 5.9 GHz Frequency Band*. RAND Corporation. Santa Monica, California.

Carns, Ann. 2020. "Even with Challenges of Pandemic, Health Benefits May Not Change Much." *New York Times* (October 16).

Carroll, Aaron E. 2016. "How Yelp Reviews Can Help Improve Patient Care." *New York Times* (September 12).

Case, Anne, and Angus Deaton. 2020. "No, Shutdowns Won't Cause a Spike in 'Deaths of Despair.'" *Washington Post* (June 7).

Casselman, Ben, and Adam Satariano. 2019. "Amazon's Latest Experiment: Retraining Its Work Force." *New York Times* (July 11).

Castaneda, Leonardo. 2020. "How One Bay Area Business Switched from Selling Holiday Wreaths to Supplying Pasta and Toilet Paper." *The Mercury News* (April 16).

Catalini, Christian, Christian Fons-Rosen, and Patrick Gaulé. 2018. "How Do Travel Costs Shape Collaboration?" NBER Working Paper 24780 (June).

Cellini, Stephanie Riegg, and Nicholas Turner. 2019. "Gainfully Employed? Assessing the Employment and Earnings of For-Profit College Students Using Administrative Data." *Journal of Human Resources* 54 (Spring), pp. 342–70.

Cengiz, Doruk, Arindrajit Dube, Attila Linder, and Ben Zipperer. 2017. "Criminal Deterrence: A Review of the Literature." *Journal of Economic Literature* 55 (March), pp. 5–48.

———. 2019. "The Effect of Minimum Wages on Low-Wage Jobs: Evidence from the United States Using a Bunching Estimator." NBER Working Paper 25434 (January).

Chalfin, Aaron, and Justin McCrary. 2017. "Are U.S. Cities Underpoliced? Theory and Evidence." *Review of Economics and Statistics* 100 (March), pp. 167–86.

———. 2018. "Criminal Deterrence: A Review of the Literature." *Journal of Economic Literature* 55, 1 (March), pp. 5–48.

Chandra, Amitabh, Amy Finkelstein, Adam Sacarny, and Chad Syverson. 2016. "Perhaps Market Forces Do Work in Health Care after All." *Harvard Business Review* (December 5).

Chase, Matt. 2015. "Paying to Get Inside the Restaurant." *The Atlantic* (April 23).

Chetty, Raj, Nathaniel Hendren, Patrick Kline, and Emmanuel Saez. 2014. "Where

Is the Land of Opportunity? The Geography of Intergenerational Mobility in the United States." NBER Working Paper 19843. National Bureau of Economic Analysis. Cambridge.

Chetty, Raj, Nathaniel Hendren, Frina Lin, Jeremy Majerovitz, and Benjamin Scuderi. 2016. "Childhood Environment and Gender Gaps in Adulthood." *American Economic Review Papers and Proceedings* 106 (May), pp. 282–88.

Christensen, Clayton. 1997. *The Innovator's Dilemma: When New Technologies Cause Great Firms to Fail*. Harvard Business Review Press.

Chung, Juliet, and Dawn Lim. 2020. "Yale's David Swensen Puts Money Managers on Notice about Diversity." *Wall Street Journal* (October 23).

Cicala, Steve. 2015. "When Does Regulation Distort Costs? Lessons from Fuel Procurement in US Electricity Generation." *American Economic Review* 105 (January), pp. 411–44.

———2017. "Imperfect Markets versus Imperfect Regulation in U.S. Electricity Generation." NBER Working Paper 23053 (January).

Clemens, Jeffrey, Lisa B. Kahn, and Jonathan Meer. 2018. "The Minimum Wage, Fringe Benefits, and Worker Welfare." NBER Working Paper 24635 (May).

Coase, Ronald. 1960. "The Problem of Social Cost." *Journal of Law and Economics* 3 (October), pp. 1–40.

Coates, John C., and Suraj Srinivasan. 2014. "SOX after Ten Years: A Multidisciplinary Review." *Accounting Horizons* 28 (September), pp. 627–71.

Coglianese, Cary, Natasha Sarin, and Stuart Shapiro. 2020. "Deregulatory Deceptions: Reviewing the Trump Administration's Claims about Regulatory Reform." Penn Program On Regulation (November 1).

Cohen, Alma, Moshe Hazan, Roberto Tallarita, and David Weiss. 2019. "The Politics of CEOs." John M. Olin Center for Law, Economics, and Business Discussion Paper 1002 (May).

Cohodes, Sarah, Elizabeth Setren, and Christopher R. Walters. 2021. "Can Successful Schools Replicate? Scaling Up Boston's Charter School Sector." *American Economic Journal: Economic Policy* 13, 1 (February), pp. 138–67.

Confessore, Nicholas. 2019. "Mick Mulvaney's Master Class in Destroying a Bureaucracy from Within." *New York Times Magazine* (April 16).

Cooper, Preston. 2016. "Government Subsidies Drive For-Profit Colleges' Failures." *Forbes* (June 2).

Cooper, Zack, Amanda E. Kowalski, Eleanor N. Powell, and Jennifer Wu. 2019. "Politics and Health Care Spending in the United States." NBER Working Paper 23748.

Correal, Annie. 2018. "Inside the Dollar Van Wars." *New York Times* (June 8).

Corrigan, Jack. 2019. "VA Released Millions of People's Personal Data Despite Known Risks." *Nextgov* (November 18).

Costinot, Armaud, and Andres Rodriguez-Clare. 2018. "The US Gains from Trade: Valuation Using the Demand for Foreign Factor Services." NBER Working Paper 24407.

Council of Economic Advisers. 2019. *The Economic Effects of Federal Deregulation since January 2017: An Interim Report* (June). www.whitehouse.gov/wp-content

/uploads/2019/06/The-Economic-Effects-of-Federal-Deregulation-Interim-Re port.pdf.

Cowen, Tyler. 2011. *The Great Stagnation: How America Ate All the Low-Hanging Fruit of Modern History, Got Sick, and Will (Eventually) Feel Better*. New York: Dutton.

Crampton, Liz. 2019. "USDA Farms Out Economists Whose Work Challenges Trump Policies." *Politico* (May 22).

Crandall, Robert W., and Clifford Winston. 2003. "Does Antitrust Policy Improve Consumer Welfare? Assessing the Evidence." *Journal of Economic Perspectives* 17 (Fall), pp. 3–26.

Crawford, Gregory S., Oleksandr Shcherbakov, and Matthew Shum. 2019. "Quality Overprovision in Cable Television Markets." *American Economic Review* 109 (March), pp. 956–95.

Cui, Ruomeng, Jun Li, and Dennis J. Zhang. 2018. "Reducing Discrimination with Reviews in the Sharing Economy: Evidence from Field Experiments on Airbnb." SSRN. https://papers.ssrn.com/sol3/papers.cfm?abstract_id=2882982.

Cunningham, Eric. 2016. "No, *Wall Street Journal*, Chinese Imports Didn't Kill My Hometown." *Wall Street Journal* (August 16).

Currie, Janet, and Maya Rossin-Slater. 2015. "Early-Life Origins of Lifecycle Well-being: Research and Policy Implications." *Journal of Policy Analysis and Management* 34 (Winter), pp. 208–42.

Currie, Janet, and Reed Walker. 2019. "What Do Economists Have to Say about the Clean Air Act 50 Years after the Establishment of the Environmental Protection Agency?" *Journal of Economic Perspectives* 33 (Fall), pp. 3–26.

Currie, Janet, Joshua Graff Zivin, Katherine Meckel, Matthew Neidell, and Wolfram Schlenker. 2013. "Something in the Water: Contaminated Drinking Water and Infant Health." *Canadian Journal of Economics* 46 (August), pp. 791–810.

Curtis, E. Mark. 2018. "Who Loses Under Cap-and-Trade Programs? The Labor Market Effects of the NOx Budget Trading Program." *Review of Economics and Statistics* 100 (March), pp. 151–66.

Curto, Vilsa, Liran Einav, Amy Finkelstein, Jonathan Levin, and Jay Bhattacharya. 2019. "Health Care Spending and Utilization in Public and Private Medicare." *American Economic Journal: Applied Economics* 11 (April), pp. 302–32.

Cutter, W. Bowman, and Sofia F. Franco. 2012. "Do Parking Requirements Significantly Increase the Area Dedicated to Parking? A Test of the Effect of Parking Requirements Values in Los Angeles County." *Transportation Research A* 46 (July), pp. 901–25.

Dai, Weijia, and Michael Luca. 2020. "Digitizing Disclosure: The Case of Restaurant Hygiene Scores." *American Economic Journal: Microeconomics* 12 (May), pp. 41–59.

Davies, Antony, and James R. Harrigan. 2018. "A Better Kind of Regulation," *US News and World Report* (January 3).

Davis, Lucas W., and Lutz Kilian. 2011. "The Allocative Cost of Price Ceilings in the U.S. Residential Market for Natural Gas." *Journal of Political Economy* 119 (April), pp. 212–41.

De Freytas-Tamura, Kimiko. 2019. "Can Scooby Doo and the Rest of the Dollar Vans go High-Tech?" *New York Times* (December 11).

De Nardi, Mariachristina, Eric French, and John Bailey Jones. 2016. "Medicaid Insurance in Old Age." *American Economic Review* 106 (November), pp. 3480–520.

Deaton, Angus. 2018. "The U.S. Can No Longer Hide from its Deep Poverty Problem." *New York Times* (June 24).

Decarolis, Francesco, Leonardo M. Giuffrida, Elisabetta Iossa, Vincenzo Mollisi, and Giancarlo Spagnolo. 2018. "Bureaucratic Competence and Procurement Outcomes." NBER Working Paper 24201 (January).

DeGood, Kevin, and Andrew Schwartz. 2016. "Can New Transportation Technologies Improve Equity and Access to Opportunity?" *Center for American Progress.* Washington, DC (April).

deHaan, Ed, Simi Kedia, Kevin Koh, and Shivaram Rajgopal. 2015. "The Revolving Door and the SEC's Enforcement Outcomes: Initial Evidence from Civil Litigation." *Journal of Accounting and Economics* 60 (November-December), pp. 65–96, https://ideas.repec.org/s/eee/jaecon.html.

Deming, David J., Michael L. Lovenheim, and Richard W. Patterson. 2016. "The Competitive Effects of Online Education." NBER Working Paper 22749 (October).

Deshpande, Manasi. 2016. "Does Welfare Inhibit Success? The Long-Term Effects of Removing Low-Income Youth from the Disability Roles." *American Economic Review* 106 (November), pp. 3300–30.

Detter, Dag, and Stefan Folster. 2017. *The Public Wealth of Cities: How to Unlock Hidden Assets to Boost Growth and Prosperity.* Brookings Institution Press.

Diamond, Rebecca, Timothy McQuade, and Franklin Qian. 2018. "The Effects of Rent Control Expansion on Tenants, Landlords, and Inequality: Evidence from San Francisco." NBER Working Paper 24181 (January).

Doleac, Jennifer L. 2017. "The Effects of DNA Databases on Crime." *American Economic Journal: Applied Economics* 9 (January), pp. 165–201.

Doleac, Jennifer L., and Benjamin Hansen. 2016. "Does 'Ban the Box' Help or Hurt Low Skilled Workers? Statistical Discrimination and Employment Outcomes When Criminal Histories Are Hidden." NBER Working Paper 22469 (July).

Doleac, Jennifer L., and Anita Mukherjee. 2018. "The Moral Hazard of Lifesaving Innovations: Naloxone Access, Opioid Abuse, and Crime." SSRN. https://ssrn.com/abstract=3135264.

Dolfin, Sarah, and Peter Z. Schochet. 2012. *The Benefits and Costs of the Trade Adjustment Assistance (TAA) Program under the 2002 Amendments.* Mathematica Policy Research final report prepared as part of the Evaluation of the Trade Adjustment Assistance Program (December).

Dorsey, Jackson. 2017. "Harnessing the Power of the Sun through Online Platforms: Evidence from the Rooftop Solar Market" (November).

Dourado, Eli. 2019. "How Do We Move the Needle on Progress?" (September 26). https://elidourado.com/blog/move-the-needle-on-progress/.

Downey, Hannah, and Holly Fretwell. 2017. "Public Lands Management." In *A New Landscape: 8 Ideas for the Interior Department.* Bozeman, Montana: PERC Public Lands Report.

Dranove, David, Christopher Ody, and Amanda Starc. 2021. "A Dose of Managed Care: Controlling Drug Spending in Medicaid," *American Economic Journal: Applied Economics*, 13 (January), pp. 170–97.

Drazen, Allan, and Nuno Limao. 2008. "A Bargaining Theory of Inefficient Redistribution Policies." *International Economic Review* 49 (May), pp. 621–57.

Drutman, Lee. 2015. "Despite Citizens United, Elections Aren't a Good Investment for a Corporation." *Washington Post* (March 27).

Dutz, Mark, Jonathan M. Orszag, and Robert D. Willig. 2012. "The Liftoff of Consumer Benefits from the Broadband Revolution." *Review of Network Economics* 11 (December), pp. 1–34.

Economides, Nicholas, Katja Seim, and V. Brian Viard. 2008. "Quantifying the Benefits of Entry into Local Phone Service." *RAND Journal of Economics* 39 (Autumn), pp. 699–730.

Edlund, Lena, and Cecilia Machado. 2019. "It's the Phone, Stupid: Mobiles and Murder." NBER Working Paper 25883 (May).

Ehley, Brianna. 2014. "Federal Government Pays Workers $5 Million to Not Work." *Fiscal Times* (August 4).

———. 2015. "Why We Can't Kill a Useless Government Agency." *Fiscal Times* (March 19).

Einav, Liran, Amy Finkelstein, and Neale Mahoney. 2018. "Long-Term Care Hospitals: A Case Study in Waste." NBER Working Paper 24946 (August).

Eisenach, Jeffrey A., and Kevin W. Caves. 2012. "What Happens When Local Phone Service Is Deregulated?" *Regulation* (Fall), pp. 34–41.

Ellin, Abby. 2018. "A High School Education and College Degree All in One." *New York Times* (November 1).

Ellickson, Robert C. 1991. *Order without Law: How Neighbors Settle Disputes*. Harvard University Press.

Eno Foundation. 2018. *Aviation Insights*. Center for Transportation (January 17).

Epple, Dennis, Richard E. Romano, and Miguel Urquiola. 2017. "School Vouchers: A Survey of the Economics Literature." *Journal of Economic Literature* 55 (June), pp. 441–92.

Epstein, Richard. 2011. "Reforms? What Reforms?" Hoover Institution Defining Ideas (May 31).

Evans, Ganon, Carter Harrison, and Nick Lindquist. 2020. "United States: A Market Environmentalist Vision for America." In *Green Market Revolution*, edited by Christopher Barnard and Kai Weiss. Vienna, Austria: Austrian Economic Center and British Conservative Alliance.

Ewing, Jack. 2019. "Nestle Says It Can Be Virtuous and Profitable. Is That Even Possible?" *New York Times* (November 15).

———. 2020. "The Age of Electric Cars Is Dawning ahead of Schedule." *New York Times* (September 20).

Fajgelbaum, Pablo D., Pinelopi K. Goldberg, Patrick J. Kennedy, and Amit K. Khandelwal. 2019. "The Return to Protectionism." NBER Working Paper 25638 (March).

Falk, Justin. 2012. "Comparing Benefits and Total Compensation in the Federal Government and the Private Sector." *BE Journal of Economic Policy and Analysis* 12 (October), pp. 1–37.

Farran, Dale C., and Mark W. Lipsey. 2017. "Misrepresented Evidence Doesn't Serve Pre-K Programs Well." Brookings Institution (February 24). www.brookings .edu/blog/education-plus-development/2017/02/24/misrepresented-evidence -doesnt-serve-pre-k-programs-well/.

Feenstra, Robert C., Hong Ma, and Yuan Xu. 2017. "US Exports and Employment." NBER Working Paper 24056 (November).

Feenstra, Robert C., and David E. Weinstein. 2017. "Globalization, Markups, and U.S. Welfare." *Journal of Political Economy* 125 (August), pp. 1040–74.

Feldstein, Martin. 2005. "Rethinking Social Insurance." *American Economic Review* 95 (March), pp. 1–24.

Ferrara, Peter J. 2018. "SEC Deregulation Would Save Shareholders Time and Money." *Investor's Business Daily* (January 19).

Feyrer, James, Erin T. Mansur, and Bruce Sacerdote. 2017. "Geographic Dispersion of Economic Shocks: Evidence from the Fracking Revolution." *American Economic Review* 107 (April), pp. 1313–34.

Figlio, David N., Cassandra M. D. Hart, and Krzysztof Karbownik. 2020. "Effects of Scaling Up Private School Choice Programs on Public School Students." NBER Working Paper 26758 (February).

Figlio, David N., Paola Giuliano, Riccardo Marchingiglio, Umut Ozek, and Paola Sapienza. 2021. "Diversity in Schools: Immigrants and the Educational Performance of U.S. Born Students." NBER working paper 28596 (March).

Finkel, Eli J., Paul W. Eastwick, Benjamin R. Karney, Harry T. Reis, and Susan Sprecher. 2012. "Online Dating: A Critical Analysis from the Perspective of Psychological Science." *Psychological Science in the Public Interest* 13 (January), pp. 3–66.

Fishman, Charles. 2020. "The System That Actually Worked." *The Atlantic* (May 6).

Flaaen, Aaron, Ali Hortacsu, and Felix Tintelnot. 2020. "The Production Relocation, and Price Effects of US Trade Policy: The Case of Washing Machines." *American Economic Review* 110 (July), pp. 2103–27.

Flanders, Will, and Collin Roth. 2017. "Land of the Free? 50 State Study on How Professional Licensing Laws Lead to Fewer Jobs." *Wisconsin Institute for Law & Liberty* (October). www.will-law.org/wp-content/uploads/2017/10/final.pdf.

Flint, Anthony. 2015. "10 Years Later, Did the Big Dig Deliver?" *Boston Globe* (December 29).

Fobosi, Siyabulela. 2020. "South Africa's Minibus Taxi Industry has been Marginalised for Too Long. This Must Change." *The Conversation* (July 14). https: //theconversation.com/profiles/siyabulela-christopher-fobosi-1131937/articles.

Foldvary, Fred E., and Daniel B. Klein. 2003. *The Half-Life of Policy Rationales: How New Technology Affects Old Policy Issues.* New York University Press.

Fone, Zachary S., Joseph J. Sabia, and Resul Cesur. 2019. "Do Minimum Wage Increases Reduce Crime?" NBER Working Paper 25647 (March).

Fowler, Anthony, Haritz Garro, and Jorg L. Spenkuch. 2020. "Quid Pro Quo? Corporate Returns to Campaign Contributions." *Journal of Politics* 82 (July), pp. 844–58.

Fowler, Geoffrey A. 2020. "My Car Was in a Hit-and-Run. Then I Learned It Recorded the Whole Thing." *Washington Post* (February 27).

Fowlie, Meredith, Michael Greenstone, and Catherine Wolfram. 2018. "Do Energy Efficiency Investments Deliver? Evidence from the Weatherization Assistance Program." *Quarterly Journal of Economics* 133 (August), pp. 1597–644.

Fox, Justin. 2017. "Maine Is Drowning in Lobsters." *Wall Street Journal* (May 18).

Frakes, Michael D., Jonathan Gruber, and Timothy Justicz. 2020. "Public and Private Options in Practice: The Military Health System," NBER Working Paper No. 28256 (December).

Francesconi, Marco, and James J. Heckman. 2016. "Child Development and Parental Investment: An Introduction." *Economic Journal* 126 (October), pp. F1–F27.

Frankel, Todd C. 2019. "Senate Report Faults Safety Commission for Failures Related to Dangerous Baby Products, Elevators." *Washington Post* (December 18).

Friedman, Milton. 1962. *Capitalism and Freedom*. University of Chicago Press.

———. 1970. "The Social Responsibility of Business Is to Increase Its Profits." *New York Times Magazine*. (September 13).

Friedman, Uri. 2014. "Bill Gates: 'The Idea That Innovation Is Slowing Down Is . . . Stupid,'" *The Atlantic* (March 12).

Fretwell, Holly Lippke. 2009. *Who Is Minding the Federal Estate?* Lanham, Maryland: Rowman and Littlefield.

Fretwell, Holly, and Shawn Regan. 2015. "Divided Lands: State vs. Federal Management in the West." PERC Public Lands Report (March).

Frakes, Michael D., and Melissa F. Wasserman. 2017. "Is the Time Allocated to Review Patent Applications Inducing Examiners to Grant Invalid Patents? Evidence from Microlevel Application Data." *Review of Economics and Statistics* 99 (July), pp. 550–63.

Freedman, David H. 2016. "The War on Stupid People." *The Atlantic* (July/August).

Ganong, Peter, and Daniel W. Shoag. 2017. "Why Has Regional Income Convergence in the U.S. Declined?" *Journal of Urban Economics* 102 (November), pp. 76–90.

Garcia, Jorge Luis, James J. Heckman, Duncan Ermini Leaf, and Maria Jose Prados. 2020. "Quantifying the Life-Cycle Benefits of an Influential Early-Childhood Program." *Journal of Political Economy* 128 (July), pp. 2502–41.

Gelber, Alexander, Timothy J. Moore, and Alexander Strand. 2017. "The Effect of Disability Insurance Payments on Beneficiaries' Earnings." *American Economic Journal: Economic Policy* 9 (August), pp. 229–61.

Gelles, David. 2018. "Businesses Look at Washington and Say, 'Never Mind, We'll Do It.'" *New York Times* (February 1).

Gelles, David, Hiroko Tabuchi, and Matthew Dolan. 2015. "Complex Car Software Becomes the Weak Spot under the Hood." *New York Times* (September 26).

General Accountability Office. 2016. *Federal Workforce: Distribution of Performance Ratings across the Federal Government, 2013*. GAO-16-520R (May).

———. 2017. *Actions Needed to Systematically Evaluate Cost and Effectiveness across Security Countermeasures*. GAO-17-794 (September).

Gillingham, Kenneth, James Bushnell, Meredith Fowlie, Michael Greenstone, Alan Krupnick, Charles Kolstad, Adele Morris, Richard Schmalensee, and James Stock. 2016. "Reforming the U.S. Coal Leasing Program." *Science* 354 (December 2).

Glaeser, Edward L. 2011. *Triumph of the City: How Our Greatest Invention Makes Us Richer, Smarter, Greener, Healthier, and Happier*. New York: Penguin Press.

————. 2017a. "Reforming Land Use Regulations," Brookings Institution (April 24). www.brookings.edu/research/reforming-land-use-regulations/.

————. 2017b. "The War on Work—and How to End It," *City Journal*. Special Issue: The Shape of Work to Come. www.city-journal.org/html/war-work-and-how-end-it-15250.html.

————. 2019. "How to Talk to Millennials about Capitalism." *City Journal* (Spring).

Glaeser, Edward L., Jed Kolko, and Albert Saiz. 2001. "Consumer City." *Journal of Economic Geography* 1 (January), pp. 27–50.

Glaeser, Edward L., and Erzo F. P. Luttmer. 2003. "The Misallocation of Housing under Rent Control." *American Economic Review* 93 (September), pp. 1027–46.

Glaeser, Edward L., and James M. Poterba. 2021. "Introduction to Economic Analysis and Infrastructure Investment." In *Economic Analysis and Infrastructure Investment*, edited by Edward L. Glaeser and James M. Poterba. University of Chicago Press.

Glaeser, Edward L., and Bryce A. Ward. 2009. "The Causes and Consequences of Land Use Regulation: Evidence from Greater Boston." *Journal of Urban Economics* 65 (May), pp. 265–78.

Glantz, Aaron. 2020. "Bailout Money Bypasses Hard-Hit New York, California for North Dakota, Nebraska." Reveal (April 23). https://www.revealnews.org/article/bailout-money-bypasses-hard-hit-new-york-california-for-north-dakota-nebraska/.

Glickman, Aaron, and Janet Weiner. 2019. "Why Deaths Continue to Rise in the Opioid Epidemic." *CHERISH* (January 22). https://cherishresearch.org/2019/01/why-deaths-continue-to-rise-in-the-opioid-epidemic/.

Gold, Russell. 2017. "Investors Are Building Their Own Green-Power Lines." *Wall Street Journal* (April 6).

Goldberg, Pinelopi Koujianou, and Giovanni Maggi. 1999. "Protection for Sale: An Empirical Investigation." *American Economic Review* 89 (December), pp. 1135–55.

Gonzalez, Tanja Artiga, Markus Schmid, and David Yermack. 2019. "Does Price Fixing Benefit Corporate Managers?" *Management Science* 65 (October), pp. 4813–40.

Goodman, John C. 2018. "Can the Market Really Work in Health Care?" *Forbes* (May 22).

Goodman, Joshua, Julia Melkers, and Amanda Pallais. 2017. "Can Online Delivery Increase Access to Education?" NBER Working Paper 22754 (September).

Goolsbee, Austan, and Peter J. Klenow. 2006. "Valuing Consumer Products by the Time Spent Using Them: An Application to the Internet." *American Economic Review Papers and Proceedings* 96 (May), pp. 108–13.

Gopnik, Adam. 2018. "The Great Crime Decline: Drawing the Right Lessons from the Fall in Urban Violence." *New Yorker* (February 12).

Gorback, Caitlin. 2020. "Ridesharing and the Redistribution of Economic Activity."

Gordon, Robert J. 2016. *The Rise and Fall of American Economic Growth: The U.S. Standard of Living Since the Civil War*. Princeton University Press.

Gowen, Annie, Juliet Eilperin, Ben Guarino, and Andrew Ba Tran. 2020. "Science Ranks Grow Thin in Trump Administration." *Washington Post* (January 23).

Gramm, Phil, and John F. Early. 2018. "Government Can't Rescue the Poor." *Wall Street Journal* (October 10).

Greene, Jay, and Aaron Gregg. 2019. "Amazon Will Challenge Pentagon's Award of $10 Billion JEDI Contract to Microsoft." *Washington Post* (November 14).

Greenspan, Alan, and Adrian Wooldridge. 2018. *Capitalism in America: A History.* New York: Penguin Press.

Greenstein, Shane, and Ryan C. McDevitt. 2011. "The Broadband Bonus: Estimating Broadband Internet's Economic Value." *Telecommunications Policy* 35 (August), pp. 617–32.

Greenstone, Michael, John A. List, and Chad Syverson, 2012. "The Effects of Environmental Regulation on the Competitiveness of US Manufacturing." MIT Center for Energy and Environmental Policy Research Working Paper 2012-013 (September).

Grimm, Curtis, and Clifford Winston. 2000. "Competition in the Deregulated Railroad Industry: Sources, Effects, and Policy Issues." In *Deregulation of Network Industries: What's Next,* edited by Sam Peltzman and Clifford Winston. Brookings Institution, pp. 41–71.

Hackman, Michelle. 2018. "Vocational Training Is Back as Firms Pair with High Schools to Groom Workers." *Wall Street Journal* (August 13).

Hahn, Robert, and Robert Metcalfe. 2017. "The Ridesharing Revolution: Economic Survey and Synthesis." In *More Equal By Design: Economic Design Responses to Inequality,* edited by Scott Duke Kominers and Alex Teytelboym. Oxford University Press.

Hakobyan, Shushanik, and John McLaren. 2016. "Looking for Local Labor Market Effects of NAFTA." *Review of Economics and Statistics* 98 (October), pp. 728–41.

Han, Suyoun, and Morris M. Kleiner. 2016. "Analyzing the Influence of Occupational Licensing Duration on Labor Market Outcomes." NBER Working Paper 22810 (November).

Hansen, Benjamin, Joseph J. Sabia, and Daniel I. Rees. 2015. "Cigarette Taxes and Youth Smoking: Updated Estimates Using YRBS Data." NBER Working Paper 21311.

Hanushek, Eric A., Paul E. Peterson, Laura M. Talpey, and Ludger Woessmann. 2019. "The Achievement Gap Fails to Close." *Education Next* 19 (Summer), pp. 1–9.

Hardman, Joshua. 2018. "Don't Choose a Degree in Four Years When You Can Be Certified in One." *E21* (April 30).

Harris, Matthew C., Jineong Park, Donald J. Bruce, and Matthew N. Murray. 2017. "Peacekeeping Force: Effects of Providing Tactical Equipment to Local Police Enforcement." *American Economic Journal: Economic Policy* 9 (August), pp. 291–313.

Hart, Oliver. 2020. "Shareholders Don't Always Want to Maximize Shareholder Value." *ProMarket* (September 14).

Hartley, Peter R., Kenneth B. Medlock III, and Olivera Jankovska. 2017. "Electricity Reform and Retail Pricing in Texas." Center for Energy Studies, Rice University (June).

Harwell, Drew. 2020. "Ring and Nest Helped Normalize American Surveillance and Turned Us into a National of Voyeurs." *New York Times* (February 18).

Hausman, Catherine, and Ryan Kellogg. 2015. "Welfare and Distributional Implications of Shale Gas." *Brookings Papers on Economic Activity* (Spring), pp. 71–139.

Hausman, Jerry A. 1997. "Valuing the Effect of Regulation on New Services in Telecommunications." *Brookings Papers on Economic Activity: Microeconomics*, pp. 1–38.

Hazlett, Thomas W. 2008. "Optimal Abolition of FCC Spectrum Allocation." *Journal of Economic Perspectives* 22 (Winter), pp. 103–28.

Heckman, James J. 2006. "Skill Formation and the Economics of Investing in Disadvantaged Children." *Science* 312 (June 30), pp. 1900–02.

Heckman, James J., and Ganesh Karapakula. 2019. "The Perry Preschoolers at Late Midlife: A Study in Design-Specific Inference." Working Paper 2019-034. Human Capital and Economic Opportunity Global Working Group.

Heckman, James J., and Gonzalo Schwartz. 2018. "Inaccurate Reporting on Social Inequality Makes Matters Worse." *The Hill* (October 8).

Heckman, James J., Jeffrey A. Smith, and Christopher Taber. 1996. "What Do Bureaucrats Do? The Effect of Performance Standards and Bureaucratic Preferences on Acceptance into the JTPA Program." In *Reinventing Government and the Problem of Bureaucracy* 7, edited by Gary Libecap. Greenwich, Connecticut: JAI Press, pp. 191–217.

Heller, Sara B., Anuj K. Shah, Jonathan Guryan, Jens Ludwig, Sendhil Mullainathan, and Harold A. Pollack. 2017. "Thinking, Fast and Slow? Some Field Experiments to Reduce Crime and Dropout in Chicago." *Quarterly Journal of Economics* 132 (February), pp. 1–54.

Hendren, Nathaniel, and Ben Sprung-Keyser. 2019. "A Unified Welfare Analysis of Government Policies." NBER Working Paper 26144 (August).

Henley, Jon. 2020. "We Should Have Done More, Admits Architect of Sweden's Covid-19 Strategy." *The Guardian* (June 3).

Herkenhoff, Kyle F., Lee E. Ohanian, and Edward C. Prescott. 2018. "Tarnishing the Golden and Empire States: Land-Use Restrictions and the U.S. Economic Slowdown." *Journal of Monetary Economics* 91 (January), pp. 89–109.

Hertel-Fernandez, Alexander, Matto Mildenberger, and Leah Stokes. 2018. "Legislative Staff and Representation in Congress." *American Political Science Review* 113 (1), pp. 1–18.

Hess, Frederick M. 2010. "Does School Choice 'Work?'" *National Affairs* (Fall), pp. 35–53.

Hilger, Nathaniel. 2016. "Upward Mobility and Discrimination: The Case of Asian Americans." NBER Working Paper 22748 (October).

Ho, Daniel E., Zoe C. Ashwood, and Cassandra Handan-Nader. 2019. "New Evidence on Information Disclosure through Restaurant Hygiene Grading." *American Economic Journal: Economic Policy* 11 (November), pp. 404–28.

Hoagland, Alex, and Trevor Woolley. 2018. "It's No Accident: Evaluating the Effectiveness of Vehicle Safety Inspections." *Contemporary Economic Policy* 36 (4), pp. 607–28.

Hoekstra, Mark, Steven L. Puller, and Jeremy West. 2017. "Cash for Corollas: When Stimulus Reduces Spending." *American Economic Journal: Applied Economics* 9 (July), pp. 1–35.

Holladay, J. Scott, A. J. Glusman, and Steven Soloway. 2011. "Internet Benefits: Consumer Surplus and Net Neutrality." Policy Brief 10. Institute for Policy Integrity, New York University School of Law (October).

Holland, Stephen P., Erin T. Mansur, Nicholas Z. Muller, and Andrew J. Yates. 2020. "Decompositions and Policy Consequences of an Extraordinary Decline in Air Pollution from Electricity Generation." *American Economic Journal: Economic Policy* 12 (November), pp. 244–74.

Houde, Sebastien, and Joseph E. Aldy. 2017. "Consumers' Response to State Energy Efficient Appliance Rebate Programs." *American Economic Journal: Economic Policy* 9 (November), pp. 227–55.

Howard, Philip. (2019). "Bureaucracy vs. Democracy: Examining the Bureaucratic Causes of Public Failure, Economic Waste, and Voter Alienation." *The American Interest* (January 31), www.the-american-interest.com/2019/01/31/bureaucracy-vs-democracy.

Howell, Sabrina T. 2017. "Financing Innovation: Evidence from R&D Grants." *American Economic Review* 107 (April), pp. 1136–64.

Hsiang, Solomon, and others. 2020. "The Effect of Large-Scale Anti-Contagion Policies on the COVID-19 Pandemic." *Nature* (June 8).

Hsieh, Chang-Tai, and Enrico Moretti. 2017. "Housing Constraints and Spatial Misallocation." NBER Working Paper 21154.

Hu, Winnie. 2017. "Taxi Medallions, Once a Safe Investment, Now Drag Owners into Debt." *New York Times* (September 10).

Hudgins, Edward. 2019. "How Extending the AIDS Drug Access Model to Other Diseases Would Save Lives." Heartland Institute Policy Brief (February).

Hufbauer, Gary Clyde, and Zhiyao Lu. 2017. "The Payoff to America from Globalization: A Fresh Look with a Focus on Costs to Workers." Policy Brief 17-16. Peterson Institute for International Economics (May).

Hughes, Charles. 2017. "Menu Labeling Requirements Would Raise Food Costs." *E21 Commentary* (September 12).

Hwang, Hyeonjun, Clifford Winston, and Jia Yan. 2020. "Measuring the Benefits of Ridesharing Services to Urban Travelers: The Case of the San Francisco Bay Area." Working Paper. Brookings Institution.

Hyman, Benjamin G. 2018. "Can Displaced Labor Be Retrained? Evidence from Quasi-Random Assignment to Trade Adjustment Assistance." University of Chicago.

Ip, Greg. 2016. "A Cure for Swelling Drug Prices: Competition." *Wall Street Journal* (August 31).

———. 2020. "Economics vs. Epidemiology: Quantifying the Trade-Off." *Wall Street Journal* (April 15).

Irwin, Neil. 2016. "How Did Walmart Get Cleaner Stores and Higher Sales? It Paid Its People More." *New York Times* (October 15).

Isen, Adam, Maya Rossin-Slater, and W. Reed Walker. 2017. "Every Breath You Take—Every Dollar You'll Make: The Long-Term Consequences of the Clean Air Act of 1970." *Journal of Political Economy* 125 (June), pp. 848–902.

Ivory, Danielle. 2015. "Federal Auditor Finds Broad Failures at NHTSA." *New York Times* (June), p. 19.

Jacobsen, Grant D. 2019. "Who Wins in an Energy Boom? Evidence from Wage Rates and Housing." *Economic Inquiry* 5 (January), pp. 9–32.

Jaeger, David A., Theodore J. Joyce, and Robert Kaestner. (2020). "A Cautionary Tale of Evaluating Identifying Assumptions: Did Reality TV Really Cause a Decline in Teenage Childbearing?" *Journal of Business and Economic Statistics* 38 (2), pp. 317–26.

James, Kevin. 2016. "Private Markets for Student Financing." *National Affairs* (Summer), pp. 21–34.

Jamison, Peter. 2017. "D.C. Has Essentially Lost Track of the Real Estate It Owns, New Report Finds." *Washington Post* (August 17).

Jardim, Ekaterina, Mark C. Long, Robert Plotnick, Emma van Inwegen, Jacob Vigdor, and Hilary Wething. 2018. "Minimum Wage Increases and Individual Employment Trajectories." NBER Working Paper 25182 (October).

Jayaratne, Jith, and Philip E. Strahan. 1996. "The Finance-Growth Nexus: Evidence from Bank Branch Deregulation." *Quarterly Journal of Economics* 111 (May), pp. 639–70.

Jin, Ginger, and Phillip Leslie. 2003. "Effect of Information on Product Quality: Evidence from Restaurant Hygiene Grade Cards." *Quarterly Journal of Economics* 118 (May), pp. 409–51.

———. 2019. "New Evidence on Information Disclosure through Restaurant Hygiene Grading: Reply." *American Economic Journal: Economic Policy* 11 (November), pp. 429–43.

Jones, Benjamin F., and Lawrence H. Summers. 2020. "A Calculation of the Social Returns to Innovation." NBER Working Paper 27863 (September).

Johnson, Janna E., and Morris M. Kleiner. 2020. "Is Occupational Licensing a Barrier to Interstate Migration?" *American Economic Journal: Economic Policy* 12 (August,) pp. 347–73.

Johnson, Matthew S. 2020. "Regulation by Shaming: Deterrence Effects of Publicizing Violations of Workplace Safety and Health Laws." *American Economic Review* 110 (June), pp. 1866–904.

Kahneman, Daniel, and Alan B. Krueger. 2006. "Developments in the Measurement of Subjective Well-Being." *Journal of Economic Perspectives* 20 (Winter), pp. 3–24.

Kalt, Joseph P., and Mark A. Zupan. 1990. "The Apparent Ideological Behavior of Legislators: Testing for Principal-Agent Slack in Political Institutions." *Journal of Law and Economics* 33 (April), pp. 103–31.

Kaplan, Sheila. 2017. "Inquiry Criticizes F.D.A. on Pace of Food Recalls." *New York Times* (December 28).

Karpoff, Jonathan M. 2001. "Public versus Private Initiative in Arctic Exploration: The Effects of Incentives and Organizational Structure." *Journal of Political Economy* 109 (February), pp. 38–78.

Kashian, Russ, Jeff Pagel, and Ike Brannon. 2017. "The Jones Act in Perspective: A Survey of Costs and Effects of the 1920 Merchant Marine Act." Grassroot Institute of Hawaii. www.grassrootinstitute.org/2017/04/the-jones-act-in-perspective/.

Kearney, Melissa S., and Phillip B. Levine. 2015. "Media Influences on Social Outcomes: The Impact of MTV's *16 and Pregnant* on Teen Childbearing." *American Economic Review* 105 (December), pp. 3597–632.

———. 2016. "Does Reality TV Induce Real Effects? A Response to Jaeger, Joyce, and Kaestner (2016)," IZA Discussion Paper 10318 (October).

———. 2018. "A Comment on Jaeger, Joyce, and Kaestner (2018) *Did Reality TV Really Cause a Decline in Teenage Childbearing?*" NBER, www.nber.org/data-appendix/w19795/KL_Response_to_JJK-JBES-July_2018_FINAL.pdf.

———. 2019. "Early Childhood Education by Television: Lessons from *Sesame Street.*" *American Economic Journal: Applied Economics* 11 (January), pp. 318–50.

Keiser, David A., and Joseph S. Shapiro. 2019. "US Water Pollution Regulation Over the Past Half Century: Burning Waters to Crystal Springs?" *American Economic Review* 33 (Fall), pp. 51–75.

Kent, Sarah, and Bradley Olson. 2017. "Exxon, Shell, BP Join Forces to Cut Emissions from Natural Gas." *Wall Street Journal* (November 22).

Kerr, Sari Pekkala, William Kerr, Caglar Ozden, and Christopher Parsons. 2016. "Global Talent Flows." *Journal of Economic Perspectives* 30 (Fall), pp. 83–106.

Kerr, William R., William F. Lincoln, and Prachi Mishra. 2014. "The Dynamics of Firm Lobbying." *American Economic Journal: Economic Policy* 6 (November) pp. 343–79.

Khullar, Dhruv. 2017. "The Unhealthy Politics of Pork: How It Increases Your Medical Costs." *New York Times* (October 25).

Klein, Matthew. 2017. "U.S. Cities Must Unlock the Value of the Land They Sit On." *Financial Times* (July 21).

Klein, Patrick, and Christopher Walters. 2016. "Evaluating Public Programs with Close Substitutes: The Case of Head Start." *Quarterly Journal of Economics* 131 (November), pp. 1795–848.

Klein, Tobias J., Christian Lambertz, and Konrad O. Stahl. 2016. "Market Transparency, Adverse Selection, and Moral Hazard." *Journal of Political Economy* 124 (December), pp. 1677–713.

Kleiner, Morris, and Evgeny S. Vorotnikov. 2018. *At What Cost? State and National Estimates of the Cost of Occupational Licensing.* Institute for Justice. https://ij.org/wp-content/uploads/2018/11/Licensure_Report_WEB.pdf.

Kleit, Andrew N. 2016. "Is It Time to Deregulate All Electric Utilities?" *Wall Street Journal* (November 13).

Kleven, Hendrik. 2019. "The EITC and the Extensive Margin: A Reappraisal." NBER Working Paper 26405 (October).

Knott, Anne Marie. 2017. "Is R&D Getting Harder, or Are Companies Just Getting Worse at It?" *Harvard Business Review* (March 21).

Krause, Sarah. 2019. "The FCC Has Fined Robocallers $208 Million. It's Collected $6,790." *Washington Post* (March 28).

Kremer, Michael. 2001. "Creating Markets for New Vaccines Part II: Design Issues." In *Innovation Policy and the Economy*, edited by Adam Jaffe, Josh Lerner, and Scott Stern. MIT Press.

Krolikowski, Marcin W., and Kevin Okoeguale. 2018. "Economic Shocks, Competition and Merger Activity." *Journal of Business Accounting and Finance Perspectives* 1, pp. 1–20.

Kroszner, Randall S., and Philip E. Strahan. 2014. "Regulation and Deregulation of the U.S. Banking Industry: Causes, Consequences, and Implications for the Future." In *Economic Regulation and Its Reform: What Have We Learned?* edited by Nancy Rose. University of Chicago Press.

Krueger, Alan B. 2015. "The Minimum Wage: How Much Is Too Much?" *New York Times* (October 9).

Krupnick, Matt. 2015. "Steep Fees and First Class Prices, But Private Jets Are Available to More." *New York Times* (February 16).

Kurtulus, Fidan Ana. 2016. "The Impact of Affirmative Action on the Employment of Minorities and Women: A Longitudinal Analysis Using Three Decades of EEO-1 Filings." *Journal of Policy Analysis and Management* 35 (Winter), pp. 34–66.

Lai, K. K. Rebecca, Troy Griggs, Max Fisher, and Audrey Carlsen. 2017. "Is America's Military Big Enough?" *New York Times* (March 22).

LaLonde, Robert J. 1995. "The Promise of Public Sector-Sponsored Training Programs." *Journal of Economic Perspectives* 9 (Spring), pp. 149–68.

Lane, Charles. 2017. "How Liberals Undermine the Food Stamp Program." *Washington Post* (February 15).

Langer, Ashley, Vikram Maheshri, and Clifford Winston. 2017. "From Gallons to Miles: A Disaggregate Analysis of Automobile Travel and Externality Taxes." *Journal of Public Economics* 152 (August), pp. 34–46.

Leard, Benjamin, and Jianwei Xing. 2020. "What Does Ridesharing Replace?" Working Paper 20-03. Resources for the Future (February).

Leeth, John, and Nathan Hale. 2013. "Evaluating OSHA's Effectiveness and Suggestions for Reform." Mercatus Center, George Mason University (April).

Leibbrandt, Andreas, and John A. List. 2018. "Do Equal Employment Opportunity Statements Backfire? Evidence from a Natural Field Experiment on Job-Entry Decisions." NBER Working Paper 25035 (September).

Leonhardt, David. 2016. "Schools That Work." *New York Times* (November 4).

———. 2018. "The Democrats Are the Party of Fiscal Responsibility." *New York Times* (April 15).

———. 2019. "A C.E.O. Who's Scared for America." *New York Times* (March 31).

Lerner, Josh. 2009. *Boulevard of Broken Dreams: Why Public Efforts to Boost Entrepreneurship and Venture Capital Have Failed—and What to Do About It.* Princeton University Press.

———. 2020. "Government Incentives for Entrepreneurship." NBER Working Paper 26884.

Levinson, Arik. 2016. "How Much Energy Do Building Energy Codes Save? Evidence from California Houses." *American Economic Review* 106 (October), pp. 2867–94.

Levin, Alan. 2016a. "Thanks to This Man, Airplanes Don't Crash into Mountains Anymore." *Wall Street Journal* (August 10).

———. 2016b. "iPad Apps Help Cut Fatal Crashes of Private Planes to New Lows." *Wall Street Journal* (August 11).

Levine, Michael E. 1989. "Comment." *Brookings Papers on Economic Activity: Microeconomics*, pp. 42–48.

Levitt, Steven D. 1994. "Using Repeat Challengers to Estimate the Effect of Campaign Spending on Election Outcomes in the U.S. House." *Journal of Political Economy* 102 (August), pp. 777–98.

Levitz, Jennifer. 2018. "Why Businesses Are Pushing for Better Child Care in America." *Wall Street Journal* (February 10).

Lewis, Michael. 2018. *The Fifth Risk*, New York: W. W. Norton.

Libecap, Gary D. 2018. "Federal Lands, Opportunity Costs, and Bureaucratic Management." NBER Working Paper 24705 (June).

Lipton, Eric. 2015. "Trucking and Rail Industries Turn State Troopers into Unwitting Lobbyists." *New York Times* (April 1).

Lipton, Eric, Abby Goodnough, Michael D. Shear, Megan Twohey, Apoorva Mandavilli, and Sheri Fink. 2020. "Built for This, CDC Shows Flaws in Crisis." *New York Times* (June 3).

Liscow, Zachary. 2018. "Is Efficiency Biased?" *University of Chicago Law Review* 85, pp. 1649–718.

Litan, Robert E. 2014. *Trillion Dollar Economists: How Economists and Their Ideas Have Transformed Business*. Hoboken, New Jersey: John Wiley and Sons.

———. 2018. "A Scalpel, Not an Axe: Updating Antitrust and Data Laws to Spur Competition and Innovation." Progressive Policy Institute, Washington, DC (September).

Litan, Robert E., and Alice M. Rivlin. 2001. *Beyond the Dot.coms*, Brookings Institution Press.

Litan, Robert E. and Peter Wallison. 2007. *Competitive Equity: A Better Way to Organize Mutual Funds*. Washington, DC: American Enterprise Institute Press.

Liu, Meng, Erik Brynjolfsson, and Jason Dowlatabadi. 2021 (forthcoming). "Do Digital Platforms Reduce Moral Hazard? The Case of Uber and Taxis." *Management Science*.

Loftus, Peter. 2019. "Fast-Track Drug Approval, Designed for Emergencies, Is Now Routine." *Wall Street Journal* (July 5).

Lohr, Steve. 2018. "This Start-Up Says It Wants to Fight Poverty. A Food Stamp Giant Is Blocking It." *New York Times* (April 23).

———. 2019. "Income Before: $18,000. After: $85,000. Does Tiny Nonprofit Hold a Key to the Middle Class?" *New York Times* (March 15).

Loutskina, Elena, and Philip E. Strahan. 2015. "Financial Integration, Housing, and Economic Volatility." *Journal of Financial Economics* 115 (January), pp. 25–41.

Luce, Edward. 2020. "Inside Trump's Coronavirus Meltdown." *Financial Times* (May 14).

Lund, Susan, James Manyika, Scott Nyquist, Lenny Mendonca, and Sreenivas Ramaswamy. 2013. *Game Changers: Five Opportunities for US Growth and Renewal*. McKinsey Global Institute (July).

Lux, Marshall, and Robert Greene. 2016. "Out of Reach: Regressive Trends in Credit Card Access." Harvard Kennedy School M-RCBG Associate Working Paper Series 54 (April).

MacKay, Alexander, and Ignacia Mercadal. 2021. "Deregulation, Market Power and

Prices: Evidence from the Electricity Sector." Harvard Business School working paper (February).

MaCurdy, Thomas. 2015. "How Effective Is the Minimum Wage at Supporting the Poor?" *Journal of Political Economy* 123 (April), pp. 497–545.

Magni-Berton, Raul, and Diego Rios. 2019. "Why do Academics Oppose the Market? A Test of Nozick's Hypothesis." *Current Sociology* 67 (6), pp. 856–78.

Mak, Tim. 2020. "Whistleblower: TSA Failed to Protect Staff, Endangered Passengers During Pandemic." *NPR* (June 19).

Makridis, Christos Andreas. 2018. "Why Is There a Public/Private Pay Gap?" MIT Sloan School of Management Working Paper (July).

Maloney, William F., and Felipe Valencia Caicedo. 2017. "Engineering Growth: Innovative Capacity and Development in the Americas." Center for Economic Studies and Ifo Institute Working Paper 6339 (February).

Maltais, Kirk. 2019. "Struggling Farmers See Bright Spot in Solar." *Wall Street Journal* (September 23).

Mankiw, N. Gregory. 2020. "C.E.O.s Are Qualified to Make Profits, Not Lead Society." *New York Times* (July 24).

Manzi, Jim. 2012. *Uncontrolled: The Surprising Payoff of Trial and Error for Business, Politics, and Society.* New York: Basic Books.

Markey-Towler, Brendan. 2018. "Monopolies Can't Survive Forever." University of Queensland Working Paper (March).

Markind, Daniel. 2020. "Will the First Test Case for Renewable Energy Come from a Small Hawaiian Island?" *Forbes* (January 30).

Masur, Jonathan S., and Eric A. Posner. 2016. "Unquantified Benefits and the Problem of Regulation under Uncertainty." *Cornell Law Review* 102, pp. 87–137.

Mathur, Aparna. 2015. "TANF Is Failing the Non-Working Poor." *Forbes* (September 14).

Mayda, Anna Marie, Francesc Ortega, Giovanni Peri, Kevin Shih, and Chad Sparber. 2017. "The Effect of the H-1B Quota on Employment and Selection of Foreign-Born Labor," NBER Working Paper 23902 (October).

McArdle, Megan. 2014. *The Up Side of Down: Why Failing Well Is the Key to Success.* New York: Penguin Books.

McCoy, Shawn. 2015. "Postmaster Warns of Myopia, New Report Shows Growing Troubles for Postal Service." *InsideSources* (January 9).

McDonnell, Simon, Josiah Madar, and Vicki Been. 2011. "Minimum Parking Requirements and Housing Affordability in New York City." *Housing Policy Debate* 21, issue 1, pp. 45–68.

McDougall, Glen, and Alasdair Roberts. 2008. "Commercializing Air Traffic Control: Have the Reforms Worked?" *Canadian Public Administration* 51 (April), pp. 45–69.

McLaughlin, Michael, and Mark R. Rank. 2018. "Estimating the Economic Cost of Poverty in the United States." *Social Work Research* 42, no. 2 (June), pp. 73–83.

Melitz, Marc J. 2003. "The Impact of Trade on Aggregate Industry Productivity and Intra-Industry Reallocations." *Econometrica* 71 (November), pp. 1695–725.

Metcalf, Gilbert E. 2019. "On the Economics of a Carbon Tax for the United States." *Brookings Papers on Economic Activity* (Spring), pp. 405–84.

Meyer, Bruce D., and Nikolas Mittag. 2019. "Using Linked Survey and Administrative Data to Better Measure Income: Implications for Poverty, Program Effectiveness, and Holes in the Safety Net." *American Economic Journal: Applied Economics* 11 (April), pp. 176–204.

Meyer, Bruce D., and James X. Sullivan. 2013. "Winning the War: Poverty from the Great Society to the Great Recession." *Brookings Papers on Economic Activity* 45 (Fall), pp. 133–200.

———. 2016. "Annual Report on U.S. Consumption Poverty: 2016." https://leo.nd .edu/assets/249750/meyer_sullivan_cpr_2016_1_.pdf.

Meyer, Bruce D., Derek Wu, Victoria R. Mooers, and Carla Medalia. 2019. "The Use and Misuse of Income Data and Extreme Poverty in the United States." NBER Working Paper 25907 May.

Meyer, Gregory. 2020. "US Offshore Wind Power Spending Has Oil In Its Sights." *Financial Times* (July 8).

Meyer, Jared. 2016. "How to Recharge the Hotel Industry." *E21* (June 13).

Miller, Ben. 2018. "The Student Debt Problem Is Worse Than We Imagined." *Wall Street Journal* (August 25).

Miller, Claire Cain. 2018. "Lowe's Joins Other Big Employers in Offering Paid Parental Leave." *New York Times* (February 1).

Miller, Conrad. 2017. "The Persistent Effect of Temporary Affirmative Action." *American Economic Journal: Applied Economics* 9 (July), pp. 152–90.

Mills, Anna, and Edward J. Timmons. 2018. "Bringing the Effects of Occupational Licensing into Focus: Optician Licensing in the United States." *Eastern Economic Journal* 44 (January), pp. 69–83.

Milyo, Jeffrey. 1998. "The Electoral Effects of Campaign Spending in House Elections: A Natural Experiment Approach." Department of Economic Discussion Paper 98-06. Tufts University.

Moffitt, Robert A. 2012. "Economics and the Earned Income Tax Credit." In *Better Living Through Economics*, edited by John J. Siegfried. Harvard University Press.

———. 2014. "The Social Safety Net in the Great Recession." *Milken Institute Review* (4th quarter), pp. 55–65.

———. 2015. "The Deserving Poor, the Family, and the U.S. Welfare System." *Demography* 52 (June), pp. 729–49.

Moore, Michael J., and W. Kip Viscusi. 1990. *Compensation Mechanisms for Job Risks: Wages, Workers' Compensation, and Product Liability.* Princeton University Press.

Moore, Travis. 2018. "Solving the Tech Deficit on Capitol Hill." Lawfare. www .lawfareblog.com/solving-tech-deficit-capitol-hill-call-applications.

Morath, Eric. 2020. "Coronavirus Relief often Pays Workers More Than Work." *Wall Street Journal* (April 28).

Morath, Eric, and Julie Jargon. 2016. "Across the U.S., Workers at the Bottom of the Ladder Get Pay Raises." *Wall Street Journal* (August 23).

Moretti, Enrico. 2017. "Fires Aren't the Only Threat to the California Dream." *New York Times* (November 3).

Morris, Loveday, and Missy Ryan. 2016. "After More Than $1.6 Billion in U.S. Aid, Iraq's Army Still Struggles." *Washington Post* (June 10).

Morrison, Steven, and Clifford Winston. 1999. "Regulatory Reform of U.S. Intercity Transportation." In *Essays in Transportation Economics and Policy: A Handbook in Honor of John R. Meyer*, edited by José A. Gómez-Ibáñez, William B. Tye, and Clifford Winston. Brookings Institution.

———. 2000. "The Remaining Role of Government Policy in Deregulated Airline Industry." In *Deregulation of Network Industries: What's Next*, edited by Sam Peltzman and Clifford Winston. Brookings Institution, pp. 1–40.

Morrison, Steven, Clifford Winston, and Tara Watson. 1999. "Fundamental Flaws of Social Regulation: The Case of Airplane Noise." *Journal of Law and Economics* 42 (October), pp. 723–44.

Mulligan, Casey B. 2012. *The Redistribution Recession: How Labor Market Distortions Contracted the Economy*. Oxford University Press.

Murphy, Kevin M., Andrei Shleifer, and Robert W. Vishny. 1991. "The Allocation of Talent: Implications for Growth." *Quarterly Journal of Economics* 106 (May), pp. 503–30.

Musgrave, Richard A. 1959. *The Theory of Public Finance: A Study in Public Economy*. New York: McGraw-Hill.

Nakashima, Ellen, and Aaron Gregg. 2018. "NSA's Top Talent Is Leaving because of Low Pay, Slumping Morale, and Unpopular Reorganization." *Washington Post* (January 2).

Neumark, David. 2018. "Experimental Research on Labor Market Discrimination." *Journal of Economic Literature* 56 (September), pp. 799–866.

Neumark, David, and Peter Shirley. 2021. "Myth or Measurement: What Does the New Minimum Wage Research Say about Minimum Wages and Job Loss in the United States?" NBER Working Paper 28388 (January).

Niquette, Mark. 2019. "Dalio Says Capitalism's Income Inequality Is National Emergency." *Bloomberg News* (April 7).

Nocera, Joe. 2018. "Thanks for Nothing, Supreme Court. You Left Patents a Mess." *Bloomberg* (April 25).

Noll, Roger G. 1989. "Comment." *Brookings Papers on Economic Activity: Microeconomics*, pp. 48–58.

Nordhaus, William D. 2004. "Schumpeterian Profits in the American Economy: Theory and Measurement." NBER Working Paper 10433 (April).

———. 2008. *A Question of Balance: Weighing the Options on Global Warming Policies*. Yale University Press.

———. 2019. "Climate Change: The Ultimate Challenge for Economics." *American Economic Review* 109 (June), pp. 1991–2014.

North, Douglas C. 1991. "Institutions." *Journal of Economic Perspectives* 5 (Winter), pp. 97–112.

Okun, Arthur M. 1975. *Equality and Efficiency, The Big Tradeoff*. Brookings Institution.

Olson, Elizabeth. 2016. "When Finding the Right Lawyer Seems Daunting, Crowdsource One." *New York Times* (December 28).

Oreskes, Naomi, and Erik M. Conway. 2018. "Fixing the Climate Requires More Than Technology." *New York Times* (October 16).

Ori, Sam. 2017. "It's Time to Let the Free Market Work for Water." *Wall Street Journal* (October 15).

Oster Jr., Clinton V. 2006. *Reforming the Federal Aviation Administration: Lessons from Canada and the United Kingdom*. IBM Center for the Business of Government. Washington, DC.

Ostrom, Elinor. 1990. *Governing the Commons: The Evolution of Institutions for Collective Action*. Cambridge University Press.

Otterman, Sharon. 2021. "N.Y.'s Vaccine Websites Weren't Working. He Built a New One for $50." *New York Times* (February 9).

Oum, Tae H., Jia Yan, and Chumyan Yu. 2008. "Ownership Forms Matter for Airport Efficiency: A Stochastic Frontier Investigation of Worldwide Airports." *Journal of Urban Economics* 64 (September), pp. 422–35.

Page, Sydney. 2020. "Extra Food Is Rotting on Farms While Americans Go Hungry. This Group Is Trying to Fix That." *Washington Post* (June 10).

Palmer, Brad. 2017. "Why Congress Just Killed a Rule Restricting Coal Companies from Dumping Waste in Streams." *Vox* (February 2).

Paris, Costas. 2018. "Energy Firms will Build U.S. Gateway for World's Biggest Tankers." *Wall Street Journal* (May 2).

Parolin, Zachary. 2018. "Race, Social Assistance, and the Risk of Child Poverty across the 50 United States." Herman Deleeck Centre for Social Policy, University of Antwerp, Working Paper 18.04 (January).

Pascrell Jr., Bill. 2019. "Why Is Congress So Dumb?" *Washington Post* (January 11).

Pei, Sen, Sasikiran Kandula, and Jeffrey Shaman. 2020. "Differential Effects of Intervention Timing on COVID-19 Spread in the United States." Department of Environmental Health Sciences, Mailman School of Public Health, Columbia University. www.medrxiv.org/content/10.1101/2020.05.15.20103655v1.full.pdf.

Peker, Emre. 2019. "Companies Go to New Depths for Ocean Plastic in Recycling Push." *Wall Street Journal* (November 4).

Peltzman, Sam. 1989. "The Economic Theory of Regulation after a Decade of Deregulation." *Brookings Papers on Economic Activity: Microeconomics*, pp. 1–41.

Peri, Giovanni. 2016. "Immigrants, Productivity, and Labor Markets." *Journal of Economic Perspectives* 30 (Fall), pp. 3–30.

Phillipon, Thomas. 2019. *The Great Reversal: How America Gave Up On Free Markets*. Cambridge, Massachusetts: Belknap Press.

Philipson, Tomas J., and Eric Sun. 2008. "Is the Food and Drug Administration Safe and Effective?" *Journal of Economic Perspectives* 22 (Winter), pp. 85–102.

Pike, Lili. 2020. "Why 15 States Suddenly Made Masks Mandatory." *Vox* (May 29).

Plumer, Brad, and Coral Davenport. 2019. "Science under Attack: How Trump Is Sidelining Researchers and Their Work." *New York Times* (December 28).

Poole Jr., Robert W., 2018. "Post-Mortem on 2017 US ATC Corporation Effort." *Air Traffic Control Reform News* 152 (March).

Porter, Eduardo. 2016. "Job Training Works. So Why Not Do More?" *New York Times* (July 6).

Posner, Eric, and Glen Weyl. 2014. "Thomas Piketty Is Wrong: America Will Never Look Like a Jane Austen Novel." *New Republic* (July 31).

———. 2018. "Sponsor an Immigrant Yourself." *Politico Magazine* (February 13).

Posner, Richard A. 2008. *How Judges Think*. Harvard University Press.

Prendergast, Canice. 2017. "How Food Banks Use Markets to Feed the Poor." *Journal of Economic Perspectives* 31 (Fall), pp. 145–62.

Quinn, Aine. 2019. "Sawdust Might Be One Answer to the World's Plastic Problem." *Bloomberg News* (July 22).

Ramnath, Shanthi P., and Patricia K. Tong. 2017. "The Persistent Reduction in Poverty from Filing a Tax Return." *American Economic Journal: Economic Policy* 9 (November), pp. 367–94.

Rauch, Jonathan. 1995. *Demosclerosis: The Silent Killer of American Government*. New York: Random House.

Rea, David, and Tony Burton. 2019. "New Evidence on the Heckman Curve." StatModeling. http://statmodeling.stat.columbia.edu/wp-content/uploads/2018/05/Heckman-curve-May-2018.pdf.

Reiley, Laura. 2019. "Trump's $16 Billion Farm Bailout will Make Rich Farmers Richer, Report Says." *Washington Post* (July 31).

Reimers, Imke, and Joel Waldfogel. 2021 (forthcoming). "Digitalization and Pre-Purchase Information: The Causal and Welfare Impacts of Reviews and Crowd Ratings." *American Economic Review*.

Rein, Lisa. 2015. "$80 Million Paid to Feds to Stay Home." *Washington Post* (December 3).

———. 2016a. "The Federal Workforce, Where Everyone's Performance Gets Rave Reviews." *Washington Post* (June 13).

———. 2016b. "Patent Lawsuits Swell and Watchdog Says the Government Is to Blame." *Washington Post* (July 20).

Rein, Lisa, and Andrew Ba Tran. 2017. "How the Trump Era Is Changing the Federal Bureaucracy." *Washington Post* (December 30).

Reinhard, Beth, and Emma Brown. 2020. "Face Masks in National Stockpile Have Not Been Substantially Replenished Since 2009." *Washington Post* (March 10).

Renn, Aaron M. 2018. "The Market Is 'Banning the Box.'" *City Journal* (August 8).

Reynolds, Alan. 2018. "The Return of Antitrust." *Regulation* 41 (Spring), pp. 24–30.

Ridley, Matt. 2015. "The Myth of Basic Science." *Wall Street Journal* (October 23).

———. 2020. *How Innovation Works and Why It Flourishes in Freedom*. New York: HarperCollins Publishers.

Roberts, Russ. 2018. "Do the Rich Get All the Gains from Economic Growth?" Russ Roberts blog (October 23). https://medium.com/@russroberts/do-the-rich-capture-all-the-gains-from-economic-growth-c96d93101f9c.

Robertson, Campbell. 2019. "We Didn't Get PhDs Just to Sit Around: Civil Servants' Good Will Erodes." *New York Times* (January 24).

Robertson, Campbell, and John Schwartz. 2015. "Decade after Katrina, Pointing Finger More Firmly at Army Corps." *New York Times* (May 23).

Rodgers, Luke P. 2018. "Give Credit Where?: The Incidence of Child Care Tax Credits." *Journal of Urban Economics* 108 (November), pp. 51–71.

Rodrik, Dani. 2014. "When Ideas Trump Interests: Preferences, Worldviews, and Policy Innovations." *Journal of Economic Perspectives* 28 (Winter), pp. 189–208.

Romer, Paul M. 1990. "Endogenous Technological Change." *Journal of Political Economy* 98 (October), pp. S71–S102.

Rosenthal, Brian M. 2017. "The Most Expensive Mile of Subway Track on Earth." *New York Times* (December 28).

Rossitti, Giuseppe. 2019. "Centres of Power: U.S. Capitals' Location and Ability Sorting of Legislators." London School of Economics Working Paper (November).

Rotherham, Andrew J. 2017. "Complex History of School Choice." *U.S. News and World Report* (July 25).

Russakoff, Dale. 2015. *The Prize: Who's in Charge of America's Schools?* Boston: Houghton-Mifflin.

Sabia, Joseph J., and Richard Burkhauser. 2010. "Minimum Wages and Poverty: Will a $9.50 Federal Minimum Wage Really Help the Working Poor?" *Southern Economic Journal* 76 (January), pp. 592–623.

Saez, Emmanuel, and Gabriel Zucman. 2019. "Alexandria Ocasio-Cortez's Tax Hike Idea Is Not about Soaking the Rich." *New York Times* (January 22).

Said, Carolyn. 2019. "On-Transit Shuttles to Serve Apple Hometown's Transit Desert." *San Francisco Chronicle* (October 7).

Sampat, Bhaven N. 2018. "A Survey of Empirical Evidence on Patents and Innovation." NBER Working Paper 25383 (December).

Samuelson, Robert J. 2019. "The Rise and Fall of America's 'Policy Entrepreneurs.'" *Washington Post* (July 14).

Schmalensee, Richard, and Robert N. Stavins. 2017. "Lessons Learned from Three Decades of Experience with Cap and Trade." *Review of Environmental Economics and Policy* 11 (January), pp. 59–79.

Schuck, Peter H. 2014. *Why Government Fails So Often and How It Can Do Better.* Princeton University Press, p. 109.

———. 2017. "The Tangle of Poverty." *National Affairs*, no. 12 (Summer).

Schwab, Klaus. 2019. "Why We Need the 'Davos Manifesto' for a Better Kind of Capitalism," World Economic Forum (December 1).

Scott Morton, Fiona. 2006. "Consumer Benefit from Use of the Internet." In *Innovation Policy and the Economy* 6, edited by Adam B. Jaffe, Josh Lerner, and Scott Stern. Cambridge, Massachusetts: NBER MIT Press.

Scott, Hal. 2020. "Dodd-Frank Worsens Covid's Risk." *Wall Street Journal* (March 11).

Seira, Enrique, Alan Elizondo, and Eduardo Laguna-Muggenburg. 2017. "Are Information Disclosures Effective? Evidence from the Credit Card Market." *American Economic Journal: Economic Policy* 9 (February), pp. 277–307.

Shapiro, Carl. 2018. "Antitrust in a Time of Populism." *International Journal of Industrial Organization* 61 (November), pp. 714–48.

Shapiro, Joseph S. 2016. "Trade Costs, CO2, and the Environment." *American Economic Journal: Economic Policy* 8 (November), pp. 220–54.

Shapiro, Joseph S., and Reed Walker. 2018. "Why Is Pollution from US Manufacturing Declining? The Roles of Environmental Regulation, Productivity, and Trade." *American Economic Review* 108 (December), pp. 3814–54.

Sharkey, Patrick. 2018. *Uneasy Peace: The Great Crime Decline, the Renewal of City Life, and the Next War on Violence.* New York: W.W. Norton.

———. 2020. "Why Do We Need the Police?" *Washington Post* (June 12).

Sharkey, Patrick, Gerard Torrats-Espinosa, and Delaram Takyara. 2017. "Community and the Crime Decline: The Causal Effect of Local Nonprofits on Violent Crime." *American Sociological Review* 82, no. 6, pp. 1214–40.

Shea, Michael B., and others. 2018. "Outdated Prescription Drug Labeling: How FDA-Approved Prescribing Information Lags Behind Real-World Clinical Practice." *Therapeutic Innovation and Regulatory Science* 52, no. 6, pp. 771–77.

Shirodkar, Shyla. 2004. "Design-Around Patent Strategies for Patentees and Competitors." *Patent Strategy & Management Law Journal Newsletters* 5 (November).

Shujiro, Urata, and Peter A. Petri. 2017. "Outcome of TPP11: Persuading the United States of the Disadvantages of Withdrawal." Research Institute of Economy, Trade, and Industry (RIETI). Tokyo, Japan. www.rieti.go.jp/en/papers/contribution/urata/10.html.

Sloan, Karen. 2018. "Experts to Law Grads: Don't Freak Out about Public Service Loan Forgiveness—Yet." *Law.Com* (October 11).

Small, Kenneth A., Clifford Winston, and Carol A. Evans. 1989. *Road Work: A New Highway Pricing and Investment Policy.* Brookings Institution.

Smith, Noah. (2021). "Interview: Patrick Collison, Co-founder and CEO of Stripe." Substack (March 8), https://noahpinion.substack.com/p/interview-patrick-collison-co-founder.

Smith, Rebecca, and Katherine Blunt. 2020. "Why California Keeps Having Blackouts." *Wall Street Journal* (August 23).

Solow, Robert M. 1957. "Technical Change and the Aggregate Production Function." *Review of Economics and Statistics* 39 (August), pp. 312–20.

———. 2010. "Hedging America." *The New Republic* (January 12).

Sommer, Kamila, and Paul Sullivan. 2018. "Implications of US Tax Policy for House Prices, Rents, and Homeownership." *American Economic Review* 108 (February), pp. 241–74.

Sorkin, Andrew Ross. 2020. "Has Business Left Milton Friedman Behind?" *New York Times* (September 11).

Stahl, Jessica Calfee. 2016. "Effects of Deregulation and Consolidation of the Broadcast Television Industry." *American Economic Review* 106 (August), pp. 2185–218.

Stange, Kevin. 2014. "How Does Provider Supply and Regulation Influence Health Care Markets? Evidence from Nurse Practitioners and Physician Assistants." *Journal of Health Economics* 33 (January), pp. 1–27.

Stecher, Brian M., and others. 2018. *Improving Teaching Effectiveness: The Intensive Partnerships for Effective Teaching Through 2015–2016, Final Report.* RAND Corporation, Santa Monica, California.

Stepan, Alfred, and Juan J. Linz. 2011. "Comparative Perspectives on Inequality and the Quality of Democracy in the United States." *Perspectives on Politics* 9 (December), pp. 841–56.

Stephens, Bret. 2020. "Covid-19 and the Big Government Problem." *New York Times* (April 10).

Stigler, George J. 1971. "The Theory of Economic Regulation." *Bell Journal of Economics* 2 (Spring), pp. 3–21.

———. 1981. "Comment." In *Studies in Public Regulation*, edited by Gary Fromm. MIT Press, pp. 73–77.

———. 1982. "The Economists and the Problem of Monopoly." *American Economic Review* 72 (May), pp. 1–11.

Stiglitz, Joseph E. 2019. *People, Power, and Profits: Progressive Capitalism for an Age of Discontent.* New York: W. W. Norton.

Stiglitz, Joseph, and Linda Bilmes. 2006. *The Economic Costs of the Iraq War: An Appraisal Three Years after the Beginning of the Conflict* (January).

Stolberg, Sheryl Gay, and Katie Thomas. 2020. "Trump to Tap New Company to Make Covid-19 Drugs in the U.S." *New York Times* (May 18).

Streitfeld, David. 2018. "Welcome to Zucktown, Where Everything Is Just Zucky." *New York Times* (March 21).

Summers, Lawrence H. 2020. *COVID-19 and Global Affairs: Prospects for Recovery in the World Economy.* Jackson Institute for Global Affairs. Yale University. https://jackson.yale.edu/video/event-recording-covid-19-and-global-affairs -prospects-for-recovery-in-the-world-economy/.

Surowiecki, James. 2016. "Unlikely Alliances." *New Yorker* (April 25).

Sutter, Daniel, and Marc Poitras. 2002. "The Political Economy of Automobile Safety Inspections." *Public Choice* 113 (December), pp. 367–87.

Tabarrok, Alexander. 2018. "How FDA-Approved Prescribing Information Lags Behind Real-World Clinical Practice." *Marginal Revolution* (March 28).

———. 2020. "Trump Stops Masks from Going to Canada." *Marginal Revolution* (April 4).

Tabakovic, Haris, and Thomas G. Wollmann. 2018. "From Revolving Doors to Regulatory Capture? Evidence from Patent Examiners." NBER Working Paper 24638 (May).

Tan, Xinlong, Clifford Winston, and Jia Yan. 2020. "Would U.S. Travelers Benefit from Entry By Foreign Airlines? Simulating the Effect of Cabotage Based on Low-Cost Carrier Competition in U.S. and European Union Markets." Working Paper (August).

Tankersley, Jim, and Michael Hirsh. 2011. "Neo-Voodoo Economics." *National Journal* (May 20).

Tarullo, Daniel K. 2019. "Financial Regulation: Still Unsettled a Decade after the Crisis." *Journal of Economic Perspectives* 33 (Winter), pp. 61–80.

Tashea, Jason. 2018. "DoNotPay App Aims to Help Users Sue Anyone in Small Claims Court—without a Lawyer." *ABA Journal* (October 10).

Taylor, Timothy. 2020. "Wearing Face-Masks: The Mixed Evidence." *Conversable Economist* (August 29).

Telford, Taylor. 2020. "Democrat Accuses OSHA of Being 'Invisible' While Infections Rise among Essential Workers." *Washington Post* (May 28).

Tepper, Jonathan, with Denise Hearn. 2019. *The Myth of Capitalism: Monopolies and the Death of Competition.* Hoboken, New Jersey: John Wiley and Sons.

Tergesen, Anne. 2019. "Employers Help Workers Build Household-Emergency Funds." *Wall Street Journal* (June 13).

Tewari, Ishani. 2014. "The Distributive Impacts of Financial Development: Evidence from Mortgage Markets during US Bank Branch Deregulation." *American Economic Journal: Applied Economics* 6 (October), pp. 175–96.

The Economist. 2019. "Lobbying in Trumpland" (April 13).

———. 2020. "The Pandemic Is Liberating Firms to Experiment with Radical New Ideas." (April 25).

Thrush, Glenn. 2018. "$1.7 Billion Federal Job Training Program Is Failing the Students." *New York Times* (August 26).

Timberg, Craig, and Ellen Nakashima. 2020. "The U.S. Government Spent Billions on a System for Detecting Hacks. The Russians Outsmarted It." *Washington Post* (December 15).

Timmons, Edward J., Ethan Bayne, and Conor Norris. 2020. "A Primer on Emergency Occupational Licensing Reforms for Combating Covid-19." Mercatus Policy Brief. George Mason University (March 26).

Tollefson, Jeff. 2018. "Sucking Carbon Dioxide from Air Is Cheaper Than Scientists Thought." *Nature*, www.nature.com/articles/d41586-018-05357-w.

Tomer, Adie. 2012. "Where the Jobs Are: Employer Access to Labor by Transit." Brookings Institution.

Tongzon, Jose, and Wu Heng. 2005. "Port Privatization, Efficiency, and Competitiveness: Some Empirical Evidence from Container Ports (Terminals)." *Transportation Research A* 39 (June), pp. 405–24.

Top, Emily. 2018. "How to Reduce Student Loan Rates and Tuition." *E21* (March 12).

Tucker, Catherine. 2014. "The Effect of Patent Litigation and Patent Assertion Entities on Entrepreneurial Activity." Sloan Working Paper 5095-14 (June).

United States Congressional Budget Office. 2018. *The Distribution of Household Income, 2014*. CBO, Washington, DC (March).

United States Department of Transportation. 2018. *FAA Needs to Strengthen Its Management Controls over the Use and Oversight of NextGen Developmental Funding*. Office of Inspector General, Report AV2018030 (March).

Varian, Hal, Robert E. Litan, Andrew Elder, and Jay Shutter. 2002. *The Net Impact Study: The Projected Economic Benefits of the Internet in the United States, United Kingdom, France, and Germany*. Brookings. (January), www.itu.int/net/wsis/stocktaking/docs/activities/1288617396/NetImpact_Study_Report_Brookings.pdf.

Vartabedian, Ralph. 2018. "Cost for California Bullet Train System Rises to $77.3 Billion." *Los Angeles Times* (March 9).

Vinik, Danny. 2017. "America's Government Is Getting Old." *Politico* (September 27).

Wadhwa, Vivek. 2017. "The Big Lesson from Amazon and Whole Foods: Disruptive Competition Comes out of Nowhere." *Wall Street Journal* (June 19).

Wallsten, Scott, and Katrina Kosec. 2005. "The Economic Costs of the War in Iraq." AEI-Brookings (September).

Wang, Hao, Israa Al-Saadi, Pan Lu, and Abbas Jasim. 2019. "Quantifying Greenhouse Gas Emission of Asphalt Pavement Preservation at Construction and Use Stages Using Lifecycle Assessment." *International Journal of Sustainable Transportation* 14 (1), pp. 25–34.

Wang, Zhi, Shang-Jin Wei, Xinding Yu, and Kunfu Zhu. 2018. "Re-Examining the Effects of Trading with China on Local Labor Markets: A Supply Chain Perspective." NBER Working Paper 24886 (August).

Weaver, R. Kent. 1986. "The Politics of Blame Avoidance." *Journal of Public Policy* 6 (October-December), pp. 371–98.

Weber, Lauren. 2020. "50,000 Jobs, 90,000 Resumes: Coronavirus Is Redeploying Workers at Record Pace." *Wall Street Journal* (April 15).

Werden, Gregory J., and Luke M. Froeb. 2018. "Don't Panic: A Guide to Claims of Increasing Concentration." *Antitrust Magazine* (Fall).

White, Lawrence J. 2017. "Regulating the Credit Rating Agencies? Less Would Be More." Money and Banking. www.moneyandbanking.com/commentary/2017/6/30/regulating-the-credit-rating-agencies-less-would-be-more.

Whitlock, Craig, and Bob Woodward. 2016. "Pentagon Buries Evidence of $125 Billion in Bureaucratic Waste." *Washington Post* (December 5).

Winship, Scott. 2016. *Poverty after Welfare Reform.* Manhattan Institute, New York City (August).

Winston, Clifford. 1998. "U.S. Industry Adjustment to Economic Deregulation." *Journal of Economic Perspectives* 12 (Summer), pp. 89–110.

———. 2006. *Government Failure versus Market Failure: Microeconomic Policy Research and Government Performance.* Brookings Institution.

———. 2008. "The Efficacy of Information Policy: A Review of Archon Fung, Mary Graham, and David Weil's *Full Disclosure: The Perils and Promise of Transparency.*" *Journal of Economic Literature* 46 (September), pp. 704–17.

———. 2010. *Last Exit: Privatization and Deregulation of the US Transportation System.* Brookings Institution.

———. 2013. "On the Performance of the U.S. Transportation System: Caution Ahead." *Journal of Economic Literature* 51 (September), pp. 773–824.

———. 2021. "Back to the Good—or Were They the Bad—Old Days of Antitrust? A Review Essay of Jonathan B. Baker's *The Antitrust Paradigm: Restoring a Competitive Economy.*" *Journal of Economic Literature* 59, 1 (March), pp. 265–84.

Winston, Clifford, David Burk, and Jia Yan. 2021. *Trouble at the Bar: An Economic Perspective on the Legal Profession and the Case for Fundamental Reform.* Brookings Institution Press.

Winston, Clifford, Thomas Corsi, Curtis M. Grimm, and Carol A. Evans. 1990. *The Economic Effects of Surface Freight Deregulation.* Brookings Institution.

Winston, Clifford, and Quentin Karpilow. 2016. "Should the US Eliminate Entry Barriers to the Practice of Law? Perspectives Shaped by Industry Deregulation." *American Economic Review Papers and Proceedings* 106 (May), pp. 171–76.

———. 2020. *Autonomous Vehicles: The Road to Economic Growth.* Brookings Institution Press.

Winston, Clifford, and Jia Yan. 2011. "Can Privatization of U.S. Highways Improve Motorists' Welfare?" *Journal of Public Economics* 95 (August), pp. 993–1005.

———. 2015. "Open Skies: Estimating Travelers' Benefits from Free Trade in Airline Services." *American Economic Journal: Economic Policy* 7 (May), pp. 370–414.

———. 2021. "Vehicle Size Choice and Automobile Externalities: A Dynamic Analysis." *Journal of Econometrics* 222, 1, part A (May), pp. 196–218.

Wolf Jr., Charles. 1979. "A Theory of Nonmarket Failure: Framework for Implementation Analysis." *Journal of Law and Economics* 22 (April), pp. 107–39.

Wu, Tim. 2017. "How to Stop Drug Price Gouging." *New York Times* (April 20).

Wu, Xi. 2020. "SEC Regulations and Firms." NYU Stern School of Business.

Xing, Jianwei, Benjamin Leard, and Shanjun Li. 2019. "What Does an Electric Vehicle Replace?" NBER Working Paper 25771 (April).

Yan, Jia, and Clifford Winston. 2014. "Can Private Airport Competition Improve Runway Pricing? The Case of San Francisco Bay Area Airports." *Journal of Public Economics* 115 (July), pp. 146–57.

Yoder, Eric. 2021. "The Federal Government Faces Wicked Problems. It Needs More Expertise, A New Report Says." *Washington Post* (March 18).

Yoder, Eric, and Lisa Rein. 2017. "Firing Federal Workers Isn't as Easy as Trump Makes It Seem in His Budget." *Washington Post* (March 16).

Zhou Ruohua, Annetta, Katherine Baicker, Sarah Taubman, and Amy N. Finkelstein. 2017. "The Uninsured Do Not Use the Emergency Department More—They Use Other Care Less." *Health Affairs* 36 (December), pp. 2115–22.

Zimmer, Carl. 2020. "Epidemics Started Later Than First Estimated." *New York Times* (May 28).

Zimmerman, Mae. 2015. "The Sweet Gig of Being a Bureaucrat." *Wall Street Journal* (November 19).

Zipkin, Amy. 2019. "GPS for Air Travel Came with Big Downsides: Noise, Then Lawsuits." *New York Times* (November 18).

INDEX

Page numbers followed by t represent tables.

www.ingramcontent.com/pod-product-compliance
Lightning Source LLC
Chambersburg PA
CBHW031408270326
41929CB00010BA/1371